Other Selves
Philosophers on Friendship

Other Selves
Philosophers on Friendship

Edited by
Michael Pakaluk

Hackett Publishing Company, Inc.

Indianapolis/Cambridge

Copyright © 1991 by Hackett Publishing Company, Inc.

Plato, *Lysis*, translated by Stanley Lombardo, copyright © 1991 by Hackett Publishing Company, Inc.

Aristotle, *Rhetoric*, translated by Terence Irwin, copyright © 1991 by Hackett Publishing Company, Inc.

Printed in the United States of America

19 18 17 16 15   6 7 8 9 10

Interior design by Dan Kirklin

For further information, please address
  Hackett Publishing Company
  P.O. Box 44937
  Indianapolis, Indiana 46244-0937

  www.hackettpublishing.com

Library of Congress Cataloging-in-Publication Data
Other selves: philosophers on friendship / edited by Michael Pakaluk.
        p.   cm.
  Includes bibliographical references.
  ISBN 0-87220-114-7: ISBN 0-87220-113-9 (pbk).
    1. Friendship.   2. Philosophy.   I. Pakaluk, Michael, 1957– .
BJ1533.F8044   1991   90-44276
177'.6—dc20   CIP

ISBN-13: 978-0-87220-114-9
ISBN-13: 978-0-87220-113-2 (pbk.)

CONTENTS

ACKNOWLEDGMENTS

Plato: *Lysis*, translated by Stanley Lombardo, copyright © 1991 by Hackett Publishing Company, Inc. reprinted by permission of Hackett Publishing Company, Inc. First published in *Other Selves*, edited by Michael Pakaluk, Hackett Publishing Company, Inc., Indianapolis: 1991.

Excerpts from Aristotle: *Nicomachean Ethics*, translated by Terence Irwin, copyright © 1985 by Terence Irwin, reprinted by permission of Hackett Publishing Company, Inc.

Excerpts from Aristotle: *Rhetoric*, translated by Terence Irwin, copyright © 1991 by Hackett Publishing Company, Inc. First published in *Other Selves*, edited by Michael Pakaluk, Hackett Publishing Company, Inc., Indianapolis: 1991.

Excerpts from Cicero: *On Old Age and Friendship*, translated by Frank Copley, copyright © 1967. Reprinted by permission of the University of Michigan Press.

Excerpts from Seneca: *Epistulae Morales*, translated by R. M. Gummere, copyright © 1917 by Harvard University Press. Reprinted by permission of the Loeb Classical Library.

Excerpts from Aelred of Rievaulx: *Spiritual Friendship*, translated by Eugenia Laker, s.s.n.d., copyright © 1974. Reprinted by permission of Cistercian Publications, Kalamazoo.

Excerpts from St. Thomas Aquinas: *Summa Theologica, First Complete American Edition*, translated by the Fathers of the English Dominican Province, copyright © 1947. Reprinted by permission of Glencoe/McGraw Hill.

Excerpts from Montaigne: *The Complete Essays of Montaigne*, translated by Donald M. Frame, copyright © 1958 by the Board of Trustees of the Leland Stanford Junior University. Reprinted by permission of Stanford University Press.

Excerpts from Immanuel Kant: *Lectures on Ethics*, translated by Louis Infield, copyright © 1930. Reprinted by permission of Methuen and Company, Ltd.

Excerpts from Søren Kierkegaard: *Works of Love*, translated by Howard and Edna Hong, copyright © 1962 by Howard Hong. Reprinted by permission of Harper & Row, Publishers, Inc.

Elizabeth Telfer: "Friendship," first published in *Proceedings of the Aristotelian Society for 1970*, copyright © 1970 by the Aristotelian Society. Reprinted by courtesy of the Editor of the Aristotelian Society.

Cover: Alinari/Art Resource, N.Y.   Anderson 3861   Raphael, det. School of Athens   Romas, Stanze

INTRODUCTION

Almost all of the central philosophical writings on friendship produced in the West are gathered in this slim anthology. And together they constitute something like a tradition. For Plato's dialogue on friendship influenced Aristotle; Aristotle influenced Cicero; and all the others were acquainted with either Aristotle or Cicero. But this is not simply a tradition of philosophers commenting upon philosophers: many of the writings in this collection, although written with a philosophical discipline, are also directed to the nonphilosopher. They aim to engage, to draw in; they propose standards for living a life and not merely for thinking. And in general they are about friendships actually observed and lived.

Despite their common topic and common heritage, they also constitute a veritable sampler of philosophical genres. Aristotle's work is the only treatise, Telfer's the only professional article. Otherwise one finds dialogues (Plato, Cicero, and Aelred); letters of advice (Seneca); a lecture (Kant); a formalized public disputation (Aquinas); an exhortation (Kierkegaard); and essays of strikingly different kinds (Montaigne, Bacon, and Emerson).

There is currently a vigorous renewal of interest in the topic of friendship among philosophers, as a glance at the bibliography at the back of the book reveals.[1] This is a striking phenomenon, when viewed against the backdrop of recent philosophical history. Between the writings of Emerson and the contemporary work of Telfer, one finds a relatively long period in which philosophers were largely silent about friendship. A topic once so central to moral philosophy that Aristotle, for example, devoted two whole books of the *Nicomachean Ethics* to it, for a while dropped out of sight altogether. Why did this happen, and why has interest in friendship now revived? There are no doubt many reasons for this; the ones I shall explore briefly have to do with developments within moral philosophy itself.

The great divide in contemporary ethical thought has been between the view that ethics is fundamentally about rights and

---

1. See especially under the heading "Telfer (Contemporary Work)."

the view that it is fundamentally about promoting human welfare generally. The former view is typically referred to as *deontology*, the latter as *consequentialism*. Both were already prominently on the scene when Emerson wrote, and for both friendship is ethically problematical.

Deontology typically identifies moral reasons for action as those that are universalizable and *impartial*, and both universalizability and impartiality make friendship ethically problematic. A reason for action is *universalizable* if it can be converted into a general law that ought to be binding on all rational agents in similar circumstances. For example, a person on a crowded beach has a reason to turn down the volume on his radio, and his reason for doing so might be thought to be universalizable in the sense that the other beachgoers, who are in a relevantly similar situation, would have the same reason to turn their radios down as well. In such cases, it is natural for the agent to view himself as one among many equal persons and to see his action as bound by a pattern of lawfulness that binds everyone equally. But the reasons that friends have for doing good for each other seem to have a different character. First, friends regard each other not simply as one among many but rather as unique individuals to whom they are related in ways in which they are not related to humanity at large. Second, because of their familiarity and shared experiences, they have reasons for acting that seem unavailable to nonfriends. And third, those reasons seem not to be straightforwardly universalizable. I might have a reason to give my friend the last crust of bread that no nonfriend, no mere rational agent, would have. To inquire whether a reason for action is universalizable is, in effect, to pose the question: "What if everyone acted like that?" But that question seems odd and even irrelevant when put in the mouth of a friend deciding how to act towards his friend.[2]

Impartiality may be understood as the viewpoint of an ideal, disinterested judge. Any emotion or attitude—such as envy or hostility—that would hinder the judgment of a judge and render him partial or biassed is to be excluded from the impartial point of view. However, friendly attachments can make a judge partial: indeed, that is the reason why judges recuse themselves from

---

2. Lawrence Blum's *Friendship, Altruism, and Morality* (see bibliography) has a very good discussion of universalizability and friendship on pp. 87–105.

cases that involve a close friend or relative. So it would seem that the impartial point of view excludes friendly feelings and attachments and that to reason about human actions impartially involves detaching oneself from motives that are characteristic of friendship. Hence when human actions are viewed impartially in this sense, friendship seems to be difficult to justify morally; for this would seem to involve the odd if not impossible project of justifying partiality with impartial reasons.[3]

Consequentialism has difficulties of a different sort in accounting for friendship. According to consequentialism, an agent ought to do whatever action produces the greatest aggregate welfare for all human beings. Thus the good deeds that a friend does for his friend would be morally justified only if they were to bring about the most good for everyone. Now, on this view the way in which friends regard the good deeds they do for each other seems difficult to explain, for true friends seem to love each other for their own sake, and they seem to regard the good that they do for each other as valuable in its own right. Yet consequentialism says that these acts are valuable only as related to something extrinsic to the friendship, the aggregate of human welfare, and thus it apparently instrumentalizes friendship.

Furthermore, a true friendship seems in some way insulated from changes in fortune and external circumstances, as is suggested, for instance, by the wedding vow "for richer or poorer, in sickness and in health." Indeed, making a commitment to another seems to involve devoting oneself to his well-being, regardless of changes outside of that relationship. Yet a friend's confidence that he ought to show this sort of commitment to his friend seems misplaced, if the acts of friends are morally justified only as related to the aggregate of human welfare, which no doubt is constantly shifting. It is not clear that the kinds of acts that promote this aggregate will always be the kinds of acts that friendship requires.

Moreover, consequentialism seems to reverse the order of moral justification that appears to fit friendship most appropriately. For it seems correct to say that regard for the welfare of others generally is a kind of extension of the regard that we have for those who are close to us. This is reflected in the proverb "charity begins at home": it seems that we love friends and

3. See Blum, pp. 46–49.

relatives first and then try to extend this sort of regard to human beings generally. But consequentialism makes regard for human beings generally the primary moral motive, and it justifies love for friends and relatives only as a means to this or at best as an instance of this more general concern. Hence it seems to imply that our attachments to friends and relatives are accidental and that our friends are in some objectionable sense replaceable.

Let me stress that I sketch these problems only to indicate some of the difficulties that have drawn moral philosophers to study friendship more thoroughly in recent years. There are evident ways in which deontologists and consequentialists might try to handle these difficulties, and whether these responses are adequate cannot be investigated here. Indeed, one of the reasons why a detailed bibliography is included in this volume is to invite the reader to examine these matters with care, after having thought about the phenomenon of friendship itself. The important point is that friendship does not straightforwardly fit into the account of morality provided either by deontology or consequentialism. Hence on both of these views, friendship has something of a dubious moral standing. This helps to explain why, during the time when these two views have dominated moral philosophy, friendship has received little attention. And it also helps to explain why in recent years interest in friendship has revived. Friendship is something like a recalcitrant moral datum, a point at which theory seems to fit reality only by being stretched and pulled. So it assumes importance when, as we see today, the received ethical theories are being reevaluated in particularly searching ways.[4]

As an alternative to deontology and consequentialism, some philosophers have recently attempted to revive the view, which dates back at least to Plato and Aristotle, that ethics is largely about human virtue and vice.[5] On this view, an act is right or wrong depending upon whether it is in accordance with or contrary to a virtue. Virtues, in turn, are states of character that, when acquired, make someone a good human being. Now,

---

4. To see the role that discussions of friendship play in contemporary critiques of deontology and consequentialism, consult the entries under the heading "Friendship, Consequentialism, and Deontology" in the bibliography.

5. Two particularly important books are Alasdair MacIntyre's *After Virtue* (Notre Dame, 1981) and Philippa Foot's *Virtues and Vices* (Berkeley, 1978).

typically this approach to ethics is developed from a first-person point of view. That is, it begins with a question such as "How ought *I* to live my life?" From there, one reasons along lines like the following: "I ought to do well with my life, but I can do well only if I am good, and I can become good only by acquiring virtues, and so I ought to act in accordance with the various virtues."

This is, of course, a very rough sketch, but it suffices to show that this approach to ethics typically takes as its starting point the individual and the individual's concern to live life well. But then it might seem problematic how, on this way of understanding ethics, one is to develop an adequate social philosophy, for how does one move from a concern for one's own life to a concern for the lives of others? And how is an individual's pursuit of his own virtue related to the pursuit of virtue by others? Now, this is where friendship would seem to come in: after all, a friend is often said to be "another self." Hence philosophers interested in virtue have turned their attention to friendship as something that seems crucial in accounting for the social character of morality. Friendship appears to be the bridge that can link together the individual and the various groups to which he belongs, once virtue is taken as fundamental in the moral life.

This point leads to an additional reason why contemporary moral philosophers have turned their attention to friendship, and that is as a possible way out of the problem of egoism and altruism. The problem takes many forms, but for our purposes it can be framed as follows. Clearly each of us is motivated by a concern for his or her own safety and well-being—call this the *egoistic motive*. Furthermore, it is possible to feel a regard for the safety and well-being of others generally. Whether this concern arises by nature or is acquired need not be taken up here— the important point is that it does indeed seem possible to be motivated in this way, which is called having 'goodwill' or 'fellow feeling' or 'love of humanity'. Call this sort of motive the *altruistic motive*.

Now, what is the relation between these two motives, when they coexist in a person? To subordinate one to the other seems to deprive it of its proper character. If the altruistic is subordinated to the egoistic motive, then one loves others for the sake of one's own good, which would seem not to be a genuine love of others at all. And if the egoistic is subordinated to the altruistic motive, then one loves oneself for the sake of others—a state of mind which, if attainable, would seem to amount to the obliteration of self-love. For similar reasons, it would hardly seem possible to convince an egoist, on egoistic grounds, to act altruistically or to convince an altruist to act egoistically.

The alternative that remains is that the motives are independent of each other and that a person, without reason, moves back and forth from acting on the one to acting on the other. Such was the view arrived at by Henry Sidgwick in his *Methods of Ethics*, a great 19th-century work on ethics which contains the classic statement of this problem. But, as Sidgwick himself recognized, this position seems unsatisfactory, for it would seem that mere chance or accident would determine which motive predominated. Furthermore, on this view it seems impossible for the moral life to have a unity, for each person becomes effectively divided into two *personae*, one selfish and the other selfless.

Contemporary moral philosophers have attempted to deal with the problem of egoism and altruism in intriguing and ingenious ways. For example, one line of thought is that it is impossible to pursue one's own self-interest rationally, without viewing oneself objectively. But to view oneself objectively implies viewing oneself as just one person among many equals. Hence, the egoistic and altruistic motives converge, as it were, in an objective understanding of oneself in relation to others.[6] Another line of thought is simply to deny that a significant distinction can be drawn between a person and others. According to this view, the problem of egoism and altruism arises from a sort of misguided metaphysical individualism: do away with the distinction between a person and others, it is claimed, and you do away with the distinction of motives.[7]

Both of these lines of thought lead back to classical discussions of friendship, though in different ways. The first is suggestive of Aristotle's argument in *Nicomachean Ethics*, book IX, chapters 4 through 9, that true self-love implies forming friendships in which the good of one's friend is esteemed as one's own. Indeed,

6. This is, in very broad outline, the argument of Thomas Nagel's *The Possibility of Altruism* (Princeton, 1970).

7. Something like this is the position taken by Derek Parfit in *Reasons and Persons* (Oxford, 1984).

claims of this sort are made by several of the writers in this collection. And in fact a friendship may be understood as a coordination of the interests of two or more persons, within a kind of objective relationship which serves as a good common to the friends. The second line of thought leads to the classical accounts of friendship as to a less desperate alternative, for the writers featured in this volume tend to view persons neither as distinct as they are claimed to be by modern forms of individualism nor as indistinct as is implied by those who reject that individualism.[8] They hold out the promise of a *via media*, between an unjustified individualism and opposing views that seem to deny the integrity of persons.

In closing it is useful to enter a *caveat:* to say that the writings included in this collection are *central* is not to say that, even taken together, they provide anything like an exhaustive or representative treatment of friendship. It is indeed an important and worthwhile exercise to ask: What types of friendship, or characteristics shared by all friendships, have been neglected by the writers included in this collection?

For example, the question of whether friendships between men and women have a distinctive character is not discussed. Even Emerson, whose closest friends were women, writes about friendship as though the gender of the friends is irrelevant. And although Aquinas departs from Aristotle in his *Summa contra Gentiles* and says that marriage is the greatest degree of friendship (III.123), in those parts of the *Summa Theologiae* where he discusses friendship and love most directly, marriage receives no special attention, and Aristotle is used without evident alteration. Another obvious shortcoming of the tradition is that none of the writers is concerned with whether there are distinctive types of friendship between women, and none seems especially interested in friendships between men that center around the responsibilities of family and home. Aristotle speaks of friends' drinking together, playing dice, doing gymnastics, hunting, and discussing philosophy (IX.12), but not clearing a field or raising a barn.

Moreover, friendships among children receive little attention.

---

8. For instance, Aristotle's claim that a human being is by nature social (see Ethics IX.9) suggests that a human individual is essentially adapted to living life in common with others.

The reasons for this neglect are familiar enough: for example, children are incapable of serious commitment; they do not fully possess virtues, and hence cannot have the types of friendship which presuppose them; their tastes are changing; they have not adopted considered principles for living their lives; they lack the independence truly to be another's equal; and so on. Nevertheless, it must be said that there is a relationship between childhood and friendship that is not explored by the writers in this collection. Children exhibit, almost paradigmatically, some of the most important characteristics of friendship, such as trust and affection. Furthermore, many of the closest friendships are those which begin in childhood.

These and other limitations in the tradition of philosophical writing about friendship provide, of course, reasons for supplementing and developing that tradition, rather than rejecting it. None of the writers included here claims comprehensiveness or completeness for his or her work. Most of the selections are essays, and essays invite other essays. Even Aristotle's work, the only treatise on friendship, displays a remarkable appreciation of the many different sorts of relationship that go by the name 'friendship'. Religious societies, familial bonds, affinities among travellers, civility among citizens, arrangements of hospitality, and tacit contractual agreements—all of these are woven into his account of friendship.

If philosophers of an earlier age have failed to discuss friendship completely, we have, throughout much of the recent past, completely failed to discuss it. The present collection provides a kind of standard, which needs to be met, before it can be surpassed.

Note: Footnotes to the general introduction and the selection introductions are those of the editor. All footnotes to the selections are those of the translators except for that of Telfer, in which case they are those of the author.

Plato

LYSIS

Introduction

Socrates, the teacher of Plato and the principal figure of the *Lysis*, had no school, no curriculum, and charged no fees. Philosophy, as he practiced it, is often the expression of friendship of a certain sort. In this regard, it is sometimes contrasted by Plato with sophistry, which is the way of the flatterer, the false and merely apparent friend (see *Gorgias* 465c, 507e–8a, 513b).

It is not surprising, then, that Plato, a follower and friend of Socrates, should himself write a dialogue on friendship. But the dialogue he writes is perplexing and is undoubtedly meant to be, for that is the way in which philosophical friendship is practiced: friends should be humbled and checked (cp. *Lysis* 210e), not flattered into thinking they are knowledgeable, when in fact they are not. When you finish the dialogue, if you agree with Socrates that you are at a loss as to what a friend is (223a), and you find yourself wanting to go back and determine where the discussion went off track and where it hit upon the truth—then you have been drawn in, and the work has achieved what is apparently one of its important purposes.

Although no doctrine on friendship advanced in the dialogue is left standing without a challenge, there are various lines of thought which Plato evidently takes seriously: for example, that it is shared goodness and not any sort of likeness that underlies friendship (214d); that the inconstancy of the bad in relation to themselves makes them unfit to befriend others (214c–d); and that affection for other persons must somehow be grounded in a desire that terminates in a primary object of love (219c–220b).

The *Lysis* is often grouped with the *Charmides, Laches, Euthyphro,* and *Hippias Major* as a 'definitional' dialogue, that is, one that attempts to find what it is that all things called by a certain term (e.g. 'courage,' 'piety') have in common. Yet the focus of the *Lysis* seems to be just as much on human action and causation. Indeed, the question that predominates in the dialogue is: How does one *become* the friend of another? (see 206c, 210d, 212a, and 214a). Plato's brief account of why genuine love tends to be reciprocated (222a) should be read in this light. If "the genuine and not the pretended lover must be befriended by his boy," then the way one becomes a friend of another is by genuinely loving that person.

We see this taking place in the action of the dialogue. Hippothales, a pretended lover who actually is in love with himself (205d–e), remains on the sidelines, while Socrates, concerned for Lysis' true good, wins the boy's affection. Plato in fact makes extraordinary use of dramatic action in the dialogue: his points are conveyed almost as much by what the characters *do* as by what they *say*. To give one example: Socrates begins his investigation of friendship by questioning a *pair* of friends (207b–c), the usual unit of friendship, and the disagreements between Lysis and Menexenus about who is older, of better birth, and so on, vividly illustrate the friends' *equality*. Looking for such clever devices is a fun game to play: I leave it to the reader to find others.

Plato

LYSIS
A DIALOGUE ON FRIENDSHIP

I was on my way from the Academy straight to the Lyceum,
following the road just outside and beneath the wall; and when
I got to the little gate by Panops spring, I happened to meet
Hippothales, Hieronymus' son, and Ctesippus of Paeonia, and
with them some other young men standing together in a group.
Seeing me coming, Hippothales said,

"Hey, Socrates, where are you coming from and where are
you going?"

"From the Academy," I said, "straight to the Lyceum."

"Well, come straight over here to us, why don't you? You
won't come? It's worth your while, I assure you."

"Where do you mean, and who all are you?"

"Over here," he said, showing me an open door and an en-
closed area just facing the wall. "A lot of us spend our time here.
There are quite a few besides ourselves—and they're all good-
looking."

"What is this, and what do you do here?"

"This is a new wrestling-school," he said, "just built. But we
spend most of our time discussing things, and we'd be glad to
have you join in."

"How very nice," I said. "And who is the teacher here?"

"Your old friend and admirer, Mikkos."

"Well, God knows, he's a serious person and a competent
instructor."

"Well, then, won't you please come in and see who's here?"

"First I'd like to hear what I'm coming in for—and the name
of the best-looking member."

Plato: *Lysis*, translated by Stanley Lombardo, copyright © 1991 by Hackett Pub-
lishing Company, Inc. reprinted by permission of Hackett Publishing Company,
Inc. First published in *Other Selves*, edited by Michael Pakaluk, Hackett Publishing
Company, Inc., Indianapolis: 1991.

"Each of us has a different opinion on who that is, Socrates."

"So tell me, Hippothales, who do you think it is?"

He blushed at the question, so I said, "Aha! You don't have to answer that, Hippothales, for me to tell whether you're in love with any of these boys or not—I can see that you are not only in love but pretty far gone too. I may not be much good at anything c else, but I have this god-given ability to tell pretty quickly when someone is in love, and who he's in love with."

When he heard this he really blushed, which made Ctesippus say, "O very cute, Hippothales, blushing and too embarrassed to tell Socrates the name. But if he spends any time at all with you he'll be driven to distraction hearing you say it so often. d We're all just about deaf, Socrates, from all the 'Lysis' he's poured into our ears. And if he's been drinking, odds are we'll wake up in the middle of the night thinking we hear Lysis' name. As bad as all this is in normal conversation, it's nothing compared to when he drowns us with his poems and prose pieces. And worst of all, he actually sings odes to his beloved in a weird voice, which we have to put up with listening to. And now when you ask him the name he blushes!"

"Lysis must be pretty young," I said. "I say that because the e name doesn't register with me."

"That's because they don't call him by his own name much. He still goes by his father's name, because his father is so famous. I'm sure you know what the boy looks like; his looks are enough to know him by."

"Tell me whose son he is," I said.

"He's the oldest son of Democrates of Aexone."

"Well, congratulations, Hippothales, on finding someone so spirited and noble to love! Now come on and perform for me 205 what you've performed for your friends here, so that I can see if you know what a lover ought to say about his boyfriend to his face, or to others."

"Do you think what *he* says really counts for anything, Socrates?"

"Are you denying that you are in love with the one he says you are?"

"No, but I am denying that I write love poems about him and all."

"The man's not well, he's raving," Ctesippus hooted.

"O.K., Hippothales," I said. "I don't need to hear any poems **b** or songs you may or may not have composed about the boy. Just give me the general sense, so I'll know how you deal with him."

"Well why don't you ask Ctesippus? He must have total recall of it all, from what he says about it being drummed into his head from listening to me."

"You bet I do," Ctesippus said, "and it's pretty ridiculous too, Socrates. I mean, here he is, completely fixated on this boy and totally unable to say anything more original to him than any child could say. How ridiculous can you get? All he can think of **c** to say or write is stuff the whole city goes around singing— poems about Democrates and the boy's grandfather Lysis and all his ancestors, their wealth and their stables and their victories at the Pythian, Isthmian, and Nemean Games in the chariot races and the horseback races. And then he gets into the really ancient history. Just the day before yesterday he was reciting some poem to us about Heracles being entertained by one of their ancestors **d** because he was related to the hero—something about him being a son of Zeus and the daughter of their deme's founding father— old women's spinning-songs, really. This is the sort of thing he recites and sings, Socrates, and forces us to listen to."

When I heard that I said, "Hippothales, you deserve to be ridiculed. Do you really compose and sing your own victory-ode before you've won?"

"I don't compose or sing victory-odes for myself, Socrates."

"You only think you don't."

"How is that?" he asked.

"You are really what these songs are all about," I said. "If you **e** make a conquest of a boy like this, then everything you've said and sung turns out to eulogize yourself as victor in having won such a boyfriend. But if he gets away, then the greater your praise of his beauty and goodness, the more you will seem to have lost and the more you will be ridiculed. This is why the **206** skilled lover doesn't praise his beloved until he has him: he fears how the future may turn out. And besides, these good-looking boys, if anybody praises them, get swelled heads and start to think they're really somebody. Doesn't it seem that way to you?"

"It certainly does," he said.

"And the more swell-headed they get, the harder they are to catch."

"So it seems."

"Well, what do you think of a hunter who scares off his game and makes it harder to catch?"

"He's pretty poor."

b   "And isn't it a gross misuse of language and music to drive things wild rather than to soothe and charm?"

"Well, yes."

"Then be careful, Hippothales, that you don't make yourself guilty of all these things through your poetry. I don't imagine you would say that a man who hurts himself, by his poetry, is at all a good poet—after all, he does hurt himself."

"No, of course not," he said. "That wouldn't make any sense at
c   all. But that's just why I'm telling you all this, Socrates. What different advice can you give me about what one should say or do so his prospective boyfriend will like him?"

"That's not easy to say. But if you're willing to have him talk with me, I might be able to give you a demonstration of how to carry on a conversation with him instead of talking and singing the way your friends here say you've been doing."

"That's easy enough," he said. "If you go in with Ctesippus here and sit down and start a conversation, I think he will come
d   up to you by himself. He really likes to listen, Socrates. And besides, they're celebrating the festival of Hermes, so the younger and older boys are mingled together. Anyway, he'll probably come up to you; but if he doesn't, he and Ctesippus know one another because Ctesippus' cousin is Menexenus, and Menexenus is Lysis' closest companion. So have Ctesippus call him if he doesn't come by himself."

e   "That's what I'll have to do," I said, and, taking Ctesippus with me, I went into the wrestling-school, followed by the others. When we got inside, we found that the boys had finished the sacrifice and the ritual and, still all dressed up, were starting to play knucklebones. Most of them were playing in the courtyard outside, but some of them were over in a corner of the dressing-room playing with a great many knucklebones, which they drew from little baskets. Still others were standing around watching
207 this group, and among them was Lysis. He stood out among the boys and older youths, a garland on his head, and deserved to be called not only a beautiful boy but a well-bred young gentleman. We went over to the other side of the room, where it was quiet, sat down, and started up a conversation among ourselves.

Lysis kept turning around and looking at us, obviously wanting to come over, but too shy to do so alone. After a while Menexenus, taking a break from his game in the court, came in, and, when he saw Ctesippus and me, he came to take a seat beside us. Lysis saw him and followed over, sitting down together with Menexenus next to him, and then all the others came too. When Hippothales (let's not forget about him) saw that a small crowd had gathered, he took up a position in the rear where he thought Lysis wouldn't see him—afraid he might annoy him—and listened from his outpost.

Then I looked at Menexenus and asked him, "Son of Demophon, which of you two is older?"

"We argue about that," he said.

"Then you probably disagree about which one has the nobler family too," I said.

"Very much so," he said.

"And likewise about which one is better looking." They both laughed.

"Naturally, I won't ask which of you two is richer. For you two are friends, isn't that so?"

"Definitely," they said.

"And friends have everything in common, as the saying goes; so in this respect the two of you won't differ, that is, if what you said about being friends is true."

They agreed.

I was about to ask them next which of them was juster and wiser when somebody came in to get Menexenus, saying that the trainer was calling him. It seemed he still had some part to play in the ceremony, and so off he went. I asked Lysis then, "Am I right in assuming, Lysis, that your father and mother love you very much?"

"Oh, yes," he said.

"Then they would like you to be as happy as possible, right?"

"Naturally."

"Well, do you think a man is happy if he's a slave and is not permitted to do whatever he likes?"

"No, by Zeus, I don't think so."

"Well, then, if your father and mother love you and want you to be happy, it's clear that they must be extremely concerned to make sure that you *are* happy."

"Well, of course," he said.

"So they allow you to do as you please, and they never scold you or stop you from doing whatever you want to do."

"Not true, Socrates. There are a whole lot of things they don't let me do."

208   "What do you mean?" I said. "They want you to be happy but they stop you from doing what you want? Well, tell me this. Suppose you have your heart set on driving one of your father's chariots and holding the reins in a race. You mean they won't let you?"

"That's right," he said. "They won't let me."

"Well, whom do they let drive it?"

"There's a charioteer who gets a salary from my father."

"What? They trust a hired hand instead of you to do whatever he likes with the horses, and they actually pay him for doing that?"

b   "Well, yes."

"But I suppose they trust you to drive the mule-team, and if you wanted to take the whip and lash them, they would let you?"

"Why ever would they?" he said.

"Is anyone allowed to whip them?"

"Sure," he said, "the muleteer."

"A slave or free?"

"A slave."

"It seems, then, that your parents think more even of a slave than their own son and trust him rather than you with their property and let him do what he wants, but prevent you. But

c   tell me one more thing. Do they allow you to be in charge of your own life, or do they not trust you even that far?"

"Are you kidding?"

"Who is in charge of you, then?"

"My guardian here."

"He's a slave, isn't he?"

"What else? He's ours, anyway."

"Pretty strange, a free man directed by a slave. How does this guardian direct you; I mean, what does he do?"

"Mostly he takes me to school."

"And your schoolteachers, they're not in charge of you too, are they?"

"They sure are!"

d   "It looks like your father has decided to put quite a few masters and dictators over you. But what about when you come home to your mother, does she let you do whatever it takes to make you happy, like playing with her wool or her loom when she's weaving? She doesn't stop you from touching the blade or the comb or any of her other wool-working tools, does she?"

"Stop me?" he laughed. "She would beat me if I laid a finger on them."   e

"Good gracious!" I said. "You must have committed some kind of terrible offense against your father or mother."

"No, I swear!"

"Then why in the world do they so strangely prevent you from being happy and doing what you like? And why are they raising you in a perpetual condition of servitude to someone or other, day in and day out? Why do you hardly ever get to do what you want to do? The upshot is, it seems, that your many and varied possessions do you no good at all. Everybody but you has charge of them, and this extends to your own person, which, well-born though it is, somebody else tends and takes care of—while you, Lysis, control nothing, and get to do nothing you want to do."   209

"Well, Socrates, that's because I haven't come of age yet."

"That can't be it, son of Democrates, since there are *some* things, I imagine, that your father and mother trust you with without waiting for you to come of age. For instance, when they want someone to read or write for them, I'll bet that you, of everyone in the household, are their first choice for the job. Right?"   b

"Right."

"And nobody tells you which letter to write first and which second, and the same goes for reading. And when you take up your lyre, I'll bet neither your father nor mother stop you from tightening or loosening whatever string you wish, or from using a plectrum or just your fingers to play."

"No, they don't."

"Then what's going on? What's the reason they let you have your way here, but not in all the cases we've been talking about?"   c

"I suppose it's because I understand these things but not those."

"Aha!" I said. "So your father isn't waiting for you to come of age before he trusts you with everything; but come the day when he thinks that you know more than he does, he'll trust you with himself and everything that belongs to him."

"I guess so," he said.

"Well, then," I said, "what about your neighbor? Would he use the same rule of thumb as your father about you? When he

d   thinks you know more about managing his estate than he does, will he trust you to do it, or will he manage it himself?"

"I suppose he will trust me to do it."

"And how about the Athenians? Do you think they will trust you with their affairs when they perceive that you know enough?"

"I sure do."

"Well, by Zeus, let's not stop here," I said. "What about the Great King? Would he trust his eldest son, crown prince of Asia,

e   to add whatever he likes to the royal stew, or would he trust us, provided we went before him and gave him a convincing demonstration of our superior culinary acumen?"

"Why, us, of course."

"And he wouldn't let his son put the least little bit into the pot, but we could throw in fistfuls of salt if we wanted to."

"Right."

"What about if his son had something wrong with his eyes,

210   would he let him treat his own eyes, knowing he wasn't a doctor, or would he prevent him?"

"Prevent him."

"But, if he thought we were doctors, he wouldn't stop us even if we pried his eyes open and smeared ashes in them, because he would think we knew what we were doing."

"True."

"So . . . he would trust us, rather than himself or his son, with all his business, as long as we seemed to him more skilled than either of them."

"He would have to, Socrates," he said.

"Then this is the way it is, my dear Lysis: in those areas where we really understand something everybody—Greeks and

b   barbarians, men and women—will trust us, and there we will act just as we choose, and nobody will want to get in our way. There we will be free ourselves, and in control of others. There things will belong to us, because we will derive some advantage from them. But in areas where we haven't got any understanding, no one will trust us to act as we judge best, but everybody will do their best to stop us, and not only strangers, but also

our mother and father and anyone else even more intimate.   c
And there we are going to be subject to the orders of others;
there things are not going to be ours because we are not going
to derive any advantage from them. Do you agree this is how
it is?"

"I agree."

"Well, then, are we going to be anyone's friend, or is anyone
going to love us as a friend in those areas in which we are good
for nothing?"

"Not at all," he said.

"So it turns out that your father does not love you, nor does
anyone love anyone else, so far as that person is useless."

"It doesn't look like it."

"But if you become wise, my boy, then everybody will be your   d
friend, everybody will feel close to you, because you will be
useful and good. If you don't become wise, though, nobody will
be your friend, not even your father or mother or your close
relatives."

"Now, tell me, Lysis, is it possible to be high-minded in areas
where one hasn't yet had one's mind trained?"

"How could anyone?" he said.

"And if *you* need a teacher, *your* mind is not yet trained."

"True."

"Then you're not high-minded either—since you don't have a
mind of your own."

"You've got me there, Socrates!"

Hearing his last answer I glanced over at Hippothales and   e
almost made the mistake of saying: "This is how you should talk
with your boyfriends, Hippothales, cutting them down to size
and putting them in their place, instead of swelling them up and
spoiling them, as you do." But when I saw how anxious and
upset he was over what we were saying, I remembered how he
had positioned himself so as to escape Lysis' notice, so I bit my
tongue. In the middle of all this, Menexenus came back and sat   211
down next to Lysis, where he had been before. Then Lysis turned
to me with a good deal of boyish friendliness and, unnoticed by
Menexenus, whispered in my ear: "Socrates, tell Menexenus
what you've been saying to me."

I said to him: "Why don't you tell him yourself, Lysis? You
gave it your complete attention."

"I certainly did," he said.

b   "Then try as hard as you can to remember it, so that you can tell it all to him clearly. But if you forget any of it, ask me about it again the next time you run into me."

"I will, Socrates; you can count on it. But talk to him about something else, so I can listen too until it's time to go home."

"Well, I guess I'll have to, since it's you who ask. But you've got to come to my rescue if he tries to refute me. Or don't you know what a debater he is?"

"Sure I do—he's very much one. That's why I want you to have a discussion with him."

c   "So that I can make a fool of myself?"

"No, so you can teach him a lesson!"

"What are you talking about? He's very clever, and Ctesippus' student at that. And look, Ctesippus himself is here!"

"Never mind about anybody else, Socrates. Just go on and start discussing with him."

"Discuss we shall," I said.

Our little tête-à-tête was interrupted by Ctesippus' asking: "Is this a private party between you two, or do we get a share of the conversation?"

d   "Of course you get a share!" I said. "Lysis here doesn't quite understand something I've been saying, but he says he thinks Menexenus knows and wants me to ask him."

"Why don't you ask him then?"

"That's just what I'm going to do," I said. "So, Menexenus, tell me something. Ever since I was a boy there's a certain thing I've always wanted to possess. You know how it is, everybody is different: one person wants to own horses, another dogs,

e   another wants money, and another fame. Well, I'm pretty luke-warm about those things, but when it comes to having friends I'm absolutely passionate, and I would rather have a good friend than the best quail or gamecock known to man, and, I swear by Zeus above, more than any horse or dog. There's no doubt in my mind, by the Dog, that I would rather possess a friend than all Darius' gold, or even than Darius himself. That's how much

212   I value friends and companions. And that's why, when I see you and Lysis together, I'm really amazed; I think it's wonderful that you two have been able to acquire this possession so quickly and easily while you're still so young. Because you have in fact, each of you, gotten the other as a true friend—and quickly too. And

here I am, so far from having this possession that I don't even know how one person becomes the friend of another, which is exactly what I want to question you about, since you have experience of it.

"So tell me: when someone loves someone else, which of the two becomes the friend of the other, the one who loves or the one who is loved? Or is there no difference?"

"I don't see any difference," he said.

"Do you mean," I said, "that they both become each other's friend when only one of them loves the other?"

"It seems so to me," he said.

"Well, what about this: Isn't it possible for someone who loves somebody not to be loved by him in return?"

"Yes, it's possible."

"And isn't it possible for him even to be hated? Isn't this how men are often treated by the young boys they are in love with? They are deeply in love, but they feel that they are not loved back, or even that they are hated. Don't you think this is true?"

"Very true," he said.

"In a case like this, one person loves and the other is loved. Right?"

"Yes."

"Then which is the friend of the other? Is the lover the friend of the loved, whether he is loved in return or not, or is even hated? Or is the loved the friend of the lover? Or in a case like this, when the two do not both love each other, is neither the friend of the other?"

"That's what it looks like anyway," he said.

"So our opinion now is different from what it was before. First we thought that if one person loved another, they were both friends. But now, unless they both love each other, neither is a friend."

"Perhaps."

"So nothing is a friend of the lover unless it loves him in return."

"It doesn't look like it."

"So there are no horse-lovers unless the horses love them back, and no quail-lovers, dog-lovers, wine-lovers, or exercise-lovers. And no lovers of wisdom, unless wisdom loves them in return. But do people really love them even though these things are not their friends, making a liar of the poet who said,

> Happy the man who has as friends his children and
>   solid-hoofed horses,
> his hunting hounds and a host abroad?"*

"I don't think so," he said.

"Then you think he spoke the truth?"

"Yes."

"So what is loved is a friend to the person who loves it, or so
it seems, Menexenus, whether it loves him or hates him. Babies,
213   for example, who are too young to show love but not too young
to hate, when they are disciplined by their mother or father, are
at that moment, even though they hate their parents then, their
very dearest friends."

"It seems so to me."

"So by this line of reasoning it is not the lover who is a friend,
but the loved."

"It looks like it."

"And so the hated is the enemy, not the hater."

"Apparently so."

"Then many people are loved by their enemies and hated by
their friends, and are friends to their enemies and enemies to
b   their friends—if the object of love rather than the lover is a friend.
But this doesn't make any sense at all, my dear friend, in fact I
think it is simply impossible to be an enemy to one's friend and
a friend to one's enemy."

"True, Socrates. I think you're right."

"Then if this is impossible, that would make the lover the
friend of the loved."

"Apparently so."

"And the hater the enemy of the hated."

"That must be."

c   "Then we are going to be forced to agree to our previous
statement, that one is frequently a friend of a nonfriend, and
even of an enemy. This is the case when you love someone who
does not love you, or even hates you. And frequently one is an
enemy to a nonenemy, or even to a friend, as happens when
you hate someone who does not hate you, or even loves you."

"Perhaps," he said.

"Then what are we going to do," I said, "if friends are not

* Solon 21.2

those who love, nor those who are loved, nor those who love and are loved? Are there any others besides these of whom we can say that they become each other's friends?"

"By Zeus," he said, "I certainly can't think of any, Socrates."

"Do you think, Menexenus," I said, "that we may have been   d
going about our inquiry in entirely the wrong way?"

"I certainly think so, Socrates," said Lysis. And as he said it, he blushed. I had the impression that the words just slipped out unintentionally because he was paying such close attention to what was being said, which he clearly had been all along.

Well, I wanted to give Menexenus a break anyway, and I was pleased with the other's fondness for philosophy, so I turned the conversation towards Lysis, and said: "I think you're right,   e
Lysis, to say that if we were looking at things in the right way, we wouldn't be so far off course. Let's not go in that direction any longer. That line of inquiry looks like a rough road to me. I think we'd better go back to where we turned off, and look for guidance to the poets, the ancestral voices of human wisdom.   214
What they say about who friends are is by no means trivial: that God himself makes people friends, by drawing them together. What they say goes something like this:

God always draws the like unto the like

and makes them acquainted. Or haven't you come across these   b
lines?"

He said he had.

"And haven't you also come across writings of very wise men saying the same thing, that the like must always be friend to the like? You know, the authors who reason and write about Nature and the Universe?"

"Yes, I have," he said.

"And do you think what they say is right?" I asked.

"Maybe," he said.

"Maybe half of it," I said, "maybe even all of it, but we don't understand it. To our way of thinking, the closer a wicked man comes to a wicked man and the more he associates with him,   c
the more he becomes his enemy. Because he does him an injustice. And it's impossible for those who do an injustice and those who suffer it to be friends. Isn't that so?"

"Yes," he said.

"Then that would make half the saying untrue, if we assume the wicked are like each other."

"You're right," he said.

"But what I think they're saying is that the good are like each other and are friends, while the bad—as another saying goes— are never alike, not even to themselves. They are out of kilter and unstable. And when something is not even like itself and is inconsistent with itself, it can hardly be like something else and be a friend to it. Don't you agree?"

"Oh, I do," he said.

"Well, my friend, it seems to me that the hidden meaning of those who say 'like is a friend to like' is that only the good is a friend, and only to the good, while the bad never enters into true friendship with either the good or the bad. Do you agree?"

He nodded yes.

"So now we've got it. We know what friends are. Our discussion indicates to us that whoever are good are friends."

"That seems altogether true to me."

"To me also," I said. "But I'm still a little uneasy with it. By Zeus, let's see why I'm still suspicious. Is like friend to like insofar as he is like, and as such is he useful to his counterpart? I can put it better this way: When something, anything at all, is like something else, how can it benefit or harm its like in a way that it could not benefit or harm itself? Or what could be done to it by its like that could not be done to it by itself? Can such things be prized by each other when they cannot give each other assistance? Is there any way?"

"No, there isn't."

"And how can anything be a friend if it is not prized?"

"It can't."

"All right, then, like is not friend to like. But couldn't the good still be friend to the good insofar as he is good, not insofar as he is like?"

"Maybe."

"What about this, though? Isn't a good person, insofar as he is good, sufficient to himself?"

"Yes."

"And a self-sufficient person has no need of anything, just because of his self-sufficiency?"

"How could he?"

"And the person who needs nothing wouldn't prize anything."

"No, he wouldn't."

"What he didn't prize he wouldn't love."

"Definitely not."

"And whoever doesn't love is not a friend."

"It appears not."

"Then how in the world are the good going to be friends to
the good? They don't yearn for one another when apart, because
even then they are sufficient to themselves, and when together
they have no need of one another. Is there any way people like
that can possibly value each other?"

"No."

"But people who don't place much value on each other
couldn't be friends."

"True."

"Now, Lysis, consider how we have been knocked off course.   c
Are we somehow completely mistaken here?"

"How?" he asked.

"Once I heard someone say—I just now remembered this—
that like is most hostile to like, and good men to good men. And
he cited Hesiod as evidence:

> Potter is angry with potter, poet with poet
> And beggar with beggar.*

And he said that it had to be the same with everything else: d
things that are most like are filled with envy, contentiousness,
and hatred for each other, and things most unlike with friendship. The poor man is forced to be friends with the rich, and the
weak with the strong—for the sake of assistance—and the sick
man with the doctor, and in general every ignorant person has
to prize the man who knows and love him. Then he went on to
make a very impressive point indeed, saying that the like is
totally unqualified to be friend to the like; that just the opposite   e
is true; that things that are completely in opposition to each other
are friends in the highest degree, since everything desires its
opposite and not its like. Dry desires wet, cold hot, bitter sweet,
sharp blunt, empty full, full empty, and so forth on the same

* Hesiod, *Works and Days*, 11. 25–26.

principle. For the opposite, he said, is food for its opposite, whereas the like has no enjoyment of its like. Well, my friend, I thought he was quite clever as he said this, for he put it all so well. But you two, what do you think of what he said?"

"It sounds fine," said Menexenus, "at least when you hear it put like that."

"Then should we say that the opposite is its opposite's best friend?"

"Absolutely."

"But Menexenus," I said, "this is absurd. In no time at all those virtuosos, the contradiction mongers, are going to jump on us gleefully and ask us whether enmity is not the thing most opposite to friendship. How are we going to answer them? Won't we have to admit that what they say is true?"

"Yes, we will."

"So then, they will continue, is the enemy a friend to the friend, or the friend a friend to the enemy?"

"Neither," he answered.

"Is the just a friend to the unjust, or the temperate to the licentious, or the good to the bad?"

"I don't think so."

"But if," I said, "something is a friend to something because it is its opposite, then these things must be friends."

"You're right, they must."

"So like is not friend to like, nor is opposite friend to opposite."

"Apparently not."

"But there's this too we still ought to consider. We may have overlooked something else, the possibility that the friend is none of these things, but something that is neither bad nor good but becomes the friend of the good just for that reason."

"What do you mean?" he asked.

"By Zeus," I said, "I hardly know myself. I'm getting downright dizzy with the perplexities of our argument. Maybe the old proverb is right, and the beautiful is a friend. It bears a resemblance, at any rate, to something soft and smooth and sleek, and maybe that's why it slides and sinks into us so easily, because it's something like that. Now I maintain that the good is beautiful. What do you think?"

"I agree."

"All right, now, I'm going to wax prophetic and say that what

is neither good nor bad is a friend of the beautiful and the good.
Listen to the motive for my mantic utterance. It seems to me that
there are three kinds of things: the good, the bad, and the neither
good nor bad. What about you?"

"It seems so to me too," he said.

"And the good is not a friend to the good, nor the bad to the   e
bad, nor the good to the bad. Our previous argument disallows
it. Only one possibility remains. If anything is a friend to anything, what is neither good nor bad is a friend either to the good
or to something like itself. For I don't suppose anything could
be a friend to the bad."

"True."

"But we just said that like is not friend to like."

"Yes."

"So what is neither good nor bad cannot be a friend to something like itself."

"Apparently not."

"So it turns out that only what is neither good nor bad is friend
to the good, and only to the good."   217

"It seems it must be so."

"Well, then, boys, are we on the right track with our present
statement? Suppose we consider a healthy body. It has no need
of a doctor's help. It's fine just as it is. So no one in good health
is friend to a doctor, on account of his good health. Right?"

"Right."

"But a sick man is, I imagine, on account of his disease."

"Naturally."

"Now, disease is a bad thing, and medicine is beneficial and
good."

"Yes."

"And the body, as body, is neither good nor bad."

"True."   b

"And because of disease, a body is forced to welcome and love
medicine."

"I think so."

"So what is neither good nor bad becomes a friend of the good
because of the presence of something bad."

"It looks like it."

"But clearly this is before it becomes bad itself by the bad it is
in contact with. Because once it has become bad, it can no longer

desire the good or be its friend. Remember we said it was impos-
c   sible for the bad to befriend the good."

"It *is* impossible."

"Now consider what I'm going to say. I say that some things
are of the same sort as what is present with them, and some are
not. For example, if you paint something a certain color, the
paint is somehow present with the thing painted."

"Definitely."

"Then is the thing painted of the same sort, as far as color
goes, as the applied paint?"

"I don't understand," he said.

d   "Look at it this way, " I said. "If someone smeared your blond
hair with white lead, would your hair then *be* white or *appear*
white?"

"Appear white," he said.

"And yet whiteness would surely be present with it."

"Yes."

"But all the same your hair would not yet be white. Though
whiteness would be present, your hair would not be white any
more than it is black."

"True."

"But when, my friend, old age introduces this same color to
e   your hair, then it will become of the same sort as what is present,
white by the presence of white."

"Naturally."

"Here at last is my question, then. When a thing has something
present with it, will it be of the same sort as what is present? Or
only when that thing is present in a certain way?"

"Only then," he said.

"And what is neither good nor bad sometimes has not yet
become bad by the presence with it of bad, but sometimes it
has."

"Certainly."

"And when it is not yet bad although bad is present, that
presence makes it desire the good. But the presence that makes
it be bad deprives it of its desire as well as its love for the good.
218   For it is no longer neither good nor bad, but bad. And the bad
can't be friend to the good."

"No, it can't."

"From this we may infer that those who are already wise no

longer love wisdom, whether they are gods or men.* Nor do
those love it who are so ignorant that they are bad, for no bad
and stupid man loves wisdom. There remain only those who
have this bad thing, ignorance, but have not yet been made
ignorant and stupid by it. They are conscious of not knowing
what they don't know. The upshot is that those who are as yet   b
neither good nor bad love wisdom, while all those who are bad
do not, and neither do those who are good. For our earlier
discussion made it clear that the opposite is not friend to the
opposite, nor is like friend to like. Remember?"

"Of course," they both answered.

"So now, Lysis and Menexenus, we have discovered for sure
what is a friend and what is not. For we maintain that in the soul
and in the body and everywhere, that which is neither good nor   c
bad itself is, by the presence of evil, a friend of the good."

The two of them heartily agreed that this was the case, and I
was pretty happy myself. I had the satisfied feeling of a successful
hunter and was basking in it, when a very strange suspicion,
from where I don't know, came over me. Maybe what we had
all agreed to wasn't true after all. What an awful thought. "Oh,
no!" I screamed out. "Lysis and Menexenus, our wealth has all
been a dream!"

"But why?" said Menexenus.   d

"I'm afraid we've fallen in with arguments about friendship
that are no better than con artists."

"How?" he asked.

"Let's look at it this way," I said. "Whoever is a friend, is he
a friend to someone or not?"

"He has to be a friend to someone," he said.

"For the sake of nothing and on account of nothing, or for the
sake of something and on account of something?"

"For the sake of something and on account of something."

"And that something for the sake of which he is a friend, is it
a friend, or is it neither friend nor foe?"

"I don't get it," he said.

---

* "Love wisdom" translates the Greek verb *philosophein*, a compound formed
from the bases *phil-*, "love", and *soph-*, "wise". This verb could also be translated
as "philosophize", but to do so would obscure the connection between love of
wisdom and the other kinds of love and friendship in the dialogue.

e   "Naturally enough," I said. "But perhaps you will if we try it this way—and I think I might better understand what I am saying myself. A sick man, we were just now saying, is a friend to the doctor. Right?"

"Yes."

"And isn't he a friend on account of disease and for the sake of health?"

"Yes."

"And disease is a bad thing?"

"Of course."

"And what about health?" I asked. "Is it a good thing or a bad thing or neither?"

"A good thing," he said.

219   "I believe we also said that the body, which is neither good nor bad, is a friend of medicine on account of disease, that is, on account of something bad. And medicine is a good thing. It is for the sake of health that medicine has received the friendship. And health is a good thing. All right so far?"

"Yes."

"Is health a friend or not a friend?"

"A friend."

"And disease is an enemy?"

"Certainly."

b   "So what is neither good nor bad is friend of the good on account of what is bad and an enemy, for the sake of what is good and a friend."

"It appears so."

"So the friend is friend of its friend for the sake of a friend, on account of its enemy."

"It looks like it."

"Well, then," I said, "since we have come this far, boys, let's pay close attention so that we won't be deceived. The fact that the friend has become friend of the friend, and so like has become friend of like, which we said was impossible—I'm going to let that pass by. But there is another point that we must examine, so that what is now being said won't deceive us. Medicine, we

c   say, is a friend for the sake of health."

"Yes."

"Health, then, is also a friend?"

"Very much a friend."

"If, therefore, it is a friend, it is for the sake of something."

"Yes."

"And that something is a friend, if it is going to accord with our previous agreement."

"Very much so."

"Will that too, then, also be a friend for the sake of a friend?"

"Yes."

"Aren't we going to have to give up going on like this? Don't we have to arrive at some first principle which will no longer bring us back to another friend, something that goes back to the first friend, something for the sake of which we say that all the rest are friends too?"

d

"We have to."

"This is what I am talking about, the possibility that all the other things that we have called friends for the sake of that thing may be deceiving us, like so many phantoms of it, and that it is that first thing which is truly a friend. Let's think of it in this way. Suppose a man places great value on something, say, a father who values his son more highly than all his other possessions. Would such a man, for the sake of his supreme regard for his son, also value something else? If, for example, he learned that his son had drunk hemlock, would he value wine if he thought it could save his son?"

e

"Why, certainly," he said.

"And also the container the wine was in?"

"Very much."

"At that time would he place the same value on the ceramic cup or the three pints of wine as on his son? Or is it the case that all such concern is expended not for things that are provided for the sake of something else, but for that something else for whose sake all the other things are provided? Not that we don't often talk about how much we value gold and silver. But that's not so and gets us no closer to the truth, which is that we value above all else that for which gold and all other provisions are provided, whatever it may turn out to be. Shall we put it like that?"

220

"Most certainly."

"And isn't the same account true of the friend? When we talk about all the things that are our friends for the sake of another friend, it is clear that we are merely using the word 'friend'. The real friend is surely that in which all these so-called friendships terminate."

b

"Yes, surely," he said.

"Then the real friend is not a friend for the sake of a friend."

"True."

"So much, then, for the notion that it is for the sake of some friend that the friend is a friend. But then is the good a friend?"

"It seems so to me," he said.

c   "And it is on account of the bad that the good is loved. Look, this is how it stands. There are three things of which we have just been speaking—good, bad, and what is neither good nor bad. Suppose there remained only two, and bad were eliminated and could affect no one in body or soul or anything else that we say is neither good nor bad in and of itself. Would the good then be of any use to us, or would it have become useless? For if nothing could still harm us, we would have no need of any

d   assistance, and it would be perfectly clear to us that it was on account of the bad that we prized and loved the good—as if the good is a drug against the bad, and the bad is a disease, so that without the disease there is no need for the drug. Isn't the good by nature loved on account of the bad by those of us who are midway between good and bad, but by itself and for its own sake it has no use at all?"

"It looks like that's how it is," he said.

e   "Then that friend of ours, the one which was the terminal point for all the other things that we called 'friends for the sake of another friend,' does not resemble them at all. For they are called friends for the sake of a friend, but the real friend appears to have a nature completely the opposite of this. It has become clear to us that it was a friend for the sake of an enemy. Take away the enemy and it seems it is no longer a friend."

"It seems it isn't," he said, "not, at least, by what we are saying now."

"By Zeus," I said, "I wonder, if the bad is eliminated, whether

221   it will be possible to be hungry or thirsty or anything like that. Or if there will be hunger as long as human beings and other animals exist, but it won't do harm. Thirst, too, and all the other desires, but they won't be bad, because the bad will have been abolished. Or is it ridiculous to ask what will be then and what will not? Who knows? But we do know this: that it is possible for hunger to do harm, and also possible for it to help. Right?"

"Certainly."

"And isn't it true that thirst or any other such desires can be

felt sometimes to one's benefit, sometimes to one's harm, and   b
sometimes to neither?"

"Absolutely."

"And if bad things are abolished, does this have anything to
do with things that aren't bad being abolished along with them?"

"No."

"So the desires that are neither good nor bad will continue to
exist, even if bad things are abolished."

"It appears so."

"And is it possible to desire and love something passionately
without feeling friendly towards it?

"It doesn't seem so to me."

"So there will still be some friendly things even if the bad is
abolished."

"Yes."

"It is impossible, if bad were the cause of something's being a   c
friend, that with the bad abolished one thing could be another's
friend. When a cause is abolished, the thing that it was the cause
of can no longer exist."

"That makes sense."

"Haven't we agreed that the friend loves something, and loves
it on account of something, and didn't we think then that it was
on account of bad that what was neither good nor bad loved the
good?"

"True."

"But now it looks like some other cause of loving and being   d
loved has appeared."

"It does look like it."

"Then can it really be, as we were just saying, that desire is
the cause of friendship, and that what desires is a friend to that
which it desires, and is so whenever it does so? And that what
we were saying earlier about being a friend was all just chatter,
like a poem that trails on too long?"

"There's a good chance," he said.

"But still," I said, "a thing desires what it is deficient in. Right?"   e
"Yes."

"And the deficient is a friend to that in which it is deficient."

"I think so."

"And it becomes deficient where something is taken away
from it."

"How couldn't it?"

"Then it is what belongs to oneself, it seems, that passionate love and friendship and desire are directed towards, Menexenus and Lysis."

They both agreed.

"And if you two are friends with each other, then in some way you naturally belong to each other."

"Absolutely," they said together.

222   "And if one person desires another, my boys, or loves him passionately, he would not desire him or love him passionately or as a friend unless he somehow belonged to his beloved either in his soul or in some characteristic, habit, or aspect of his soul."

"Certainly," said Menexenus, but Lysis was silent.

"All right," I said, "what belongs to us by nature has shown itself to us as something we must love."

"It looks like it," he said.

"Then the genuine and not the pretended lover must be be-
b   friended by his boy."

Lysis and Menexenus just managed a nod of assent, but Hippothales beamed every color in the rainbow in his delight.

Wanting to review the argument, I said, "It seems to me, Lysis and Menexenus, that if there is some difference between belonging and being like, then we might have something to say about what a friend is. But if belonging and being like turn out to be the same thing, it won't be easy to toss out our former argument that like is useless to like insofar as they are alike. And
c   to admit that the useless is a friend would strike a sour note. So if it's all right with you, I said, since we are a little groggy from this discussion, why don't we agree to say that what belongs is something different from what is like?"

"Certainly."

"And shall we suppose that the good belongs to everyone, while the bad is alien? Or does the bad belong to the bad, the good to the good, and what is neither good nor bad to what is neither good nor bad?"

They both said they liked this latter correlation.

d   "Well, here we are again, boys," I said. "We have fallen into the same arguments about friendship that we rejected at first. For the unjust will be no less a friend to the unjust, and the bad to the bad, as the good will be to the good."

"So it seems," he said.

"Then what? If we say that the good is the same as belonging, is there any alternative to the good being a friend only to the good?"

"No."

"But we thought we had refuted ourselves on this point. Or don't you remember?"

"We remember."

"So what can we still do with our argument? Or is it clear that there is nothing left? I do ask, like the able speakers in the law courts, that you think over everything that has been said. If neither the loved nor the loving, nor the like nor the unlike, nor the good, nor the belonging, nor any of the others we have gone through—well, there have been so many I certainly don't remember them all any more, but if none of these is a friend, then I have nothing left to say."

Having said that, I had a mind to get something going with one of the older men there. But just then, like some kind of divine intermediaries, the guardians of Menexenus and Lysis were on the scene. They had the boys' brothers with them and called out to them that it was time to go home. It actually was late by now. At first our group tried to drive them off, but they didn't pay any attention to us and just got riled up and went on calling in their foreign accents. We thought they had been drinking too much at the Hermaea and might be difficult to handle, so we capitulated and broke up our party. But just as they were leaving I said, "Now we've done it, Lysis and Menexenus— made fools of ourselves, I, an old man, and you as well. These people here will go away saying that we are friends of one another—for I count myself in with you—but what a friend is we have not yet been able to find out."

Aristotle

NICOMACHEAN ETHICS

Introduction

Aristotle's treatment of friendship, like his treatments of so many other subjects, constituted a great advance over anything produced by his predecessors and was to serve as a kind of reference point for future work on the subject. Much of the subsequent work on friendship in the Western tradition can be understood either as building upon and supplementing Aristotle's views or as reacting against them.

Aristotle's indebtedness to the *Lysis* is obvious: there are numerous parallels and correspondences.[1] Yet he goes far beyond the tentative proposals of Plato: Aristotle's treatise on friendship is comprehensive and confident, as well as undeniably profound.

The treatise, which constitutes about one-fifth of the *Ethics*, divides roughly into three sections. Aristotle first distinguishes and contrasts three species of friendship (VIII.2–5). His focus here is on friendships voluntarily entered into, what might be called 'companionships'. But the Greek word for friendship, *philia*, has a very wide extension, and Aristotle in the next major section of the treatise discusses the relationship between friendship and justice in the family and in society (VIII.9–12).

The last and longest part of the treatise is a discussion of a

---

1. For example: *Ethics* 1159b31 with *Lysis* 207c10; 1168b35–36 with 210b3; 1155b29–30 with 212d7; 1159a27–33 with 213a1–3; 1155a34 with 214a6; 1155b6–8 with 214b2–3; 1159b9 and 1166b7 with 214c7–d1; 1155a35 with 215c9; and 1159b19–23 with 215e1–7.

series of disputed questions on friendship (VIII.13–IX.12). Of greatest importance here is the section from IX.4 to 9, in which Aristotle examines the relationship between friendship and self-love. Aristotle's central claim is that "a friend is another self," which he explains by the analogy: as a good person is related to himself, so he is related to his friend (11bba30–32). In IX.4 and 8 Aristotle redescribes moral goodness (his topic in the preceding books of the *Ethics*) as self-love, whereas vice becomes a kind of self-hatred. In IX.8 Aristotle maintains that no one loves another more than himself. His argument seems to be that this would be impossible, because the good that is gained in giving to another is necessarily greater than the good that is received. Chapter 9 of book IX contains a series of arguments, of increasing difficulty, for the thesis that friends are necessary for happiness.

These chapters tend to raise for the modern reader the question of whether there is not, in the end, something objectionably egoistic about Aristotle's account of friendship. How can we love a friend because he is necessary for our happiness, and also love that friend *for his own sake*? And, if friendship is an extension of self-love, then isn't it *really* self-love, and what appears to be love for another is in fact love for oneself?

That these difficulties were not, it seems, troublesome to Aristotle in turn raises an additional set of questions. Is our sense that there should be something more, some sort of 'altruism' in friendship, a coherent one? What is friendship actually like? (Is Aristotle's account true to life, even if in some sense troublesome?) If Aristotle is understood as having the view, not that friendship is an extension of self-love, but rather that self-love is inherently and by nature social, then does the view remain objectionable?

Aristotle

NICOMACHEAN ETHICS
BOOKS VIII AND IX

viii 1
1155a
5

After that the next topic to discuss is friendship; for it is a virtue, or involves virtue, and besides is most necessary for our life.

For no one would choose to live without friends even if he had all the other goods. For in fact rich people and holders of powerful positions, even more than other people, seem to need friends. For how would one benefit from such prosperity if one had no opportunity for beneficence, which is most often displayed, and most highly praised, in relation to friends? And how would one guard and protect prosperity without friends, when it is all the more precarious the greater it is? In poverty also, and in the other misfortunes, people think friends are the only refuge.

Moreover, the young need it to keep them from error. The old need it to care for them and support the actions that fail because of weakness. And those in their prime need it, to do fine actions; for 'when two go together . . .', they are more capable of understanding and acting.

Further, a parent would seem to have a natural friendship for a child, and a child for a parent, not only among human beings but also among birds and most kinds of animals. Members of the same race, and human beings most of all, have a natural friendship for each other; that is why we praise friends of humanity. And in our travels we can see how every human being is akin and beloved to a human being.

Moreover, friendship would seem to hold cities together, and legislators would seem to be more concerned about it than about justice. For concord would seem to be similar to friendship and they aim at concord above all, while they try above all to expel civil conflict, which is enmity.

Further, if people are friends, they have no need of justice,

10

15

20

25

Excerpts from Aristotle: *Nicomachean Ethics*, translated by Terence Irwin, copyright © 1985 by Terence Irwin, reprinted by permission of Hackett Publishing Company, Inc.

but if they are just they need friendship in addition; and the justice that is most just seems to belong to friendship.

However, friendship is not only necessary, but also fine. For we praise lovers of friends, and having many friends seems to   30
be a fine thing. Moreover, people think that the same people are good and also friends.

Still, there are quite a few disputed points about friendship.

For some hold it is a sort of similarity and that similar people are friends. Hence the saying 'Similar to similar', and 'Birds of a feather', and so on. On the other hand it is said that similar   35
people are all like the proverbial potters, quarrelling with each other.

On these questions some people inquire at a higher level, more   1155b
proper to natural science. Euripides says that when earth gets dry it longs passionately for rain, and the holy heaven when filled with rain longs passionately to fall into the earth; and Heracleitus says that the opponent cooperates, the finest har-   5
mony arises from discordant elements, and all things come to be in struggle. Others, e.g. Empedocles, oppose this view, and say that similar aims for similar.

Let us, then, leave aside the puzzles proper to natural science, since they are not proper to the present examination; and let us examine the puzzles that concern human [nature], and bear on characters and feelings.   10

For instance, does friendship arise among all sorts of people, or can people not be friends if they are vicious?

Is there one species of friendship, or are there more? Some people think there is only one species because friendship allows more and less. But here their confidence rests on an inadequate sign; for things of different species also allow more and less.   15

Perhaps these questions will become clear once we find out   viii 2
what it is that is lovable. For, it seems, not everything is loved, but [only] what is lovable, and this is either good or pleasant or useful. However, it seems that what is useful is the source of some good or some pleasure; hence what is good and what is   20
pleasant are lovable as ends.

Do people love what is good, or what is good for them? For sometimes these conflict; and the same is true of what is pleasant. Each one, it seems, loves what is good for him; and while what is good is lovable unconditionally, what is lovable for each one is what is good for him. In fact each one loves not what *is* good   25 for him, but what *appears* good for him; but this will not matter, since [what appears good for him] will be what appears lovable.

Hence there are these three causes of love.

Love for a soulless thing is not called friendship, since there is no mutual loving, and you do not wish good to it. For it would presumably be ridiculous to wish good things to wine; the most

30   you wish is its preservation so that you can have it. To a friend, however, it is said, you must wish goods for his own sake.

If you wish good things in this way, but the same wish is not returned by the other, you would be said to have [only] goodwill for the other. For friendship is said to be *reciprocated* goodwill.

But perhaps we should add that friends are aware of the recip-

35   rocated goodwill. For many a one has goodwill to people whom

1156a he has not seen but supposes to be decent or useful, and one of these might have the same goodwill towards him. These people, then, apparently have goodwill to each other, but how could we call them friends when they are unaware of their attitude to each other?

Hence, [to be friends] they must have goodwill to each other,

5   wish goods and be aware of it, from one of the causes mentioned above.

viii 3   Now since these causes differ in species, so do the types of loving and types of friendship. Hence friendship has three species, corresponding to the three objects of love. For each object of love has a corresponding type of mutual loving, combined with awareness of it, and those who love each other wish goods

10   to each other in so far as they love each other.

Those who love each other for utility love the other not in himself, but in so far as they gain some good for themselves from him. The same is true of those who love for pleasure; for they like a witty person not because of his character, but because he is pleasant to themselves.

And so those who love for utility or pleasure are fond of a

15   friend because of what is good or pleasant for themselves, not in so far as the beloved is who he is, but in so far as he is useful or pleasant.

Hence these friendships as well [as the friends] are coincidental, since the beloved is loved not in so far as he is who he is, but in so far as he provides some good or pleasure.

And so these sorts of friendships are easily dissolved, when the

friends do not remain similar [to what they were]; for if someone   20
is no longer pleasant or useful, the other stops loving him.

What is useful does not remain the same, but is different at
different times. Hence, when the cause of their being friends is
removed, the friendship is dissolved too, on the assumption
that the friendship aims at these [useful results]. This sort of
friendship seems to arise especially among older people, since
at that age they pursue what is advantageous, not what is pleas-   25
ant, and also among those in their prime or youth who pursue
what is expedient.

Nor do such people live together very much. For sometimes
they do not even find each other pleasant. Hence they have no
further need to meet in this way if they are not advantageous [to
each other]; for each finds the other pleasant [only] to the extent
that he expects some good from him. The friendship of hosts   30
and guests is taken to be of this type too.

The cause of friendship between young people seems to be
pleasure. For their lives are guided by their feelings, and they
pursue above all what is pleasant for themselves and what is
near at hand. But as they grow up [what they find] pleasant
changes too. Hence they are quick to become friends, and quick   35
to stop; for their friendship shifts with [what they find] pleasant,
and the change in such pleasure is quick. Young people are   1156b
prone to erotic passion, since this mostly follows feelings, and
is caused by pleasure; that is why they love and quickly stop,
often changing in a single day.

These people wish to spend their days together and to live
together; for this is how they gain [the good things] correspond-   5
ing to their friendship.

But complete friendship is the friendship of good people similar in virtue; for they wish goods in the same way to each other
in so far as they are good, and they are good in themselves.
[Hence they wish goods to each other for each other's own sake.]
Now those who wish goods to their friend for the friend's own   10
sake are friends most of all; for they have this attitude because
of the friend himself, not coincidentally. Hence these people's
friendship lasts as long as they are good; and virtue is enduring.

Each of them is both good unconditionally and good for his
friend, since good people are both unconditionally good and
advantageous for each other. They are pleasant in the same ways

15   too, since good people are pleasant both unconditionally and for
       each other. [They are pleasant for each other] because each per-
       son finds his own actions and actions of that kind pleasant, and
       the actions of good people are the same or similar.

       It is reasonable that this sort of friendship is enduring, since
       it embraces in itself all the features that friends must have. For
20   the cause of every friendship is good or pleasure, either uncondi-
       tional or for the lover; and every friendship reflects some similar-
       ity. And all the features we have mentioned are found in this
       friendship because of [the nature of] the friends themselves. For
       they are similar in this way [i.e. in being good]. Moreover, their
       friendship also has the other things—what is unconditionally
       good and what is unconditionally pleasant; and these are lovable
       most of all. Hence loving and friendship are found most of all
       and at their best in these friends.

25   These kinds of friendships are likely to be rare, since such
       people are few. Moreover, they need time to grow accustomed
       to each other; for, as the proverb says, they cannot know each
       other before they have shared the traditional [peck of] salt, and
       they cannot accept each other or be friends until each appears
       lovable to the other and gains the other's confidence. Those who
30   are quick to treat each other in friendly ways wish to be friends,
       but are not friends, unless they are also lovable, and know this.
       For though the wish for friendship comes quickly, friendship
       does not.

viii 4   This sort of friendship, then, is complete both in time and in
       the other ways. In every way each friend gets the same things
35   and similar things from each, and this is what must be true of
1157a friends. Friendship for pleasure bears some resemblance to this
       complete sort, since good people are also pleasant to each other.
       And friendship for utility also resembles it, since good people
       are also useful to each other.

       With these [incomplete friends] also, the friendships are most
       enduring when they get the same thing—e.g. pleasure—from
5   each other, and, moreover, get it from the same source, as witty
       people do. They must not be like the erotic lover and the boy he
       loves. For these do not take pleasure in the same things; the
       lover takes pleasure in seeing his beloved, while the beloved
       takes pleasure in being courted by his lover. When the beloved's
       bloom is fading, sometimes the friendship fades too; for the lover

no longer finds pleasure in seeing his beloved, while the beloved
is no longer courted by the lover.   10

Many, however, remain friends if they have similar characters
and come to be fond of each other's characters from being accustomed to them. Those who exchange utility rather than pleasure
in their erotic relations are friends to a lesser extent and less
enduring friends.

Those who are friends for utility dissolve the friendship as
soon as the advantage is removed; for they were never friends   15
of each other, but of what was expedient for them.

Now it is possible for bad people as well [as good] to be friends
to each other for pleasure or utility, for decent people to be
friends to base people, and for someone with neither character
to be a friend to someone with any character. Clearly, however,
only good people can be friends to each other because of the
other person himself; for bad people find no enjoyment in one
another if they get no benefit.   20

Moreover, it is only the friendship of good people that is
immune to slander. For it is hard to trust anyone speaking against
someone whom we ourselves have found reliable for a long time;
and among good people there is trust, the belief that he would
never do injustice [to a friend], and all the other things expected
in a true friendship. But in the other types of friendship [distrust]
may easily arise.   25

[These must be counted as types of friendship.] For people
include among friends [not only the best type, but] also those
who are friends for utility, as cities are—since alliances between
cities seem to aim at expediency—and those who are fond of
each other, as children are, for pleasure. Hence we must presumably also say that such people are friends, but say that there are
more species of friendship than one.   30

On this view, the friendship of good people in so far as they are
good is friendship in the primary way, and to the full extent; and
the others are friendships by similarity. They are friends in so far
as there is something good, and [hence] something similar to
[what one finds in the best kind]; for what is pleasant is good to
lovers of pleasure. But these [incomplete] types of friendship are
not very regularly combined, and the same people do not become
friends for both utility and pleasure. For things that [merely] coin-   35
cide with each other are not very regularly combined.

1157b   Friendship has been assigned, then, to these species. Base
people will be friends for pleasure or utility, since they are similar
in that way. But good people will be friends because of themselves, since they are friends in so far as they are good. These,
5   then, are friends unconditionally; the others are friends coincidentally and by being similar to these.

viii 5   Just as with the virtues some people are called good in their
state of character, others good in their activity, the same is true
of friendship. For some people find enjoyment in each other by
living together, and provide each other with good things. Others,
however, are asleep or separated by distance, and so are not
10   active in these ways, but are in the state that would result in the
friendly activities; for distance does not dissolve the friendship
unconditionally, but only its activity. But if the absence is long,
it also seems to cause the friendship to be forgotten; hence the
saying, 'Lack of conversation has dissolved many a friendship'.

Older people and sour people do not appear to be prone to
15   friendship. For there is little pleasure to be found in them, and
no one can spend his days with what is painful or not pleasant,
since nature appears to avoid above all what is painful and to
aim at what is pleasant.

Those who welcome each other but do not live together would
20   seem to have goodwill rather than friendship. For nothing is as
proper to friends as living together; for while those who are
in want desire benefit, blessedly happy people [who want for
nothing], no less than the others, desire to spend their days
together, since a solitary life fits them least of all. But people
cannot spend their time with each other if they are not pleasant
and do not enjoy the same things, as they seem to in the friendship of companions.

25   It is the friendship of good people that is friendship most of
all, as we have often said. For what is lovable and choiceworthy
seems to be what is unconditionally good or pleasant, and what
is lovable and choiceworthy for each person seems to be what is
good or pleasant for him; and both of these make one good
person lovable and choiceworthy for another good person.

Loving would seem to be a feeling, but friendship a state. For
30   loving occurs no less towards soulless things, but reciprocal
loving requires decision, and decision comes from a state; and
what makes [good people] wish good to the beloved for his own
sake is their state, not their feeling.

Moreover, in loving their friend they love what is good for themselves; for when a good person becomes a friend he becomes a good for his friend. Each of them loves what is good for himself, and repays in equal measure the wish and the pleasantness of his friend; for friendship is said to be equality. And this is true above all in the friendship of good people.

Among sour people and older people friendship is found less often, since they are worse tempered and enjoy meeting people less, [and so lack] what seems to be most typical and most productive of friendship. That is why young people become friends quickly, but older people do not, since they do not become friends with people in whom they find no enjoyment— nor do sour people. These people have goodwill to each other, since they wish goods and give help in time of need; but they scarcely count as friends, since they do not spend their days together or find enjoyment in each other, and these things seem to be above all typical of friendship.

No one can have complete friendship for many people, just as no one can have an erotic passion for many at the same time; for [complete friendship, like erotic passion,] is like an excess, and an excess is naturally directed at a single individual. Moreover, just as it is hard for the same person to please many people intensely at the same time, it is also hard, presumably, to be good towards many people at the same time.

Besides, he must gain experience of the other too, and become accustomed to him, which is very difficult.

It is possible, however, to please many people when the friendship is for utility or pleasure, since many people can be pleased in these ways, and the services take little time.

Of these other two types of friendship the friendship for pleasure is more like [real] friendship; for they get the same thing from each other, and they find enjoyment in each other or in the same things. This is what friendships are like among young people; for a generous [attitude] is found here more [than among older people], whereas it is mercenary people who form friendships for utility.

Moreover, blessedly happy people have no need of anything useful, but do need sources of pleasure. For they want to spend their lives with companions, and though what is painful is borne for a short time, no one could continuously endure even The Good Itself if it were painful to him; hence they seek friends who

35

1158a

viii 6

5

10

15

20

are pleasant. But, presumably, they must also seek friends who are good as well [as pleasant], and good for them too; for then they will have everything that friends must have.

Someone in a position of power appears to have separate groups of friends; for some are useful to him, others pleasant, but the same ones are not often both. For he does not seek friends who are both pleasant and virtuous, or useful for fine actions, but seeks one group to be witty, when he pursues pleasure, and the other group to be clever in carrying out instructions; and the same person rarely has both features.

Though admittedly, as we have said, an excellent person is both pleasant and useful, he does not become a friend to a superior [in power and position] unless the superior is also superior in virtue; otherwise he does not reach [proportionate] equality by having a proportionate superior. And this superiority both in power and in virtue is not often found.

The friendships we have mentioned involve equality, since both friends get the same and wish the same to each other, or exchange one thing for another, e.g. pleasure for benefit. But, as we have said, they are friendships to a lesser extent, and less enduring. Because they are both similar and dissimilar to the same thing they seem both to be and not to be friendships. For in so far as they are similar to the friendship of virtue, they appear to be friendships; for that type of friendship includes both utility and pleasure, and one of these types includes utility, the other pleasure. On the other hand, since the friendship of virtue is enduring and immune to slander, while these change quickly and differ from it in many other ways as well, they do not appear to be friendships, in so far as they are dissimilar to that [best] type.

A different species of friendship is the one that corresponds to superiority, e.g. of a father towards his son, and in general of an older person towards a younger, of a man towards a woman, and of any sort of ruler towards the one he rules.

These friendships also differ from each other. For friendship of parents to children is not the same as that of rulers to ruled; nor is friendship of father to son the same as that of son to father, or of man to woman as that of woman to man.

For each of these friends has a different virtue and a different function, and there are different causes of love. Hence the ways of loving are different, and so are the friendships. Each does not

get the same thing from the other, then, and must not seek it; but   20
whenever children accord to their parents what they must accord
to those who gave them birth, and parents accord what they must
to their children, their friendship is enduring and decent.

In all the friendships corresponding to superiority, the loving
must also be proportional, e.g. the better person, and the more   25
beneficial, and each of the others likewise, must be loved more
than he loves; for when the loving reflects the comparative worth
of the friends, equality is achieved in a way, and this seems to
be proper to friendship.

Equality, however, does not appear to be the same in friend-   30
ship as in justice. For in justice equality is equality primarily in
worth and secondarily in quantity; but in friendship it is equality
primarily in quantity and secondarily in worth.

This is clear if friends come to be separated by some wide gap
in virtue, vice, wealth, or something else; for then they are
friends no more, and do not even expect to be. This is most   35
evident with gods, since they have the greatest superiority in all
goods. But it is also clear with kings, since far inferior people do   1159a
not expect to be their friends; nor do worthless people expect to
be friends to the best or wisest.

Now in these cases there is no exact definition of how long
people are friends. For even if one of them loses a lot, the friendship still endures; but if one is widely separated [from the other],   5
as a god is [from a human being], it no longer endures.

Hence there is this puzzle: do friends really wish their friend
to have the greatest good, e.g. to be a god? For [if he becomes a
god], *he* will no longer have friends, and hence no longer have
goods, since friends are goods.

If, then, we have been right to say that one friend wishes good
things to the other for the sake of the other *himself*, the other   10
must remain whatever sort of being he is. Hence it is to the other
as a human being that a friend will wish the greatest goods—
though presumably not all of them, since each person wishes
goods most of all to himself.

It is because they love honour that the many seem to prefer   viii 8
being loved to loving; that is why they love flatterers. For the   15
flatterer is a friend in an inferior position, or [rather] pretends to
be one, and pretends to love more than he is loved; and being
loved seems close to being honoured, which the many do indeed
pursue.

It would seem, however, that they choose honour coincidentally, not in itself. For the many enjoy being honoured by power-
20   ful people because they expect to get whatever they need from
them, and so enjoy the honour as a sign of this good treatment.
Those who want honour from decent people with knowledge
are seeking to confirm their own view of themselves, and so they
are pleased because the judgment of those who say they are
good makes them confident that they are good.

25   Being loved, on the contrary, they enjoy in itself. Hence it
seems to be better than being honoured, and friendship seems
choiceworthy in itself.

But friendship seems to consist more in loving than in being
loved. A sign of this is the enjoyment a mother finds in loving.
For sometimes she gives her child away to be brought up, and
30   loves him as long as she knows about him; but she does not seek
the child's love, if she cannot both [love and be loved]. She would
seem to be satisfied if she sees the child doing well, and she
loves the child even if ignorance prevents him from according to
her what befits a mother.

Friendship, then, consists more in loving; and people who
35   love their friends are praised; hence, it would seem, loving is the
virtue of friends. And so friends whose love corresponds to
1159b   their friends' worth are enduring friends and have an enduring
friendship. This above all is the way for unequals as well as
equals to be friends, since this is the way for them to be equalized.

Equality and similarity, and above all the similarity of those
who are similar in being virtuous, is friendship. For virtuous
people are enduringly [virtuous] in themselves, and enduring
5   [friends] to each other. They neither request nor provide assistance that requires base actions, but, you might even say, prevent
this. For it is proper to good people to avoid error themselves
and not to permit it in their friends.

Vicious people, by contrast, have no firmness, since they do
not even remain similar to what they were, but become friends
10   for a short time, enjoying each other's vice.

Useful or pleasant friends, however, last longer, for as long as
they supply each other with pleasures or benefits.

The friendship that seems to arise most from contraries is
friendship for utility, e.g. of poor to rich or ignorant to knowledgeable; for we aim at whatever we find we lack, and give
15   something else in return.

Here we might also include the erotic lover and his beloved, and the beautiful and the ugly. Hence an erotic lover also sometimes appears ridiculous, when he expects to be loved in the same way as he loves; that would presumably be a proper expectation if he were lovable in the same way, but it is ridiculous when he is not.

Presumably, however, contrary seeks contrary coincidentally, not in itself, and desire is for the intermediate. For what is good, e.g., for the dry is to reach the intermediate, not to become wet, and the same is true for the hot and so on. Let us, then, dismiss these questions, since they are rather extraneous to our concern.

As we said at the beginning, friendship and justice would seem to have the same area of concern and to be found in the same people. For in every community there seems to be some sort of justice, and some type of friendship also. At any rate, fellow-voyagers and fellow-soldiers are called friends, and so are members of other communities. And the extent of their community is the extent of their friendship, since it is also the extent of the justice found there. The proverb 'What friends have is common' is correct, since friendship involves community. But while brothers and companions have everything in common, what people have in common in other types of community is limited, more in some communities and less in others, since some friendships are also closer than others, some less close.

What is just is also different, since it is not the same for parents towards children as for one brother towards another, and not the same for companions as for fellow-citizens, and similarly with the other types of friendship. Similarly, what is unjust towards each of these is also different, and becomes more unjust as it is practised on closer friends. It is more shocking, e.g., to rob a companion of money than to rob a fellow-citizen, to fail to help a brother than a stranger, and to strike one's father than anyone else. What is just also naturally increases with friendship, since it involves the same people and extends over an equal area.

All communities would seem to be parts of the political community. For people keep company for some advantage and to supply something contributing to their life. Moreover, the political community seems both to have been originally formed and to endure for advantage; for legislators also aim at advantage, and the common advantage is said to be just.

The other types of community aim at partial advantage. Sea-

20

viii 9
25

30

35
1160a

5

10

15   travellers, e.g. seek the advantage proper to a journey, in making
money or something like that, while fellow-soldiers seek the
advantage proper to war, desiring either money or victory or
a city; and the same is true of fellow tribesmen and fellow-
demesmen. Some communities—religious societies and dining
20   clubs—seem to arise for pleasure, since these are, respectively,
for religious sacrifices and for companionship.

All these communities would seem to be subordinate to the
political community, since it aims not at some advantage close
at hand, but at advantage for the whole of life . . . [For] in
performing sacrifices and arranging gatherings for these, people
25   both accord honours to the gods and provide themselves with
pleasant relaxations. For the long-established sacrifices and gatherings appear to take place after the harvesting of the crops, as
a sort of first-fruits, since this was the time when people used to
be most at leisure [and the time when relaxation would be most
advantageous for the whole of life].

All the types of community, then, appear to be parts of the
30   political community, and these sorts of communities imply the
appropriate sorts of friendships.

viii 10   There are three species of political system (*politeia*), and an
equal number of deviations, which are a sort of corruption of
them. The first political system is kingship; the second aristoc-
racy; and since the third rests on property (*timēma*) it appears
proper to call it a timocratic system, though most people usually
35   call it a polity (*politeia*). The best of these is kingship and the
worst timocracy.

1160b   The deviation from kingship is tyranny. For, though both are
monarchies, they show the widest difference, since the tyrant
considers his own advantage, but the king considers the advantage of his subjects. For someone is a king only if he is self-
5   sufficient and superior in all goods; and since such a person
needs nothing more, he will consider the subjects' benefit, not
his own. For a king who is not like this would be only some sort
of titular king. Tyranny is contrary to this; for the tyrant pursues
his own good.

It is more evident that [tyranny] is the worst [deviation than
that timocracy is the worst political system]; but the worst is
contrary to the best; [hence kingship is the best].

10   The transition from kingship is to tyranny. For tyranny is the

degenerate condition of monarchy, and the vicious king becomes a tyrant.

The transition from aristocracy [rule of the best people] is to oligarchy [rule of the few], resulting from the badness of the rulers. They distribute the city's goods in conflict with people's worth, so that they distribute all or most of the goods to themselves, and always assign ruling offices to the same people, counting wealth for most. Hence the rulers are few, and they are vicious people instead of the most decent.

The transition from timocracy is to democracy [rule by the people], since these border on each other. For timocracy is also meant to be rule by the majority, and all those with the property-qualification are equal; [and majority-rule and equality are the marks of democracy]. Democracy is the least vicious [of the deviations]; for it deviates only slightly from the form of a [genuine] political system.

These, then, are the most frequent transitions from one political system to another, since they are the smallest and easiest.

Resemblances to these—indeed, a sort of pattern of them—can also be found in households. For the community of a father and his sons has the structure of kingship, since the father is concerned for his children. Indeed that is why Homer also calls Zeus father, since kingship is meant to be paternal rule.

Among the Persians, however, the father's rule is tyrannical, since he treats his sons as slaves. The rule of a master over his slaves is also tyrannical, since it is the master's advantage that is achieved in it. This, then, appears a correct form of rule, whereas the Persian form appears erroneous, since the different types of rule suit different subjects.

The community of man and woman appears aristocratic. For the man's rule in the area where it is right corresponds to the worth [of each], and he commits to the woman what is fitting for her. If, however, the man controls everything, he changes it into an oligarchy; for then his action conflicts with the worth [of each], and does not correspond to his superiority. Sometimes, indeed, women rule because they are heiresses; and these cases of rule do not reflect virtue, but result from wealth and power, as is true in oligarchies.

The community of brothers is like a timocratic [system], since they are equal except in so far as they differ in age; and hence, if they differ very much in age, the friendship is no longer brotherly.

Democracy is found most of all in dwellings without a master, since everyone there is on equal terms; and also in those where viii 11 the ruler is weak and everyone is free [to do what he likes].

10   Friendship appears in each of the political systems, to the extent that justice appears also. A king's friendship to his subjects involves superior beneficence. For he benefits his subjects, since he is good and attends to them to ensure that they do well, as a shepherd attends to his sheep; hence Homer also called Aga-
15   memnon shepherd of the peoples.

Paternal friendship resembles this, but differs in conferring a greater benefit, since the father is the cause of his children's being, which seems to be the greatest benefit, and of their nurture and education. These benefits are also ascribed to ancestors; and by nature father is ruler over sons, ancestors over descendants, and king over subjects.

20   All these are friendships of superiority; that is why parents are also honoured. And what is just in these friendships is not the same in each case, but corresponds to worth; for so does the friendship.

The friendship of man to woman is the same as in an aristoc-racy. For it reflects virtue, in assigning more good to the better,
25   and assigning what is fitting to each. The same is true for what is just here.

The friendship of brothers is similar to that of companions, since they are equal and of an age, and such people usually have the same feelings and characters. Friendship in a timocracy is similar to this. For there the citizens are meant to be equal and
30   decent, and so rule in turn and on equal terms. The same is true, then, of their friendship.

In the deviations, however, justice is found only to a slight degree; and hence the same is true of friendship. There is least of it in the worst deviation; for in a tyranny there is little or no friendship.

For where ruler and ruled have nothing in common, they have no friendship, since they have no justice either. This is true for
35   a craftsman in relation to his tool, and for the soul in relation to
1161b the body. For in all these cases the user benefits what he uses, but there is neither friendship nor justice towards soulless things.

Nor is there any towards a horse or cow, or towards a slave, in so far as he is a slave. For master and slave have nothing in common, since a slave is a tool with a soul, while a tool is a slave without a soul. In so far as he is a slave, then, there is no 5 friendship with him.

But there is friendship with him in so far as he is a human being. For every human being seems to have some relations of justice with everyone who is capable of community in law and agreement. Hence there is also friendship, to the extent that a slave is a human being.

Hence there are friendships and justice to only a slight degree in tyrannies also, but to a much larger degree in democracies; for there people are equal, and so have much in common. 10

As we have said, then, every friendship is found in a commu- viii 12 nity. But we should set apart the friendship of families and that of companions. The friendship of citizens, tribesmen, voyagers and suchlike are more like friendships in a community, since they appear to reflect some sort of agreement; and among these 15 we may include the friendship of host and guest.

Friendship in families also seems to have many species, but they all seem to depend on paternal friendship. For a parent is fond of his children because he regards them as something of himself; and children are fond of a parent because they regard themselves as coming from him.

A parent knows better what has come from him than the 20 children know that they are from the parent; and the parent regards his children as his own more than the product regards the maker as its own. For a person regards what comes from him as his own, as the owner regards his tooth or hair or anything; but what has come from him regards its owner as its own not at all, or to a lesser degree.

The length of time also matters. For a parent becomes fond of 25 his children as soon as they are born, while children become fond of the parent when time has passed and they have acquired some comprehension or [at least] perception. And this also makes it clear why mothers love their children more [than fathers do].

A parent loves his children as [he loves] himself. For what has come from him is a sort of other himself; [it is other because] it is separate. Children love a parent because they regard them- selves as having come from him.

Brothers love each other because they have come from the 30 same [parents]. For the same relation to the parents makes the

same thing for both of them; hence we speak of the same blood, the same stock and so on. Hence they are the same thing in a way, in different [subjects]. Being brought up together and being of an age contributes largely to friendship; for 'two of an age'
35   [get on well], and those with the same character are companions.
1162a That is why the friendship of brothers and that of companions are similar.

Cousins and other relatives are akin by being related to brothers, since that makes them descendants of the same parents [i.e. the parents of these brothers]. Some are more akin, others less, by the ancestor's being near to or far from them.

The friendship of children to a parent, like the friendship of
5   human beings to a god, is friendship towards what is good and superior. For the parent conferred the greatest benefits, since he is the cause of their being and nurture and of their education once they have been born. This sort of friendship also includes pleasure and utility, more than the friendship of unrelated people does, to the extent that [parents and children] have more of a life in common.

10   Friendship between brothers has the features of friendship between companions, especially when [the companions] are decent, or in general similar. For brothers are that much more akin to each other [than ordinary companions], and are fond of each other from birth; they are that much more similar in character when they are from the same parents, nurtured together and educated similarly; and the proof of their reliability over time is
15   fullest and firmest.

Among other relatives too the features of friendship are proportional [to the relation].

The friendship of man and woman also seems to be natural. For human beings naturally tend to form couples more than to form cities, to the extent that the household is prior to the city, and more necessary, and child-bearing is shared more widely among the animals.

20   With the other animals this is the extent of the community. Human beings, however, share a household not only for child-bearing, but also for the benefits in their life. For from the start their functions are divided, with different ones for the man and the woman; hence each supplies the other's needs by contributing a special function to the common good. Hence their friendship seems to include both utility and pleasure.

And it may also be friendship for virtue, if they are decent. 25
For each has a proper virtue, and this will be a source of enjoyment for them. Children seem to be another bond, and that is
why childless unions are more quickly dissolved; for children
are a common good for both, and what is common holds them
together.

How should a man conduct his life towards his wife, or, in 30
general, toward a friend? That appears to be the same as asking
what the just conduct of their lives is. For what is just is not the
same for a friend towards a friend as towards a stranger, or the
same towards a companion as towards a classmate.

There are three types of friendship, as we said at the beginning; viii 13
and within each type some friendships rest on equality, while 35
others correspond to superiority. For equally good people can
be friends, but also a better and a worse person; and the same is 1162b
true of friends for pleasure or utility, since they may be either
equal or unequal in their benefits. Hence equals must equalize
in loving and in the other things, because of their equality; and
unequals must make the return that is proportionate to the types
of superiority.

Accusations and reproaches arise only or most often in friend- 5
ship for utility. And this is reasonable. For friends for virtue are
eager to benefit each other, since this is proper to virtue and to
friendship; and if this is the achievement they compete for, there
are no accusations or fights. For no one objects if the other loves
and benefits him; if he is gracious, he retaliates by benefiting the 10
other. And if the superior gets what he aims at, he will not accuse
his friend of anything, since each of them desires what is good.

Nor are there many accusations among friends for pleasure.
For both of them get what they want at the same time if they
enjoy spending their time together; and someone who accused 15
his friend of not pleasing him would appear ridiculous, when he
is free to spend his days without the friend's company.

Friendship for utility, however, is liable to accusations. For
these friends deal with each other in the expectation of gaining
benefits. Hence they always require more, thinking they have
got less than is fitting; and they reproach the other because they
get less than they require and deserve. And those who confer
benefits cannot supply as much as the recipients require. 20

There are two ways of being just, one unwritten, and one
governed by rules of law. And similarly one type of friendship

of utility would seem to depend on character, and the other on
25   rules. Accusations arise most readily if it is not the same sort of
friendship when they dissolve it that it was when they formed
it.

Friendship dependent on rules is the type that is on explicit
conditions. One type of this is entirely mercenary and requires
immediate payment. The other is more generous and postpones
the time [of repayment], but conforms to an agreement [requir-
ing] one thing in return for another. In this sort of friendship it
is clear and unambiguous what is owed, but the postponement
is a friendly aspect of it. That is why some cities do not allow
30   legal actions in these cases, but think that people who have
formed an arrangement on the basis of trust must put up with
the outcome.

Friendship [for utility] that depends on character is not on
explicit conditions. Someone makes a present or whatever it is,
as to a friend, but expects to get back as much or more, since he
assumes that it is not a free gift, but a loan. And if he does not
dissolve the friendship on the terms on which he formed it, he
will accuse the other.

35   This happens because all or most people wish for what is fine,
but decide to do what is beneficial; and while it is fine to do
1163a someone a good turn without the aim of receiving one in return,
it is beneficial to receive a good turn.

We should, if we can, make a return worthy of what we have
received, [if the other has undertaken the friendship] willingly.
For we should never make a friend of someone who is unwilling,
but must suppose that we were in error at the beginning, and
received a benefit from the wrong person; for since it was not
5   from a friend, and this was not why he was doing it, we must
dissolve the arrangement as though we had received a good turn
on explicit conditions. And we will agree to repay if we can. If
we cannot repay, the giver would not even expect it. Hence we
should repay if we can. We should consider at the beginning
who is doing us a good turn, and on what conditions, so that we
can put up with it on these conditions, or else decline it.

10   It is disputable whether we must measure [the return] by the
benefit accruing to the recipient, and make the return proportional to that, or instead by the good turn done by the benefactor.
For a recipient says that what he got was a small matter for the
benefactor, and that he could have got it from someone else

instead, and so he belittles it. But the benefactor says it was the biggest thing he had, that it could not be got from anyone else, and that he gave it when he was in danger or similar need. 15

Since the friendship is for utility, surely the benefit to the recipient must be the measure [of the return]. For he was the one who required it, and the benefactor supplies him on the assumption that he will get an equal return. Hence the aid has been as great as the benefit received, and the recipient should 20 return as much as he gained, or still more, since that is finer.

But in friendships of virtue, there are no accusations. Rather, the decision of the benefactor would seem to be the measure, since the controlling element in virtue and character is found in decision.

There are also disputes in friendships that correspond to supe- viii 14 riority, since each friend expects to have more than the other, 25 but whenever this happens the friendship is dissolved.

For the better person thinks it is fitting for him to have more, on the ground that more is fittingly accorded to the good person. And the more beneficial person thinks the same. For it is wrong, people say, for someone to have an equal share when he is useless; a public service, not a friendship, is the result if the benefits from the friendship do not correspond to the worth of 30 the actions. [Each superior party says this] because he notices that in a financial association the larger contributors gain more, and he thinks the same thing is right in a friendship.

But the needy person, the inferior party in the friendship, takes the opposite view, saying it is proper to a virtuous friend to supply his needy [friends]. For what use is it, as they say, to be an excellent or powerful person's friend if you are not going 35 to gain anything by it?

Well, each of them would seem to be correct in what he ex-pects, and it is right for each of them to get more from the 1163b friendship—but not more of the same thing. Rather, the superior person should get more honour, and the needy person more profit, since honour is the reward of virtue and beneficence, while profit is what supplies need.

This also appears to be true in political systems. For someone 5 who provides nothing for the community receives no honour, since what is common is given to someone who benefits the community, and honour is something common. For it is impossi-ble both to make money off the community and to receive honour

from it at the same time; for no one endures the smaller share of
10 everything. Hence someone who suffers a monetary loss [by
holding office] receives honour in return, while someone who
accepts bribes [in office] receives money [but not honour]; for
distribution that corresponds to worth equalizes and preserves
the friendship, as we have said.

This, then, is how we should treat unequals. If we are benefited
in virtue or in money, we should return honour, and thereby
15 make what return we can. For friendship seeks what is possible,
not what corresponds to worth, since that is impossible in some
cases, e.g. with honour to gods and parents. For no one could
ever make a return corresponding to their worth, but someone
who attends to them as far as he is able seems to be a decent
person.

That is why it seems that a son is not free to disavow his father,
20 but a father is free to disavow his son. For a debtor should return
what he owes, and since no matter what a son has done he has
not made a worthy return for what his father has done for him,
he is always the debtor. But the creditor is free to remit the debt,
and hence the father is free to remit.

At the same time, however, it presumably seems that no one
would ever withdraw from a son who was not far gone in vice.
For, quite apart from their natural friendship, it is human not to
25 repel aid. The son, however, if he is vicious, will want to avoid
helping his father, or will not be keen on it. For the many wish
to receive benefits, but they avoid doing them because they
suppose it is unprofitable. So much, then, for these things.

ix 1 In all friendships of friends with dissimilar aims it is proportion
that equalizes and preserves the friendship, as we said; e.g. in
35 political friendship the cobbler receives a worthy exchange for
his shoes, and so do the weaver and the others. Here money is
1164a supplied as a common measure; everything is related to this and
measured by it.

In erotic friendships, however, sometimes the lover charges
that he loves the beloved deeply and is not loved in return; and
5 in fact perhaps he has nothing lovable in him. The beloved,
however, often charges that previously the lover was promising
him everything, and now fulfils none of his promises.

These sorts of charges arise whenever the lover loves his beloved for pleasure while the beloved loves his lover for utility,
and they do not both provide these. For when the friendship has

these causes, it is dissolved whenever they do not get what they
were friends for; for each was not fond of the other himself, but   10
only of what the other had, and since this was unstable, the
friendships are unstable too.

Friendship of character, however, is friendship in itself, and
endures, as we have said.

Friends quarrel when they get results different from those they
want; for when someone does not get what he aims at, it is like
getting nothing. It is like the person who promised the lyre   15
player a reward, and a greater reward the better he played; in
the morning, when the player asked him to deliver on his promise, the other said he had paid pleasure for pleasure. Now if this
was what each of them had wished, it would be quite enough.
But if one wished for delight and the other for profit, and one
has got his delight and the other has not made his profit, the   20
association is in no good state. For each person sets his mind on
what he finds he requires, and this will be his aim when he gives
what he gives.

Who should fix the worth [of a benefit], the giver or the receiver? The giver would seem to leave it to the receiver, as
Protagoras is said to have done. For whenever he taught any-   25
thing at all, he used to tell the pupil to estimate how much the
knowledge was worth, and that amount would be his payment.
In such cases, however, some prefer the rule 'A man should
have his payment'.

But those who take the money first, and then do nothing that
they said they would do, because their promises were excessive,
are predictably accused, since they do not carry out what they   30
agreed to. And presumably the sophists are compelled to make
excessive promises. For no one would pay them money for the
knowledge they really have; hence they take the payment, and
then do not do what they were paid to do, and predictably are
accused.

But where no agreement about services is made, friends who
give services because of the friend himself are not open to accusa-   35
tion, as we have said, since this is the character of the friendship
that reflects virtue. And the return should reflect the decision [of   1164b
the original giver], since decision is proper to a friend and to
virtue.

And it would seem that the same sort of return should also be
made to those who have shared philosophy in common with us.

For its worth is not measured by money, and no equivalent
5   honour can be paid; but it is enough, presumably, to do what
we can, as we do towards gods and parents.

If the giving is not of this sort, but on some specified condition,
then presumably the repayment must be, ideally, what each of
them thinks matches the worth of the gift. But if they do not
agree on this, then it would seem not merely necessary, but also
just, for the party who benefits first to fix the repayment. For if
10   the other receives in return as much benefit as the first received,
or as much as he would have paid for the pleasure, he will have
got the worthy return from him.

Indeed this is also how it appears in buying and selling. For
in some cities there are actually laws prohibiting legal actions in
voluntary bargains, on the assumption that if we have trusted
someone we must dissolve the association with him on the same
15   terms on which we formed it. The law does this because it
supposes that it is more just for the recipient to fix repayment
than for the giver to fix it.

For usually those who have something and those who want it
do not put the same price on it, since what they own and what
they are giving appears to givers to be worth a lot. But nonetheless the return is made in the amount fixed by the initial recipient.
20   Presumably, however, the price must be not what it appears to
be worth when he has got it, but the price he put on it before he
got it.

ix 2   Here are some other questions that raise a puzzle. Must one
accord [authority in] everything to his father, and obey him in
everything? Or must he trust the doctor when he is sick, and
should he vote for a military expert to be general? Similarly,
25   should someone serve his friend rather than an excellent person,
and return a favour to a benefactor rather than do a favour for a
companion, if he cannot do both?

Surely it is not easy to define all these matters exactly. For
they include many differences of all sorts—in importance and
unimportance and in what is fine and what is necessary. Clearly,
30   however, not everything should be given to the same person,
and usually we should return favours rather than do favours for
our companions, just as we should return a loan to a creditor
rather than lend to a companion.

But presumably this is not always true. If, e.g., someone has
35   rescued you from pirates, should you ransom him in return, no

matter who he is? Or if he does not need to be ransomed, but asks for his money back, should you return it, or should you ransom your father instead? Here it seems that you should ransom your father, rather than even yourself. 1165a

As we have said, then, generally speaking we should return what we owe. But if making a gift [to B] outweighs [returning the money to A] by being finer or more necessary, we should incline to [making the gift to B] instead.

For sometimes even a return of a previous favour is not fair [but an excessive demand], whenever [the original giver] knows he is benefiting an excellent person, but [the recipient] would be returning the benefit to someone he thinks is vicious. 5

For sometimes you should not even lend in return to someone who has lent to you. For he expected repayment when he lent to a decent person, whereas you have no hope of it from a bad person. If that is really so, then, the demand [for reciprocity] is not fair; and even if it is not so, but you think it is so, your refusal of the demand seems not at all absurd. 10

As we have often said, then, arguments about acting and being affected are no more definite than their subject matter.

Clearly, then, we should not give the same thing to everyone, and we should not give our fathers everything, just as we should not make all our sacrifices to Zeus. And since different things should be given to parents, brothers, companions and benefactors, we should accord to each what is proper and suitable. This is what actually appears to be done; e.g. kinsfolk are the people invited to a wedding, since they share the same family, and hence share in actions that concern it; and for the same reason it is thought that kinsfolk more than anyone must come to funerals. 15

20

It seems that we must supply means of support to parents more than anyone. For we suppose that we owe them this, and that it is finer to supply those who are the causes of our being than to supply ourselves in this way. And we should accord honour to our parents, just as we should to the gods, but not every sort of honour; for we should not accord the same honour to father and to mother, nor accord them the honour due a wise person or a general. We should accord a father's honour to a father, and likewise a mother's to a mother. 25

We should accord to every older person the honour befitting his age, by standing up, giving up seats and so on. With companions and brothers we should speak freely, and have everything

30   in common. To kinsfolk, fellow-tribesmen, fellow-citizens and
          all the rest we should always try to accord what is proper, and
          should compare what belongs to each, as befits closeness of
          relation, virtue or usefulness. Comparison is easier with people
          of the same kind, and more difficult with people of different
          kinds, but the difficulty is no reason for giving up the compari-
35   son; rather, we should define as far as we can.

ix 3   There is also a puzzle about dissolving or not dissolving friend-
1165b   ships with friends who do not remain the same. With friends for
          utility or pleasure perhaps there is nothing absurd in dissolving
          the friendship whenever they are no longer pleasant or useful.
          For they were friends of pleasure or utility; and if these give out,
          it is reasonable not to love.

5   However, we might accuse a friend if he really liked us for
          utility or pleasure, and pretended to like us for our character.
          For, as we said at the beginning, friends are most at odds when
          they are not friends in the way they think they are. And so, if
          we mistakenly suppose we are loved for our character, when our
          friend is doing nothing to suggest this, we must hold ourselves
10   responsible. But if we are deceived by his pretence, we are justi-
          fied in accusing him—even more justified than in accusing de-
          basers of the currency, to the extent that his evildoing debases
          something more precious.

             But if we accept a friend as a good person, and then he becomes
          vicious, and seems so, should we still love him? Surely we can-
          not, if not everything, but only what is good, is lovable. What is
15   bad is not lovable, and must not be loved; for we ought neither
          to love what is bad nor to become similar to a bad person, and
          we have said that similar is friend to similar.

             Then should the friendship be dissolved at once [as soon as
          the friend becomes bad]? Surely not with everyone, but only
          with an incurably vicious person. If someone can be set right,
          we should try harder to rescue his character than his property,
20   in so far as character is both better and more proper to friendship.

             However, the friend who dissolves the friendship seems to be
          doing nothing absurd. For he was not the friend of a person of
          this sort; hence, if the friend has altered, and he cannot save
          him, he leaves him.

             But if one friend stayed the same and the other became more
          decent and far excelled his friend in virtue, should the better
          person still treat the other as a friend? Surely he cannot. This

becomes clear in a wide separation, such as we find in friendships   25
beginning in childhood. For if one friend still thinks as a child,
while the other becomes a most superior man, how could they
still be friends, when they neither approve of the same things
nor find the same things enjoyable or painful? For they do not
even find it so in their life together and without that they cannot   30
be friends, since they cannot live together—we have discussed
this.

Then should the better person regard the other as though he
had never become his friend? Surely he must keep some memory
of the familiarity they had; and just as we think we must do
kindnesses for friends more than for strangers, so also we should
accord something to past friends because of the former friend-   35
ship, whenever excessive vice does not cause the dissolution.   ix 4

The defining features of friendship that are found in friend-   1166a
ships to one's neighbours would seem to be derived from features of friendship towards oneself.

For a friend is taken to be (1) someone who wishes and does
goods or apparent goods to his friend for the friend's own sake;
or (2) one who wishes the friend to be and to live for the friend's
own sake—this is how mothers feel towards their children, and   5
how friends who have been in conflict feel [towards each other].
(3) Others take a friend to be one who spends his time with his
friend, and (4) makes the same choices; or (5) one who shares
his friend's distress and enjoyment—and this also is true especially of mothers. And people define friendship by one of these
features.

Each of these features is found in the decent person's relation   10
to himself, and it is found in other people in so far as they
suppose they are decent. As we have said, virtue and the excellent person would seem to be the standard in each case.

(4) The excellent person is of one mind with himself, and
desires the same things in his whole soul.

(1) Hence he wishes goods and apparent goods to himself,   15
and does them in his actions, since it is proper to the good person
to achieve the good. He wishes and does them for his own sake,
since he does them for the sake of his thinking part, and that is
what each person seems to be.

(2) He wishes himself to live and to be preserved. And he
wishes this for the part by which he has intelligence more than
for any other part. For being is a good for the good person, and

20   each person wishes for goods for himself. And no one chooses
        to become another person even if that other will have every good
        when he has come into being; for, as it is, the god has the good
        [but no one chooses to be replaced by a god]. Rather [each of us
        chooses goods] on condition that he remains whatever he is; and
        each person would seem to be the understanding part, or that
        most of all. [Hence the good person wishes for goods for the
        understanding part.]

        (3) Further, such a person finds it pleasant to spend time with
        himself, and so wishes to do it. For his memories of what he has
25   done are agreeable, and his expectations for the future are good,
        and hence both are pleasant. And besides, his thought is well
        supplied with topics for study.

        (5) Moreover, he shares his own distresses and pleasures,
        more than other people share theirs. For it is always the same
        thing that is painful or pleasant, not different things at different
        times. This is because he practically never regrets [what he has
        done].

30   The decent person, then, has each of these features in relation
        to himself, and is related to his friend as he is to himself, since
        the friend is another himself. Hence friendship seems to be one
        of these features, and people with these features seem to be
        friends.

        Is there friendship towards oneself, or is there not? Let us
        dismiss that question for the present. However, there seems to
35   be friendship in so far as someone is two or more parts. This
        seems to be true from what we have said, and because an extreme
1166b   degree of friendship resembles one's friendship to oneself.

        The many, base though they are, also appear to have these
        features. But perhaps they share in them only in so far as they
        approve of themselves and suppose they are decent. For no one
5   who is utterly bad and unscrupulous either has these features or
        appears to have them.

        Indeed, even base people hardly have them.

        (4) For they are at odds with themselves, and, like incontinent
        people, have an appetite for one thing and a wish for another.

        (1) For they do not choose things that seem to be good for them,
        but instead choose pleasant things that are actually harmful. And
10   cowardice or laziness causes others to shrink from doing what
        they think best for themselves.

(2) Those who have done many terrible actions hate and shun life because of their vice, and destroy themselves.

(3) Besides, vicious people seek others to pass their days with, and shun themselves. For when they are by themselves they remember many disagreeable actions, and expect to do others in the future; but they manage to forget these in other people's company. These people have nothing lovable about them, and so have no friendly feelings for themselves.

(5) Hence such a person does not share his own enjoyments and distresses. For his soul is in conflict, and because he is vicious one part is distressed at being restrained, and another is pleased [by the intended action]; and so each part pulls in a different direction, as though they were tearing him apart. Even if he cannot be distressed and pleased at the same time, still he is soon distressed because he was pleased, and wishes these things had not become pleasant to him; for base people are full of regret.

Hence the base person appears not to have a friendly attitude even towards himself, because he has nothing lovable about him.

If this state is utterly miserable, everyone should earnestly shun vice and try to be decent; for that is how someone will have a friendly relation to himself and will become a friend to another.

Goodwill would seem to be a feature of friendship, but still it is not friendship. For it arises even towards people we do not know, and without their noticing it, whereas friendship does not. We have said this before also.

Nor is it loving, since it lacks intensity and desire, which are implied by loving. Moreover, while loving requires familiarity, goodwill can also arise in a moment, as it arises, e.g., [in a spectator] for contestants. For [the spectator] acquires goodwill for them, and wants what they want, but would not cooperate with them in any action; for, as we said, his good will arises in a moment and his fondness is superficial.

In fact goodwill would seem to originate friendship in the way that pleasure coming through sight originates erotic passion. For no one has erotic passion for another without previous pleasure in his appearance. But still enjoyment of his appearance does not imply erotic passion for him; passion consists also in longing for him in his absence and an appetite for his presence. Similarly, though people cannot be friends without previous goodwill, goodwill does not imply friendship; for when they have goodwill

15

20

25

ix 5
30

35
1167a

5

10   people only wish goods to the other, and will not cooperate with
      him in any action, or go to any trouble for him.

      Hence we might transfer [the name 'friendship'], and say that
      goodwill is inactive friendship, and that when it lasts some time
      and they grow accustomed to each other, it becomes friendship.

      It does not, however, become friendship for utility or pleasure,
      since these aims do not produce goodwill either.

15   For a recipient of a benefit does what is just when he returns
      goodwill for what he has received. But those who wish for anoth-
      er's welfare because they hope to enrich themselves through him
      would seem to have goodwill to themselves, rather than to him.
      Likewise, they would seem to be friends to themselves rather
      than to him, if they attend to him because he is of some use to
      them.

      But in general goodwill results from some sort of virtue and
      decency, whenever one person finds another to be apparently
20   fine or brave or something similar. As we said, this also arises
      in the case of contestants.

ix 6 Now concord also appears to be a feature of friendship. Hence
      it is not merely sharing a belief, since this might happen among
      people who do not know each other. Nor are people said to
25   be in concord when they agree about just anything, e.g. on
      astronomical questions, since concord on these questions is not
      a feature of friendship. Rather, a city is said to be in concord
      when [its citizens] agree about what is advantageous, make the
      same decision, and act on their common resolution.

      Hence concord concerns questions for action, and, more ex-
30   actly, large questions where both or all can get what they want.
      A city, e.g., is in concord whenever all the citizens resolve to
      make offices elective, or to make an alliance with the Spartans,
      or to make Pittacus ruler, when he is willing too.

      Whenever each person wants the same thing all to himself, as
      the people in the *Phoenissae* do, they are in conflict. For it is not
      concord when each merely has the same thing in mind, whatever
35   it is, but each must also have the same thing in mind for the same
      person; this is true, e.g., whenever both the common people and
1167b the decent party want the best people to rule, since when that is
      so both sides get what they seek.

      Concord, then, is apparently political friendship, as indeed it
      is said to be; for it is concerned with advantage and with what
      affects life [as a whole].

This sort of concord is found in decent people. For they are in   5
concord with themselves and with each other, since they are
practically of the same mind; for their wishes are stable, not
flowing back and forth like a tidal strait. They wish for what is
just and advantageous, and also seek it in common.

Base people, however, cannot be in concord, except to a small   10
extent, just as they can be friends only to a small extent; for
they are greedy for more benefits, and shirk labours and public
services. And since each wishes this for himself, he interrogates
and obstructs his neighbour; for when people do not look out
for the common good, it is ruined. The result is that they are in
conflict, trying to compel each other to do what is just, but not   15
wishing to do it themselves.

Now benefactors seem to love their beneficiaries more than   ix 7
the beneficiaries love them [in return], and this is discussed as
though it were an unreasonable thing to happen.

Here is how it appears to most people. It is because the benefi-   20
ciaries are debtors and the benefactors creditors: the debtor in a
loan wishes the creditor did not exist, while the creditor even
attends to the safety of the debtor. So also, then, a benefactor
wants the beneficiary to exist because he expects gratitude in
return, while the beneficiary is not attentive about making the   25
return.

Now Epicharmus might say that most people say this because
they 'take a bad person's point of view'. Still, it would seem to
be a human point of view, since the many are indeed forgetful,
and seek to receive benefits more than to give them.

However, it seems that the cause is more proper to [human]
nature, and the case of creditors is not even similar. For they do
not love their debtors, but in wishing for their safety simply seek   30
repayment; whereas benefactors love and like their beneficiaries
even if they are of no present or future use to them.

The same is true with craftsmen; for each likes his own product
more than it would like him if it acquired a soul. Perhaps this is   35
true of poets most of all, since they dearly like their own poems,   1168a
and are fond of them as though they were their children. This,
then, is what the case of the benefactor resembles; here the
beneficiary is his product, and hence he likes him more than the   5
product likes its producer.

The cause of this is as follows:

1. Being is choiceworthy and lovable for all.

2. We are in so far as we are actualized, since we are in so far as we live and act.

3. The product is, in a way, the producer in his actualization.

4. Hence the producer is fond of the product, because he loves his own being. And this is natural, since what he is potentially is what the product indicates in actualization.

10   At the same time, the benefactor's action is fine for him, so that he finds enjoyment in the person he acts on; but the person acted on finds nothing fine in the agent, but only, at most, some advantage, which is less pleasant and lovable.

    What is pleasant is actualization in the present, expectation for the future, and memory of the past; but what is pleasantest is

15 the [action we do] in so far as we are actualized, and this is also most lovable. For the benefactor, then, his product endures, since what is fine is long-lasting; but for the person acted on, what is useful passes away.

    Besides, memory of something fine is pleasant, while memory of [receiving] something useful is not altogether pleasant, or is less pleasant—though the reverse would seem to be true for expectation.

20   Moreover, loving is like production, while being loved is like being acted on; and [the benefactor's] love and friendliness is the result of his greater activity.

    Besides, everyone is fond of what has needed effort to produce it; e.g. people who have made money themselves are fonder of it than people who have inherited it. And while receiving a benefit seems to take no effort, giving one is hard work.

25   This is also why mothers love their children more [than fathers do], since giving birth is more effort for them, and they know better that the children are theirs. And this also would seem to be proper to benefactors.

ix 8   There is also a puzzle about whether one ought to love oneself or someone else most of all; for those who like themselves most

30 are criticized and denounced as self-lovers, as though this were something shameful.

    Indeed, the base person does seem to go to every length for his own sake, and all the more the more vicious he is; hence he is accused, e.g., of doing nothing of his own accord. The decent person, on the contrary, acts for what is fine, all the more the

35 better he is, and for his friend's sake, disregarding his own good.

The facts, however, conflict with these claims, and that is not 1168b unreasonable.

For it is said that we must love most the friend who is most a friend; and one person is most a friend to another if he wishes goods to the other for the other's sake, even if no one will know about it. But these are features most of all of one's relation to oneself; and so too are all the other defining features of a friend, since we have said that all the features of friendship extend from 5 oneself to others.

All the proverbs agree with this too, e.g. speaking of 'one soul', 'what friends have is common', 'equality is friendship' and 'the knee is closer than the shin'. For all these are true most of all in someone's relations with himself, since one is a friend to himself most of all. Hence he should also love himself most of all. 10

It is not surprising that there is a puzzle about which view we ought to follow, since both inspire some confidence; hence we must presumably divide these sorts of arguments, and distinguish how far and in what ways those on each side are true.

Perhaps, then, it will become clear, if we grasp how those on 15 each side understand self-love.

Those who make self-love a matter for reproach ascribe it to those who award the biggest share in money, honours and bodily pleasures to themselves. For these are the goods desired and eagerly pursued by the many on the assumption that they are best; and hence they are also contested.

Those who are greedy for these goods gratify their appetites and in general their feelings and the non-rational part of the soul; 20 and since this is the character of the many, the application of the term ['self-love'] is derived from the most frequent [kind of self-love], which is base. This type of self-lover, then, is justifiably reproached.

And plainly it is the person who awards himself these goods whom the many habitually call a self-lover. For if someone is always eager to excel everyone in doing just or temperate actions 25 or any others expressing the virtues, and in general always gains for himself what is fine, no one will call him a self-lover or blame him for it.

However, it is this more than the other sort of person who seems to be a self-lover. At any rate he awards himself what is

30   finest and best of all, and gratifies the most controlling part of
     himself, obeying it in everything. And just as a city and every
     other composite system seems to be above all its most controlling
     part, the same is true of a human being; hence someone loves
     himself most if he likes and gratifies this part.

35   Similarly, someone is called continent or incontinent because
1169a   his understanding is or is not the master, on the assumption that
        this is what each person is. Moreover, his own voluntary actions
        seem above all to be those involving reason. Clearly, then, this,
        or this above all, is what each person is, and the decent person
        likes this most of all.

         Hence he most of all is a self-lover, but a different kind from
     the self-lover who is reproached, differing from him as much as
5   the life guided by reason differs from the life guided by feelings,
     and as much as the desire for what is fine differs from the desire
     for what seems advantageous.

         Those who are unusually eager to do fine actions are welcomed
     and praised by everyone. And when everyone competes to
     achieve what is fine and strains to do the finest actions, every-
10   thing that is right will be done for the common good, and each
     person individually will receive the greatest of goods, since that
     is the character of virtue.

         Hence the good person must be a self-lover, since he will both
     help himself and benefit others by doing fine actions. But the
     vicious person must not love himself, since he will harm both
     himself and his neighbours by following his base feelings.

15   For the vicious person, then, the right actions conflict with
     those he does. The decent person, however, does the right ac-
     tions, since every understanding chooses what is best for itself
     and the decent person obeys his understanding.

         Besides, it is true that, as they say, the excellent person labours
     for his friends and for his native country, and will die for them if
20   he must; he will sacrifice money, honours and contested goods in
     general, in achieving what is fine for himself. For he will choose
     intense pleasure for a short time over mild pleasure for a long time;
     a year of living finely over many years of undistinguished life; and
25   a single fine and great action over many small actions.

         This is presumably true of one who dies for others; he does
     indeed choose something great and fine for himself. He is ready
     to sacrifice money as long as his friends profit; for the friends
     gain money, while he gains what is fine, and so he awards

himself the greater good. He treats honours and offices the same way; for he will sacrifice them all for his friends, since this is fine and praiseworthy for him. It is not surprising, then, that he seems to be excellent, when he chooses what is fine at the cost of everything. It is also possible, however, to sacrifice actions to his friend, since it may be finer to be responsible for his friend's doing the action than to do it himself. In everything praiseworthy, then, the excellent person awards himself what is fine.

In this way, then, we must be self-lovers, as we have said. But in the way the many are, we ought not to be.

There is also a dispute about whether the happy person will need friends or not.

For it is said that blessedly happy and self-sufficient people have no need of friends. For they already have [all] the goods, and hence, being self-sufficient, need nothing added. But your friend, since he is another yourself, supplies what your own efforts cannot supply. Hence it is said, 'When the god gives well, what need is there of friends?'

However, in awarding the happy person all the goods it would seem absurd not to give him friends; for having friends seems to be the greatest external good.

And it is more proper to a friend to confer benefits than to receive them, and proper to the good person and to virtue to do good; and it is finer to benefit friends than to benefit strangers. Hence the excellent person will need people for him to benefit. Indeed, that is why there is a question about whether friends are needed more in good fortune than in ill-fortune; for it is assumed that in ill-fortune we need people to benefit us, and in good fortune we need others for us to benefit.

Surely it is also absurd to make the blessed person solitary. For no one would choose to have all [other] goods and yet be alone, since a human being is political, tending by nature to live together with others. This will also be true, then, of the happy person; for he has the natural goods, and clearly it is better to spend his days with decent friends than with strangers of just any character. Hence the happy person will need friends.

Then what are the other side saying, and in what way is it true? Surely they say what they say because the many think that it is the useful people who are friends. Certainly the blessedly happy person will have no need of these, since he has [all] goods. Similarly, he will have no need, or very little, of friends for pleasure; for since his life is pleasant, it has no need of imported pleasures. Since he does not need these sorts of friends, he does not seem to need friends at all.

However, this conclusion is presumably not true:

(1) For we said at the beginning that happiness is a kind of activity; and clearly activity comes into being, and does not belong [to someone all the time], as a possession does. Being happy, then, is found in living and being active.

(2) The activity of the good person is excellent, and [hence] pleasant in itself, as we said at the beginning.

(3) Moreover, what is our own is pleasant.

(4) We are able to observe our neighbours more than ourselves, and to observe their actions more than our own.

(5) Hence a good person finds pleasure in the actions of excellent people who are his friends, since these actions have both the naturally pleasant [features, i.e. they are good, and they are his own].

(6) The blessed person decides to observe virtuous actions that are his own; and the actions of a virtuous friend are of this sort.

(7) Hence he will need virtuous friends.

Further, it is thought that the happy person must live pleasantly. But the solitary person's life is hard, since it is not easy for him to be continuously active all by himself; but in relation to others and in their company it is easier, and hence his activity will be more continuous. It is also pleasant in itself, as it must be in the blessedly happy person's case. For the excellent person, in so far as he is excellent, enjoys actions expressing virtue, and objects to actions caused by vice, just as the musician enjoys fine melodies and is pained by bad ones.

Further, good people's life together allows the cultivation of virtue, as Theognis says.

If we examine the question more from the point of view of [human] nature, an excellent friend would seem to be choiceworthy by nature for an excellent person.

(1) For, as we have said, what is good by nature is good and pleasant in itself for an excellent person.

(2) For animals life is defined by the capacity for perception; for human beings it is defined by the capacity for perception or understanding.

(3) Every capacity refers to an activity, and a thing is present to its full extent in its activity.

(4) Hence living to its full extent would seem to be perceiving or understanding.

(5) Life is good and pleasant in itself. For it has definite order,   20
which is proper to the nature of what is good.

(6) What is good by nature is also good for the decent person. That is why life would seem to be pleasant for everyone. Here, however, we must not consider a life that is vicious and corrupted, or filled with pains; for such a life lacks definite order, just as its proper features do. (The truth about pain will be more   25
evident in what follows.)

(7) Life itself, then, is good and pleasant. So it looks, at any rate, from the fact that everyone desires it, and decent and blessed people desire it more than others do; for their life is most choiceworthy for them, and their living is most blessed.

(8) Now someone who sees perceives that he sees; one who hears perceives that he hears; and one who walks perceives that   30
he walks.

(9) Similarly in the other cases also there is some [element] that perceives that we are active.

(10) Hence, if we are perceiving, we perceive that we are perceiving; and if we are understanding, we perceive that we are understanding.

(11) Now perceiving that we are perceiving or understanding is the same as perceiving that we are, since we agreed [in (4)] that being is perceiving or understanding.

(12) Perceiving that we are alive is pleasant in itself. For life is   1170b
by nature a good [from (5)], and it is pleasant to perceive that something good is present in us.

(13) And living is choiceworthy, for a good person most of all, since being is good and pleasant for him; for he is pleased to perceive something good in itself together [with his own being].   5

(14) The excellent person is related to his friend in the same way as he is related to himself, since a friend is another himself.

(15) Therefore, just as his own being is choiceworthy for him, his friend's being is choiceworthy for him in the same or a similar way.

   We agreed that someone's own being is choiceworthy because he perceives that he is good, and this sort of perception is pleasant in itself. He must, then, perceive his friend's being together   10
[with his own], and he will do this when they live together and share conversation and thought. For in the case of human beings

what seems to count as living together is this sharing of conversation and thought, not sharing the same pasture, as in the case of grazing animals.

15   If, then, for the blessedly happy person, being is choiceworthy, since it is naturally good and pleasant; and if the being of his friend is closely similar to his own; then his friend will also be choiceworthy. Whatever is choiceworthy for him he must possess, since otherwise he will to this extent lack something, [and hence will not be self-sufficient]. Anyone who is to be

ix 10 happy, then, must have excellent friends.

20   Then should we have as many friends as possible? Or is it the same as with the friendship of host and guest, where it seems to be good advice to 'have neither many nor none'? Is this also good advice in friendship, to have neither no friends nor many?

25   With friends for utility the advice seems very apt, since it is hard work to return many people's services, and life is too short for it. Indeed, more [such] friends than are adequate for one's own life are superfluous, and a hindrance to living finely; hence we have no need of them. A few friends for pleasure are enough also, just as a little seasoning on food is enough.

Of excellent people, however, should we have as many as

30   possible as friends, or is there some proper measure of their number, as of the number in a city? For a city could not be formed from ten human beings, but it would be a city no longer if it had ten myriads; presumably, though, the right quantity is not just

1171a one number, but anything between certain defined limits. Hence there is also some limit defining the number of friends.

Presumably, this is the largest number with whom you could live together, since we found that living together seems to be most characteristic of friendship. And clearly you cannot live with many people and distribute yourself among them.

Besides, these many people must also be friends to each other,

5   if they are all to spend their days together; and this is hard work for many people to manage. It also becomes difficult for many to share each other's enjoyments and distresses as their own, since you are quite likely to find yourself sharing one friend's pleasure and another friend's grief at the same time.

Presumably, then, it is good not to seek as many friends as possible, and good to have no more than enough for living

10   together; indeed it even seems impossible to be an extremely close friend to many people. For the same reason it also seems

impossible to be passionately in love with many people, since passionate erotic love tends to be an excess of friendship, and one has this for one person; hence also one has extremely close friendship for a few people.

This would seem to be borne out in what people actually do. For the friendship of companions is not found in groups of many people, and the friendships celebrated in song are always   15 between two people. By contrast, those who have many friends and treat everyone as close to them seem to be friends to no one, except in a fellow-citizen's way. These people are regarded as ingratiating.

Certainly it is possible to be a friend of many in a fellow-citizen's way, and still to be a truly decent person, not ingratiating; but it is impossible to be many people's friend for their virtue and for themselves. We have reason to be satisfied if we can find   20 even a few such friends.

Have we more need of friends in good fortune or in ill fortune?   ix 11 For in fact we seek them in both, since in ill fortune we need assistance, while in good fortune we need friends to live with and to benefit, since then we wish to do good.

Certainly it is more necessary to have friends in ill fortune, and hence useful friends are needed here. But it is finer to have   25 them in good fortune, and hence we also seek decent friends; for it is more choiceworthy to do good to them and spend our time with them.

The very presence of friends is also pleasant, in ill fortune as well as good fortune; for we have our pain lightened when our friends share our distress. Hence indeed one might be puzzled   30 about whether they take a part of it from us, as though helping us to lift a weight, or, alternatively, their presence is pleasant and our awareness that they share our distress makes the pain smaller. Well, we need not discuss whether it is this or something else that lightens our pain; at any rate, what we have mentioned does appear to occur.

However, the presence of friends would seem to be a mixture   35 [of pleasure and pain]. For certainly the sight of our friends in   1171b itself is pleasant, especially when we are in ill fortune, and it gives us some assistance in removing our pain. For a friend consoles us by the sight of him and by conversation, if he is dexterous, since he knows our character and what gives us pleasure and pain. Nonetheless, awareness of his pain at our ill

5   fortune is painful to us, since everyone tries to avoid causing pain to his friends.

That is why someone with a manly nature tries to prevent his friend from sharing his pain. Unless he is unusually immune to pain, he cannot endure pain coming to his friends; and he does not allow others to share his mourning at all, since he is not prone
10 to mourn himself either. Females, however, and effeminate men enjoy having people to wail with them; they love them as friends who share their distress. But in everything we clearly must imitate the better person.

In good fortune, by contrast, the presence of friends makes it pleasant to pass our time and to notice that they take pleasure in our own goods.

15 Hence it seems that we must eagerly call our friends to share our good fortune, since it is fine to do good. But we must hesitate to call them to share our ill fortune, since we must share bad things with them as little as possible; hence the saying 'My misfortune is enough'. We should invite them most of all when-
20 ever they will benefit us greatly, with little trouble to themselves.

Conversely, it is presumably appropriate to go eagerly, without having to be called, to friends in misfortune. For it is proper to a friend to benefit, especially to benefit a friend in need who has not demanded it, since this is finer and pleasanter for both friends. In good fortune he should come eagerly to help him, since friends are needed for this also; but he should be slow to
25 come to receive benefits, since eagerness to be benefitted is not fine. Presumably, though, one should avoid getting a reputation for being a killjoy, as sometimes happens, by refusing benefits.

Hence the presence of friends is apparently choiceworthy in all conditions.

ix 12   What the erotic lover likes most is the sight of his beloved,
30 and this is the sort of perception he chooses over the others, supposing that this above all is what makes him fall in love and remain in love. In the same way, surely, what friends find most choiceworthy is living together. For friendship is community, and we are related to our friend as we are related to ourselves. Hence, since the perception of our own being is choiceworthy, so is the perception of our friend's being. Perception is active
35 when we live with him; hence, not surprisingly, this is what we
1172a   seek.

Whatever someone [regards as] his being, or the end for which he chooses to be alive, that is the activity he wishes to pursue in his friend's company. Hence some friends drink together, others play dice, while others do gymnastics and go hunting, or do philosophy. They spend their days together on whichever pursuit in life they like most; for since they want to live with their friends, they share the actions in which they find their common life.

Hence the friendship of base people turns out to be vicious. For they are unstable, and share base pursuits; and by becoming similar to each other, they grow vicious. But the friendship of decent people is decent, and increases the more often they meet. And they seem to become still better from their activities and their mutual correction. For each moulds the other in what they approve of, so that '[you will learn] what is noble from noble people'.

So much, then, for friendship. The next task will be to discuss pleasure.

Aristotle

RHETORIC

Introduction

Aristotle disclaims precision for the definitions of the various emotions that he proposes in the *Rhetoric* (1359b2–17); nonetheless, his brief discussion of friendship and friendliness in II.4 illuminates the more formal discussion of the *Ethics* and is an indispensable supplement to it.

Perhaps the chief interest of this passage is its depiction of friendliness as based on reasons. In the *Ethics*, Aristotle had distinguished love *for* (or 'on account of') what is good, useful, or pleasant, suggesting that the emotion constituting friendship is responsive to reasons. A view of this sort is developed in the *Rhetoric*, where Aristotle provides a kind of catalogue of the reasons why we might be well disposed to others.

He is much more interested in detail here than in the *Ethics*. In the *Ethics*, for example, Aristotle speaks broadly of loving someone for his goodness of character. And what he says in the *Rhetoric* about feeling friendly towards those who have various virtues (1381a20–30) might help us to see what form, for Aristotle, that sort of love took in ordinary life. Again, in the *Ethics* Aristotle remarks in passing that we cannot easily be friends with those who are unpleasant to live with (1158b23–27). But in the *Rhetoric*, Aristotle describes, with a shrewd sense of human nature, specific traits that make someone a pleasant or unpleasant companion (1381a30–b10).

As suits the purposes of the *Rhetoric*, Aristotle seems more concerned here with what might be called 'formal characteristics' of friendly relations. After Aristotle it became proverbial that friendly regard is transitive: 'friends of friends are themselves friends.' But here we find a full catalogue: we love

those who are friends of friends, lovers of friends, loved by
friends, enemies of enemies, haters of enemies, and hated by
enemies (1381a15–20).

Although he promises a definition of *friendship*, Aristotle instead defines *friend* (1381a1–2). As in the *Ethics*, reciprocity is
necessary. However, unlike the *Ethics*, a practical tendency to
act on goodwill is built into the definition; the reason for this
may simply be that, in the *Rhetoric*, *friend* is defined in terms
of *friendliness*, which involves a tendency to act (1381a1),
whereas in the *Ethics* Aristotle defines friendship merely in
terms of goodwill (1156a3–5), which need not imply action
(1167a1–10, but see VIII.5). Furthermore, in the *Ethics*, being
aware of one's mutual goodwill for another is an essential
component of friendship (1155b34–56a4). But Aristotle somewhat sharply distinguishes in the *Rhetoric* between being a
friend and thinking oneself a friend (1381a1–4). This certainly
suggests that persons can think themselves friends without
being such, and it possibly implies, against the *Ethics*, that
persons who do not think themselves friends can *discover* that
they are.

One further point: that a friend is related to another as to
his own self is a fundamental theme of the *Ethics* (1166a30–31,
1170b5–6, 1171b33–34). In the *Rhetoric*, emphasis is placed instead merely on what might be described as *coincidence of wills*
(1381a10–11, 19–20, 32–34). This would seem to be a kind of
friendly relation that one *finds oneself in*, not a friendship that
one *makes*.

Aristotle

RHETORIC
II 4

1380b35 Let us say what sorts of people we are friendly to or hate, and why, but first let us define friendship and friendliness.[1]

1381a Let us take friendliness to be wishing to another what one thinks good,[2] for his sake and not for one's own, and also being disposed to do these things as far as one can. One person is a friend to another if he is friendly to the other and the other is friendly to him in return; and we think we are friends if we think that this is our relation to each other.

If these assumptions are accepted, then necessarily one is a friend to another person if one shares the other's pleasure in good 5 things and his distress at painful things, not because of something else, but because of the other person himself. For we all enjoy getting what we wish for, and we suffer pain in the contrary cases, so that pains and pleasures are signs of what we wish. People are also friends[3] if the same things are good and bad for them, or if they are friends to the same people and enemies to the same people. Necessarily these people wish the same things, and so, since

1. **friendship:** *philia*. **friendliness:** *philein*. Sometimes *philein* would appropriately be rendered 'love', and this seems the best rendering for the discussion of *philia* in the *Ethics*, where Aristotle is primarily concerned with relatively close and stable relations between people. His focus in the *Rhetoric*, however, is somewhat different; the *Rhetoric* is a book of advice to public speakers in political and legal contexts; and in Book ii Aristotle describes the different feelings, emotions, and attitudes that orators might try to arouse in their audience. His discussion of *philia* is not concerned primarily with ways of establishing close and lasting affectionate relations between individuals, but with arousing friendly or hostile feelings or attitudes. In this context 'friendliness' seems the best rendering. The rendering 'love' runs the risk of misleading the reader (and even of making Aristotle's claims sound quite odd—e.g. his remark that we tend to *philein* people who dress neatly, 1381b1).

2. **thinks good:** i.e. what A thinks good for B.

3. **People are also friends:** Read *êdê* (OCT: *dê*).

one wishes the same things for the other as one wishes for one-   10
self, one appears to be a friend to him.

We are also friendly to those who have benefited us or those
we care about; or if the benefits were great or given eagerly, or
if they were given on some difficult occasion, and for our own
sake, or if we think the other person wishes to benefit us.

Also to those who are friends of our friends and those who
are friendly to the people to whom we ourselves are friendly,
and also to those to whom the people we ourselves are friendly   15
to are friendly.

Also to those who are enemies to and hate the people we hate,
and the ones who are hated by the people we hate. For it appears
to us that what is good for these people is the same as what is
good for ourselves, so that we wish what is good for them,[4]
which is characteristic of a friend.

Also to those who tend to benefit us by providing money or   20
safety; that is why we honour generous, brave, and just people.
We suppose that these are people who do not make their living
from other people; these are the ones who make their living by
their own work, and among these the ones who make their living
by farming, especially those who work with their own hands.
We are also friendly to temperate people because they are not
unjust, and to people who are not busybodies, for the same   25
reason.

We are also friendly to those to whose friends we wish to be,
if they appear to wish to be our friends. These are good by having
virtue or have a good reputation, either among all or among the
best people, or among those whom we admire, or among those
who admire us.

Also to those who are pleasant to pass the time with and spend
our days with. These are good tempered, not eager to expose   30
our mistakes, not competitive, and not quarrelsome (for all such
people easily start fights, and people who are fighting appear to
have contrary wishes). They are also dexterous in making jokes
and taking them, for in both ways they have the same aims as
their neighbour, since they are both able to take a joke and able   35
to make the appropriate sort of joke.

---

4. **For it appears . . . what is good for them:** Or: 'For the same things appear
good to these people as appear good to ourselves, so that they wish the things
that are good for us'.

We are also friendly to people who praise the good points we
1381b have, especially those who praise the ones we are afraid we lack.

Also to people who are neat in their appearance, their dress,
and their way of life in general.

Also to those who do not reproach us either because of ⟨our⟩
mistakes or because of the good turns ⟨they have done for us⟩,
for both sorts of people are eager to expose shortcomings.

5   Also to those who do not bear grudges or keep track of griev-
ances, but are easily reconciled, for we suppose they will treat
us in the way they treat others.

Also to those who do not slander and who know good things,
not the bad things, about their neighbours or about ourselves;
for this is what the good person does.

Also to those who do not pick quarrels with[5] someone who is
10   angry or eager for something, for people who pick such quarrels
are the sort who are prone to fight.

We are also friendly to those who have some favourable attitude towards us—if, for instance, they admire us, take us to be
virtuous, or enjoy our company. This is especially true if they
take this attitude towards the qualities for which we ourselves
most of all wish to be admired or to be thought virtuous or
pleasant.

15   Also to those who are similar to us and who engage in the
same pursuits, provided that they do not obstruct us or make
their living from the same sort of work—for that is a case of
'potter ⟨quarrels with⟩ potter'. We are also friendly to those who
desire the same things as we desire, provided that it is possible
for both us and them to get these things; if it is not possible, the
same thing happens here as in the previous case.

Also to those who do not make us feel ashamed of doing
20   something unconventional—provided that this is not because
we look down on them—and to those who make us feel ashamed
of doing what is really wrong.

Also to those who wish to be friends, to rivals, or those whom
we want to feel emulation rather than spite towards us, and to
those with whom we cooperate in securing some benefit to them,
provided that a worse harm to ourselves will not result.

Also to those who remain friends to someone when he is

5. lit. 'oppose'.

absent as well as when he is present. That is why everyone is   25
also friendly to someone who is loyal to a dead friend. And in
general we are friendly to those who have intense friendships
and do not abandon their friends, for among good people we
are friendly most of all to those who are good friends.

Also to those who do not put on a false front towards us.
These are people who admit their own faults to us—for we have   30
said that we are not ashamed in front of our friends of doing
something unconventional. If, then, one who is ashamed ⟨in
these cases⟩ is not friendly to us, one who is not ashamed is like
someone who is friendly to us.

Also to those whom we do not find frightening and those who
give us confidence, for no one is friendly to someone he is afraid
of.

The species of friendship are companionship, intimacy, kinship, and so on. The causes of friendship are doing kindnesses,   35
doing them without being asked, and doing them without an-
nouncing it afterwards, for in this way someone appears to be
doing something for our own sake and not because of something
else.

It is evident that we must study enmity and hatred from the   1382a
things contrary to those we have described. The causes of enmity
are anger, malicious opposition, and slander.

Now anger is provoked by offences against oneself, but enmity
may arise without them; for we hate someone if we ⟨simply⟩
suppose that he has a bad character. Moreover, anger is always   5
directed at a particular, e.g. at Callias or Socrates, whereas hatred
may also be directed at kinds of people, for everyone hates the
thief and the informer. Further, anger is curable by lapse of time,
whereas hatred is incurable. Anger is a desire to inflict pain,
whereas hatred is a desire to inflict evil; for if we are angry, we
want someone to suffer and to be aware of it,[6] but if we hate
him, we do not care about that. Everything painful is something   10
that the person who has it is aware of, but the worst evils,
injustice and foolishness, are those that the unjust or foolish
person is least aware of, since the presence of the evil gives him
no pain. Again, anger involves pain, whereas hatred does not,
for if we are angry, we feel pain, but this is not true for hatred.

---

6. **we want . . . aware of it:** Or 'we want to be aware of his suffering'.

Moreover, if the person we are angry with suffers a great deal, we may take pity[7] on him, but no amount of suffering changes
15 our mind if we hate someone; for if we are angry with someone, we ⟨only⟩ want him to suffer in return, but if we hate ⟨some type of person⟩, we want ⟨that type of person⟩ not to exist at all.

It is evident from this, then, that it is possible, when people are enemies or friends, to prove that they are; when they are not, to make them out to be so;[8] when they say they are, to refute the assertion;[9] and if they are disputing about whether anger or enmity ⟨was the source of some offence⟩, to trace it back to whichever source one decides.

7. **if the person . . . we may take pity:** Or 'in many circumstances an angry person may take pity'.

8. **to make them out to be so:** Or 'to make them so'.

9. **to refute the assertion:** Or 'to dissolve the friendship'.

Cicero

ON FRIENDSHIP
(*DE AMICITIA*)

Introduction

"Please put me out of your mind for a little while and believe that Laelius himself is talking," Cicero writes in the introduction to his dialogue-treatise on friendship. Gaius Laelius (b. 186 B.C.), the principal speaker of the dialogue, had been trained in philosophy under the Stoics Diogenes and Panaetius. Hence Cicero's request may well contain a recognition of his own limitations, for Cicero was not an original philosopher—in philosophical circles, he is remembered today chiefly as someone who transmitted Greek philosophical thought to Roman culture. By speaking in the person of Laelius and by relying on the friendship of the reader, who he hopes will find something of himself in the dialogue, Cicero seems to succeed in transcending some of his own limitations.

After a consideration of how a virtuous man should be affected by the death of a close friend (II–IV), Laelius' discourse on friendship proper begins. We are given first of all an encomium on friendship (V–VII), which enumerates the many ways in which friendship is a good. Next the origin of friendship is discussed (VIII–IX), and then various threats to the stability of a friendship (X–XX). In this part of the dialogue and in the final section, in which friendship among ordinary men is considered (XXI–XXVI), Cicero moves from topic to topic somewhat unsystematically, evidently not wishing to sacrifice detail to some scheme of organization. The movement of the dialogue as a whole is from the general and theoretical to the particular and practical. It begins with definition and argument and ends with precepts, warnings, and examples.

Cicero's own philosophical talent lay in formulating images that reveal the force of a philosophical idea. He invents not arguments but rather turns of phrase worth contemplating. An example of this is his striking explanation of the strength of a bond of friendship: he says that it is a kind of concentration and focussing on a single person of the natural and (in principle) unlimited affection we have for any member of the human race (V.20).

The central idea of the dialogue is that "friendship springs rather from nature than from need" (VIII.27). Need is not the cause, Cicero holds, since a certain kind of self-sufficiency, a recognition that all of one's goods are within oneself (II.7; VIII.30; XXI.79), is a precondition of entering into true friendship. It is rather that nature spurs us to friendship, through an innate principle which causes us to love anyone who manifests virtue, without a regard for our own benefit (VII.28–IX.29).

Cicero

ON FRIENDSHIP
(*DE AMICITIA*)

Quintus Mucius Scaevola the Augur, out of the rich fund of his 1.1
memories, used to tell many delightful tales about his father-
in-law, Gaius Laelius, and, no matter what the subject of his
discourse, he invariably called him "Laelius the Wise." My own
father, on the day when I put on the toga of manhood, took me
to Scaevola with the understanding that insofar as I could, and
he would permit me, I should never leave the old gentleman's
side. Many a wise discourse did Scaevola hold, and many a
pointed and timely saying did he utter; these I persistently committed to memory, and was ever eager to profit by his wisdom.
After he died, I attached myself to Scaevola the Pontifex, a man
whom I may well call the one figure in our State who was truly
outstanding for his intellectual qualities and his sense of justice.
But of him, some other time. I return to Scaevola the Augur.

I have, of course, a great many memories of him, but I particu-   2
larly recall one occasion when he was sitting on a bench in his
garden, as he frequently did, in the company of a few close
friends, I among them. At that time he hit upon a topic of
conversation which was then on many people's lips. You remember it, certainly, Atticus. I'm sure you must, for in those days
you were a close friend of Publius Sulpicius. He was tribune of
the plebs, and had become the sworn enemy of Quintus Pompeius, who was then consul, after having lived on the most
intimate and cordial terms with him. You remember how people
felt: so amazed! so distressed!

Well, it happened that Scaevola, having hit upon that topic,   3
went on to recount for us a discourse on the subject of friendship
which Laelius had held in the presence of Scaevola himself and

Excerpts from Cicero: *On Old Age and Friendship*, translated by Frank Copley,
copyright © 1967. Reprinted by permission of the University of Michigan Press.

of Laelius' other son-in-law, Gaius Fannius, a few days after the death of Africanus. The ideas which Laelius had put forth I have never forgotten, and in this essay I have tried to represent them in the way I judged best—that is to say, I have depicted these individuals as actually speaking, so that I should not constantly have to stop to say "I said" and "he said," and so that we might get the feeling of their being right here and conversing with us.

4　　　You have suggested to me a great many times that I write an essay on friendship, and I quite agree that it is a subject that everyone ought to think about, and that it is particularly deserving of the consideration of men who have been as close friends as you and I. Accordingly, I have not been at all loth to adopt, at your suggestion, a procedure which may well benefit many. Now, in my "Cato the Elder," an essay on old age which I addressed to you, I represented Cato in his later years and put the discourse in his mouth. My reason for doing this was that I could think of no person better suited for discussing that period of life than one who had lived many years beyond the point at which one becomes old and in those very later years had distinguished himself beyond other men. Well, then! We have heard from our elders how truly remarkable was the friendship between Laelius and Publius Scipio, and accordingly I have judged that the figure of Laelius was the right one to utter those very sentiments which Scaevola recalled had been expressed by him. It is a fact that discourses of this kind, when placed in the mouths of men of an earlier day—especially if they be men of distinction—carry with them, somehow, a greater degree of conviction. Yes, indeed! Sometimes, when I am reading what I myself wrote, I get the strange feeling that it is actually Cato, and not I, who is doing the talking!

5　　　On that occasion I wrote as one old man to another on the subject of old age; in exactly the same way, in this present essay, I have written as one dear friend to another on the subject of friendship. In the earlier work, Cato was the speaker. I doubt if there were many men older than he at the time at which the dialogue was represented as having taken place; I am sure there was no one better acquainted with the ways of the world. In the present essay, Laelius will be the speaker—Laelius the Wise, for that is what everyone called him—and not only was he wise, but also famous for his splendid qualities as a friend. It is he who will discourse for us on the subject of friendship. Do you think that you could put me out of your mind for the moment, and imagine that Laelius himself is the actual speaker? I should like it so. See, here come Gaius Fannius and Quintus Mucius to call on their father-in-law just after the death of Africanus. They will begin the conversation, and Laelius will reply to them. His will be the whole discourse on friendship: read it, and you will recognize yourself.

FANNIUS. What you say is true, Laelius: there never was a finer   II.6
man than Africanus nor a more distinguished one, either. But you must realize that the eyes of every one of us are fastened on you, and on you alone. You are the one whom men not only call "wise" but truly deem so. This same tribute was paid not many years ago to Marcus Cato; we are well aware that Lucius Acilius, among men of an earlier day, was called "the Wise." However, they received this appellation for somewhat different reasons, Acilius, because he was accounted well-versed in the law, Cato, because of his rich fund of experience. Men were always telling stories of his conduct in Senate or forum—of the astuteness with which he laid his plans, the courage with which he carried them out, the acuity with which he replied to his opponents. It was for these reasons that in his later years he bore, virtually as part of his name, the sobriquet of "the Wise."

In your case, however, the matter is rather different. Men   7
judge you to be wise not only because of your natural endowments and your habitual ways of acting and thinking, but also because of your zeal for learning and because of your accomplishments in that field. And they apply the term not in the casual manner of the ignorant, but after the fashion of truly cultivated men. Of this kind of wise man, so they tell us, there was in all the rest of Greece not a single example (for the "Seven Wise Men," so-called, are not counted in the number of the wise by those who investigate such matters with real precision), and at Athens there was only one—the one, that is, who had been adjudged wisest of men by Apollo's oracle. This is the kind of wisdom men deem you to possess; it leads you to conclude that your whole life lies in your own hands, and that the fortunes of human existence are inferior, in power and in worth, to virtue. It is for this reason that people keep asking me—and Scaevola, here, too, I imagine—how you are taking the death of Africanus. They are all the more anxious because at the last Nones, when, as is our custom, we had gathered in the garden of Decimus

Brutus the Augur, for consultation, you did not appear, although you had habitually been very conscientious in your attention to that date and those duties.

8   SCAEVOLA. Yes, indeed, Gaius Laelius, many people, as Fannius has just said, have been making inquiry. But in answer I recount what I have simply observed. I tell them that you are grieved at the death of Africanus—a great man, and your very dear friend—but that you are bearing your grief with due restraint; that you could not be otherwise than deeply moved, for that would be inconsistent with your warm-hearted nature. As for your absence from the meeting of our College on the Nones, I tell them that your reason was illness, not grief.

LAELIUS. Good, Scaevola; you were right. That is an engagement I have always kept, and as long as I was well, I have never thought it right to absent myself from it because of personal inconvenience. In my opinion, nothing can happen to a man of principle that could cause him to fail in the discharge of any duty.

9   Fannius, when you say that people credit me with so much— with far more than I have any right to expect or even to acknowledge—that is very kind of you. But it seems to me that you are wrong in your judgment about Cato. For either no man was ever truly wise—and I am inclined to think that this is the sounder position—or else Cato was. To say nothing of other matters, how well he bore the death of his son! And I didn't forget Paulus, either, and I actually saw Gallus; but these men lost mere boys, while Cato's son was a man, already tried and tested.

10   Be careful, then, about putting anyone ahead of Cato— even that very man you mentioned, whom Apollo, as you say, judged to be wisest of men; for Cato's reputation is based on what he did, the other's on what he said. As for myself, to speak now to the two of you together, this is how I should like you to think of me.

III.   If I should say that I felt no sorrow at the loss of Scipio, I should leave it to the philosophers to judge whether I was doing right; but I should certainly not be telling the truth. I do indeed grieve! After all, I have been bereaved of a friend such as the world will never see again—at least, so it seems to me. One thing I am sure of: there never was such a one before. But I am in no need of panaceas; I am quite capable of consoling myself, and I am particularly comforted by the fact that I am free of that error which in most men is the usual cause of anguish at the passing of friends. I do not feel that Scipio has suffered any misfortune; I am the one who has suffered misfortune, if any has occurred. But to be crushed by grief at one's own misfortunes is the act not of a man who loves his friend, but of one who loves himself.

Now in Scipio's case, who would say that life had not treated him extraordinarily well? For unless he had had the temerity to want to live forever—a thought that never crossed his mind— what did he not achieve that a mere human being may rightly pray for? His fellow-countrymen began to pin the greatest hopes on him even while he was a mere lad. He never disappointed them, and when he reached manhood his greatness surpassed even their fondest expectations. He never sought the consulship, yet he was twice elected to it, the first time before the legal age, the second at an hour virtually tailor-made for him, but very nearly too late for his country. Two cities were most resolutely opposing and endangering the onward march of our power; these he laid level with the ground, and in so doing wiped war from the face of the earth, now and for all time to come. Why should I speak of his wondrously kind and gentle ways—of his deep devotion to his mother, his generosity to his sisters, his benevolence toward his relatives, his justice toward all men? You know all that. How beloved he was of his fellow-citizens was made clear by the mourning at his funeral. Well, then, what would a man like that have stood to gain from the addition of a few more years of life? Even if old age be not burdensome, as I recall Cato argued—it was the year before he died, and Scipio and I were both present—yet even so, it does take away those "green and salad days" that Scipio was still enjoying at the time of his recent death.

His life, then, was so blessed by fortune and so distinguished by achievement that little, if anything, could have been added to it; as for his death, it happened so quickly that he could scarcely have noticed it. About the manner of his death, it is difficult to say a great deal, but you know what people suspect. This much, however, I may assert with complete assurance: Scipio had known many days in the course of his life when the people had thronged about him and filled him with joy, but of all those days, his last was his most glorious; for on that occasion, after the Senate had adjourned, he was escorted home as evening came on by the Senators, by the whole citizen-body, and by our

11

12

Latin allies—on the day that was his last on this earth. To so lofty a pinnacle, in fact, had he been exalted, that we may rightly imagine him to have made his way to the gods above rather than to those of the underworld.

IV.13   For I cannot agree with those who in the last few years have begun to discuss such matters and to say that the soul dies with the body and that death is the end of all things. I am more inclined to accept the point of view expressed by men of earlier days—by our own ancestors, for example, who so scrupulously observed the honors due the dead. This they would most certainly not have done, if they had thought that the dead had no interest in anything at all. There is the view, too, of those men who lived here in Italy, in the section called "Greater Greece"—now it lies in ruins, but in those days it was rich and powerful—and it was they who by their principles and precepts gave it true intellectual distinction. Nor should we omit the opinion of that man who was adjudged wisest of men by Apollo's oracle. In this matter he did not waver from one point of view to another, as he did in many instances, but always consistently maintained that the souls of men were divine, and that when they had departed from the body, they found the road back to heaven lying open before them, and that, the better and more just a man had been, the smoother and easier this road was for him.

14   Now this was always Scipio's opinion, too. As a matter of fact, he might be said to have had a presentiment of what was to come. Only a very few days before his death, Philus and Manilius were with him, and a number of others had come, too, including you, Scaevola, and me, and on that occasion he discoursed for three days on the subject of the State. Near the very end of his discussion, he turned to the topic of the immortality of the soul, relating what he said he had heard from Africanus in a dream. If it is indeed correct that when a truly good man dies his soul takes flight, so to speak, with the greatest of ease from the emprisonment of the flesh, for whom do we imagine that passage to the realm of the divine would have been easier than for Scipio? For this reason I am afraid that to mourn at what has happened to him would come more naturally to one who hated him than to one who loved him. If on the other hand the opposite view is sounder, that is, that body and soul both perish together, and no sensation at all is left, then, to be sure, there is nothing good in death, but equally surely there is nothing bad. For once all

sensation has been lost, a man's state is exactly the same as if he had never been born at all. But still, the fact that Scipio was born makes all of us, here, very happy, and will be cause for rejoicing to this State, too, as long as it exists.

And so, as I said before, life has dealt very well with him, and 15 not so satisfactorily with me, for it would have been fairer that I, since I entered on life earlier than he, should also have departed earlier from it. Still, the joy that I gain from looking back upon our friendship causes me to conclude that my life has been rich and good, simply because I spent it in Scipio's company. He and I stood side by side in our concern for affairs of state and for personal matters; we shared a citizen's home and a soldier's tent; we shared the one element indispensable to friendship, a complete agreement in aims, ambitions, and attitudes. Therefore I do not take so much delight in that reputation for wisdom which Fannius mentioned a moment ago—and it isn't deserved, anyway—as I do in the hope that for all time to come men will remember my friendship with Scipio. And I cherish this hope the more because in all the course of history men can name scarcely three or four pairs of friends; to this category, I venture to hope, men will assign the friendship of Scipio and Laelius.

FANNIUS. That, Laelius, is bound to happen. But you have just 16 made mention of friendship. Well, we are at leisure: would you like to do a favor for me, and for Scaevola, too, I'm sure? You are always ready to talk about other questions that are raised with you: would you now in like fashion tell us what you think about friendship? How would you define it? What principles would you lay down for it?

SCAEVOLA. I shall certainly regard that as a favor. As a matter of fact, I was just about to bring up that question with you, when Fannius anticipated me. Indeed, yes; you would be doing a great favor for both of us.

LAELIUS. I should undertake such an assignment with the v.17 greatest willingness, if I were sure of my ability to handle it. Friendship is a wonderful thing, and, as Fannius has remarked, we are at leisure. But who am I? What qualifications have I? It is learned men, and Greeks at that, who are in the habit of doing the kind of thing you propose—having questions laid before them for discussion at a mere moment's notice. That is a big undertaking, and requires no small amount of practice. And so, if you want a philosophical disquisition on friendship, I suggest that you ask it of those who make a profession of such things. All I can do is to urge you to put friendship ahead of all other human concerns, for there is nothing so suited to man's nature, nothing that can mean so much to him, whether in good times or in bad.

18   In any case, I want to say first of all that friendship can exist only between good men. Now I am not going to split hairs on this question, as do those who inquire into such matters with fine precision; they say, you know, that no one can be a good man unless he is possessed of perfect wisdom. Perhaps so, but they are talking about a kind of wisdom that no man to this day has ever acquired. Our task is to look at conditions which actually exist in human life, not at those that men dream about or pray for. I should never say that even Gaius Fabricius, Manius Curius, and Tiberius Coruncanius, whom our forefathers always judged to be men of true wisdom, were wise by any such standard as that. Well then, let them keep that term "wisdom" for their own uses: it is productive of nothing but ill-will and misunderstanding; let them grant only that men such as I have just mentioned were good men. Of course they won't do it; they will insist that such a concession can be made only in the case of their "truly wise" man.

19   As for us, I suggest that we pursue the matter with our own crude mother wit, as the saying goes. There are men who behave and live in such a way that they are regarded as models of honor, integrity, justice, and generosity, men who have no vestige of avarice, lustfulness, or insolence, men of unwavering conviction, men, in short, like those whose names I just mentioned. Such men are commonly regarded as good men; by the same sign, let us decide to call them so, for, as far as men can, it is they who follow nature as the best guide to the good life. For I believe I see quite clearly that all men are meant by nature to have some sort of companionship one with another, and that the depth and significance of this companionship varies according to the degree of relationship between them. Thus it is stronger between citizen and citizen than between citizen and foreigner, between those who are related by blood than between those who are not. In the latter case, at least, nature herself brings about a friendship, but it is not quite as firmly based as it ought to be. For the friend has this advantage over the relative: relatives may lose their

goodwill, friends cannot, for once goodwill has been lost, the friend is no longer a friend, but the relative is still a relative.|

We can best comprehend the power of friendship by consider-   20
ing the fact that nature has established social contact between countless numbers of men; yet friendship is so concentrated and restricted a thing that all the true affection in the world is shared by no more than a handful of individuals.

| Now friendship is just this and nothing else: complete sympa-   VI.
thy in all matters of importance, plus goodwill and affection| and I am inclined to think that with the exception of wisdom, the gods have given nothing finer to men than this. Some people place wealth ahead of it, some good health, some power, some honors, a good many even pleasure. This last, of course, is on the mere animal level; the others are unstable things that one can never be sure of, since they depend not upon our own efforts, but upon fickle Fortune. Those who say that virtue is man's highest good, are of course very inspiring; but it is to this very virtue that friendship owes its beginning and its identity: without virtue friendship cannot exist at all.

But now let us define virtue in terms of our own way of life   21
and in words that we can understand, and let us not measure it by the degree to which we can speak of it in grandiose terms, as some professional philosophers do. Let us count as good men those who are commonly so considered—men like Paulus, Cato, Galus, Scipio, Philus. Ordinary people are quite content with them; let us forget about individuals who never existed anywhere on the face of the earth.

In the first place, how can there be a "life worth living," as   22
Ennius puts it, unless it rest upon the mutual love of friends? What could be finer than to have someone to whom you may speak as freely as to yourself? How could you derive true joy from good fortune, if you did not have someone who would rejoice in your happiness as much as you yourself? And it would be very hard to bear misfortune in the absence of anyone who would take your sufferings even harder than you. Finally, the other things on which we set our hearts have each of them a strictly limited utility: money, that we may spend it; power, that we may acquire a following; honors, that we may gain praise; pleasure, that we may enjoy it; health, that we may be free of pain and make full use of our physical endowments; friendship,

on the other hand, brings with it many advantages. Wherever you turn, it is at your side; there is no place not open to it; it is never untimely, never in the way. In short, not even water and fire, as the saying goes, are as universally essential to us as friendship. And I am not now speaking of the friendships of everyday folk, or of ordinary people—although even these are a source of pleasure and profit—but of true and perfect friendship, the kind that was possessed by those few men who have gained names for themselves as friends. For when fortune smiles on us, friendship adds a luster to that smile; when she frowns, friendship absorbs her part and share of that frown, and thus makes it easier to bear.

vii.23   Now friendship possesses many splendid advantages, but of course the finest thing of all about it is that it sends a ray of good hope into the future, and keeps our hearts from faltering or falling by the wayside. For the man who keeps his eye on a true friend, keeps it, so to speak, on a model of himself. For this reason, friends are together when they are separated, they are rich when they are poor, strong when they are weak, and—a thing even harder to explain—they live on after they have died, so great is the honor that follows them, so vivid the memory, so poignant the sorrow. That is why friends who have died are accounted happy, and those who survive them are deemed worthy of praise. Why, if the mutual love of friends were to be removed from the world, there is no single house, no single state that would go on existing; even agriculture would cease to be. If this seems a bit difficult to understand, we can readily see how great is the power of friendship and love by observing their opposites, enmity and ill will. For what house is so firmly established, what constitution is so unshakable, that it could not be utterly destroyed by hatred and internal division? From this we may judge how much good there is in friendship.

24   Why, at Agrigentum, so men say, there was a certain literary man who composed a poem in Greek in which, like some prophet of old, he declared that in all the universe everything that was firm-fixed and everything that was in motion was brought into union by friendship and scattered to fragments by discord. And, for that matter, every man alive understands that principle and has experienced the truth of it. For if ever an instance comes to light of a friend who showed his loyalty and devotion by risking his life or by sharing such a risk, who would not extoll him to

the skies? How the whole audience burst into a roar of applause not so long ago during the performance of my old friend Pacuvius' most recent play: the king did not know which man was Orestes; thereupon, Pylades declared that he was Orestes, so that he might die in Orestes' place; but Orestes insisted that *he* was Orestes, as indeed he was. The people leaped to their feet and applauded, although it was only a play; what do you think they would have done if it had been an incident in real life? It was easy to see what nature prompts men to do. Although they were not capable of doing such a thing themselves, they correctly judged its rightness when they saw it done by someone else. This, I believe, is all I can tell you of my feelings about friendship. If there are other things to say on the subject—and I have no doubt there are a great many—I think you had better direct your inquiries about them to those who make a practice of such disquisitions.

FANNIUS. But we, sir, would rather direct them to you. To be sure, I have often put the question to the sort of men you mention, and, for my part, have been very glad to hear what they had to say. But what you are saying seems to run in a quite different direction. 25

SCAEVOLA. You would say that even more, Fannius, if you had been with us a few days ago in Scipio's garden when we were talking about the State. How splendidly on that occasion did Laelius support the concept of justice against the fine-spun logic of Philus!

FANNIUS. That can't have been very difficult: the world's most just man standing up for justice!

SCAEVOLA. What, then, of friendship? Wouldn't the defense of it be easy for one who has gained his greatest glory from having maintained a friendship over the years in perfect loyalty, constancy, and justice?

LAELIUS. Here, here, now! This is compulsion! For what difference does it make what means you may take to compel me? You *are* compelling me, you know. For when one's sons-in-law are interested in something, especially in a serious and worthwhile matter, it is not only difficult but downright improper to hold out against them. Well, I have done a lot of thinking about friendship, and over and over again in the course of my reflections it has seemed to me that the most important question arising in connection with it is this: do men desire friendship VIII.26

because of their own feebleness and inadequacy, with the idea that by exchanging mutual services they may be able to give and to receive things that would be beyond their individual and separate powers? Or is this only a *result* of friendship, and there should be some other reason for it, something deeper and finer, and lying closer to man's very nature? For it is love (*amor*), the thing that gives us our word for friendship (*amicitia*), that provides the first impulse toward mutual regard. Advantages, you see, are garnered in many cases even by men who are the objects of simulated friendship, who are esteemed only for the sake of convenience. But in friendship there can be no element of show or pretense; everything in it is honest and spontaneous.

27   And so I should say that friendship takes its beginning from our very nature rather than from our sense of inadequacy, that it is due to an inclination of the heart together with a feeling of affection rather than to a consideration of the advantages which we might derive from the relation. What I mean by this can be observed even in the case of some animals: up to a certain time, they so love their young and are so loved by them that it is easy to see what their feelings are. In the case of the human being, this is even more obvious, first of all from the love that exists between children and parents—a love that can be destroyed only by the foulest crimes; second, when there arises a mutual feeling of affection—the sort of thing that occurs when we find someone with whose character and nature we feel ourselves in sympathy, because we think we see in him a bright and shining light, so to speak, of probity and virtue.

28   For there is nothing so worthy of love as virtue, nothing that offers stronger incentive to affection. Consider only the fact that we feel a kind of love even for men whom we have never seen, simply because of their virtue and probity. What man does not have a feeling of love and goodwill when he calls to mind Gaius Fabricius or Manius Curius—men whom he has never seen? What man, on the other hand, does not detest Tarquinius Superbus, Spurius Cassius, or Spurius Maelius? There were two generals against whom we fought for our very lives right here in Italy, Pyrrhus and Hannibal. For the one, because he was an upright man, we have no great feelings of enmity; the other, because he was bloodthirsty, this nation will never cease to hate.

IX.29   But if the force of probity is so great that we cherish it even in men whom we have never seen, yes—and this is still more impressive—even in an enemy, why is it surprising if the hearts of men are stirred when they find themselves observing the virtue and probity of individuals with whom they have been closely associated? It is true, of course, that such a feeling of affection is placed on a firm basis only after they have received kindnesses from these persons, have seen evidence of their interest in them, and have come to be on a footing of intimacy with them; when that first affectionate impulse of the heart has been augmented by these considerations, then there bursts forth a great and wonderful glow of love. If anyone thinks that this is to be attributed to a mere sense of inadequacy—that it exists solely to provide men with assistance in the achieving of their ambitions—he surely leaves friendship with a very humble beginning, with a base and ignoble birth, so to speak. Why! He wants it to be the child of insufficiency and poverty! If this were so, the less confidence a man had in himself, the better suited would he be for friendship—but this is far from the truth.

For the more confidence a man has in himself, the more he finds himself so fortified by virtue and wisdom that he is completely self-sufficient and believes that his destiny is in his own hands, so much the better will he be both at making and at keeping friends. Just think! Did Africanus have some "need" of me? Of course not, nor I of him. Why, no! I cherished him because, in a way, I looked up to his virtue; he, me, because of an opinion not altogether low, perhaps, that he had formed of my character; and our affection for each other grew as we were thrown more and more together. To be sure, many great advantages came to us both from our association, but it was not in expectation of these that we first began to feel drawn toward each other. 30

For we do not exercise kindness and generosity in order that we may put in a claim for gratitude; we do not make our feelings of affection into a business proposition. No, there is something in our nature that impels us to the open hand and heart. Thus it is that we are not led to friendship by the hope of material gain; rather, we judge it desirable because all its profits are encompassed by the feeling of love which it generates. 31

A very different opinion from this is held by those who, like mere animals, measure everything in terms of pleasure. And no wonder! To what lofty, splendid, god-like ideals can they look up, when they have placed all their thinking on so low and 32 contemptible a basis? However, let us exclude such men from our present deliberation. Let us keep clearly in mind that feelings of affection spring from our very nature, and that goodwill and charity come into being when we have seen clear signs of virtue. Men who make virtue their goal in life turn toward each other and grow closer and closer, that they may both enjoy the company of those they love, and derive profit from their character, that they may share and share alike in their affection for one another, that they may be more inclined to do favors than to receive them: this is the kind of competition—and an honorable kind it is—that will exist between them. This is the way in which we shall obtain the greatest advantages from friendship, and the impulse that leads us to it, being ascribed to our very nature rather than to our mere inadequacy, will be the more worthy of serious consideration and the more likely to be genuine. For if we put friendship together through the expectation of advantage, a change in our expectations would also rend it apart. But our essential nature cannot be changed, and for that reason true friendship endures forever. You see, now, what the origin of friendship is—or do you wish something further on this subject?

FANNIUS. No, Laelius. Please go on. As for our friend here, he is younger than I, and I stand on my rights as the elder in speaking for him.

33   SCAEVOLA. I quite agree, Fannius. Let's hear what you have to say, Laelius.

x.   LAELIUS. Well, then, dear friends, you shall hear what Scipio and I between us used to say on those many, many occasions when we were discussing friendship. You know, of course, that he always insisted that there was nothing harder than to maintain a friendship all the way to the last day of life, so often did it happen that interests did not agree, or there was a difference of opinion on political matters; he used to remark, too, that men's characters frequently suffer change, sometimes through ill fortune, sometimes with the increasing burden of years. As proof of these statements he used to take the analogy of boyhood, remarking that the friendships of boys were often laid aside along with the toga of childhood.

34   In cases where they were continued on into adulthood, he noted that they were still sometimes broken up by rivalry, either for a wife, or for some other advantage which the two could not obtain simultaneously. Even if some individuals remained

friends for quite a long time, their friendships were likely to be severely shaken if they should happen to become rivals for political office; for, he remarked, there was no greater danger to friendship, for ordinary men, than greed for money, and, for truly good men, than ambition for public office and distinction; from these sources, said he, the bitterest enmities had arisen, again and again, between the closest friends.

He used to say, too, that friendships were violently and in many cases quite properly broken up when men demanded of their friends something that was morally reprehensible, for example, that they assist in immorality, or aid in an illegal act. In these instances, men who refused their help, however honorable such refusal might be, nonetheless could be charged with violating the laws of friendship by those they refused to go along with; and these latter, who made bold to demand complete compliance from their friends, would say that they were showing, by the very fact of such a demand, that they themselves would do anything whatever for a friend's sake. This sort of complaint, he said, not only frequently destroyed friendships of long standing, but even became the source of enduring enmity. These, he declared, were the deadly perils, so to speak, that overhung friendship, and they were so numerous that, as he said it appeared to him, the avoiding of them required not only wisdom but also sheer good luck. 35

For all these reasons, let us first consider, if you please, how far a man ought to allow his devotion to a friend to take him. Assuming that Coriolanus had any friends, you don't suppose, do you, that they felt themselves bound to associate themselves with him in bearing arms against his own country? Or that Vecellinus' friends, or Maelius', felt themselves bound to aid these individuals in their attempts to set themselves up as monarchs? xi.36

Tiberius Gracchus tried to stir up trouble for the government; we saw how he was deserted by Quintus Tubero and by those of his own age who were his friends. Of course there is Gaius Blossius of Cumae, an old friend of your family's, Scaevola; he came to me when I was conferring with the consuls Laenas and Rupilius, on whose behalf I was to speak, and tried to beg off Gracchus. He wanted me to pardon him for doing so, and offered as his excuse that he was so devoted to Gracchus that he felt himself bound to do whatever Gracchus wanted. At that point I 37

asked him, "What? Even if he wanted to set fire to the Capitol?"
"Why!" said he, "Gracchus would never have wanted to do a
thing like that!" "But," said I, "if he had?" "I would have obeyed
his orders," said Blossius. You see what a vicious idea he expressed. Yes, and he did what he said he'd do, too—or even
more than he said. He did not fall in behind the wild schemes
of Gracchus, he led them; he made himself not merely the associate of that madman, but his champion. This was sheer insanity,
and when a court of investigation was promptly set up, Blossius
became terrified and fled to Asia, where he joined our enemies.
In the end he paid due penalty to the State—a heavy and a just
penalty. Wrongdoing, then, is not excused if it is committed for
the sake of a friend; after all, the thing that brings friends together
is their conviction of each other's virtue; it is hard to keep up a
friendship, if one has deserted virtue's camp.

38   But if we have decided that it is right to grant to friends
whatever they may wish, or to get from them whatever we may
wish, then if we should be possessed of perfect wisdom, such a
relation would have no degree of wrong in it; however, we are
talking of the sort of friends who are within our purview, whom
we have actually seen or whom we have heard people tell
about—the sort of people whom we have come to know in the
ordinary course of life. It is from their ranks that we must take our
examples, and especially from among those who come closest to
true wisdom.

39   We observe that Aemilius Papus was a close friend of Gaius
Luscinus; our forefathers have told us so, and have added that
they were twice elected together to the consulship and were
colleagues in the censorship. Furthermore, it is related that Manius Curius and Tiberius Coruncanius were in very intimate association with them and with each other. Surely, now, we may not
even suspect that any one of these men would have demanded
of his friend anything that would have been disloyal, or in viola-
tion of an oath, or unpatriotic. For in the case of men like these,
what point is there in saying that if they had demanded such a
thing they would have been refused? Why! these were men of
positively sacrosanct character, and it would be as wrong to
request such a thing as it would be to do it upon being requested!
And who were Tiberius Gracchus' followers? Gaius Carbo, Gaius
Cato! At that time his brother Gaius Gracchus was one of his

followers, too, though not at all an enthusiastic one; nowadays he has become his zealous partisan.

Let us, then, lay down this law for friendship: we must not ask wrongful things, nor do them, if we are asked to. For if a man should declare that he has done a thing of this kind for a friend's sake, the excuse does him no honor and is absolutely unacceptable even in ordinary affairs, and especially so if the act was treasonable. For you see, Fannius and Scaevola, we are so circumstanced that we are obligated to take a long view of this problem and to try to foresee what kinds of things may later happen to our State. Already there has been some turning away from the straight and narrow course prescribed by the standards of our forefathers. XII.40

Tiberius Gracchus tried to set himself up as a monarch, or, better, actually did function like one for a few months. Was this not something the like of which the Roman people had never before heard of, much less seen? After his death, his friends and relatives still followed in his path, and what they did in Publius Scipio's case I cannot relate without tears coming to my eyes. Carbo, you know, we put up with as best we could in view of the immediately preceding murder of Tiberius Gracchus; as for Gaius Gracchus, I prefer not to try to guess what to expect from his tribuneship. For the contagion is still creeping on, day after day, and once such a thing has got started, it becomes harder and harder to stop, short of complete disaster. You see in the matter of the ballot how serious a breach has already been made, first by the *lex Gabinia,* and two years later by the *lex Cassia.* I already have visions of a split between Senate and Assembly, and of the most serious questions being settled by the whim of the mob. For many more people will learn how to effect such things than how to prevent them. 41

What is my point? Simply this, that such movements can never be set afoot by one man without the aid of friends. It is our duty, therefore, to teach good men, who might unwittingly and accidentally have drifted into friendships of this kind, that they must not consider themselves so bound that they may not abandon their friends when they go wrong in matters of state. As for the wrongdoers, they must be subjected to penalties—penalties no less severe for those who follow someone else than for those who were themselves the leaders in wickedness. Who, in all 42

Greece, was more famous than Themistocles, who more powerful? As commander-in-chief in the Persian War he freed Greece
from slavery, but he became unpopular and was driven into
exile. True, his country was ungrateful and did him wrong, but
he ought to have borne that wrong, yet he did not. Instead, he
did exactly what Coriolanus had done in this country twenty
years earlier. Neither of these men found anyone to aid and abet
him in his attack on his native land; the end result was that both
committed suicide.

43   And so a community of interest with wicked men like these
must not be glossed over by the plea of friendship; rather it must
be suppressed with every stern measure at our command, so
that no man may deem it lawful to stand by a friend even when
he bears arms against his country. And this, by the way, is
altogether too likely to happen, the way things are going. For
my own part, I am no less concerned with the way the government will be after my death than with the way it is today.

XIII.44   Well then, let this be passed as our first law of friendship: that
we ask of our friends what is honorable and do what is honorable
for the sake of our friends. Let us not even so much as wait to
be asked; let us always be ready and eager, and never hang back;
and as for our advice, let us make bold to offer it freely. It is in
the friendships of men who urge upon each other what is good
and worthy that personal influence carries the greatest weight;
let us employ that influence to make our advice not only frank,
but—if the circumstances so demand—pointed, and if such influence is brought to bear upon ourselves, let us pay heed to it.

45   There are certain individuals, you know, who, I hear, are
adjudged wise men in Greece, and who—so it seems to me—
have arrived at some very remarkable conclusions—but there is
no question which they cannot solve with those razor-sharp wits
of theirs! In part, these thinkers have concluded that men should
shun too intimate friendships, for fear that one man might find
himself in difficulties on behalf of more individuals than just
himself; after all, each of us has more than enough troubles of
his own, and, say they, it is not comfortable to be too deeply
involved in the troubles of others. The most expeditious course,
they assert, is to keep the reins of friendship as slack as possible,
so that one may pull up on them or loosen them at will; for the
key to the happy life is freedom from care, and the soul cannot

enjoy this if, so to speak, a man is required to produce it for others besides himself.

Others of these wise men, so they tell us, express an idea that 46 shows even less regard for human nature. They say—and this is a topic which I briefly touched on a bit earlier—that friendship is desirable for the sake of protection and assistance, not of good-will and charity; thus the less any individual has of moral and physical strength, the more he demands friendship. This, they say, is why mere weak women are more anxious for the protection afforded by friendship than are men, poor men more anxious than rich men, and the unfortunate more than those who would be considered lucky.

What a magnificent philosophy! Why! They take the very sun 47 from the heavens, I should say, when they take friendship from life, for of all the gifts the gods have given us, this is our best source of goodness and of happiness. What, after all, is this "freedom from care" that they talk about? In appearance, it is seductive indeed, but in actual fact it is something that in many circumstances deserves only contempt. For it is not in accord with sound principle to refuse to undertake any honorable pro-posal or course of action, or having once undertaken any such thing, to refuse to go through with it, for fear one may lose one's peace of mind. If we run away from trouble, we shall have to run away from virtue, too, for it is impossible for virtue to avoid trouble in some degree when she shows her contempt and en-mity toward things incompatible with herself, when kindness stands out against malice, self-control against wantonness, brav-ery against cowardice. One may observe, for example, that it is the just who suffer most deeply at injustice, the brave at submissiveness, the temperate at concupiscence. In short, it is a distinctive characteristic of the well-regulated soul to feel joy at the good, and sorrow at the evil.

And so, if pain does touch the heart of the wise man—and it 48 certainly does, unless we are of the opinion that every vestige of human feeling has been rooted out of him—what earthly reason can be offered for excising friendship, root and branch, from life, for fear that it may become the cause of some slight hardship on our part? For if we remove all feeling from the heart, what difference is there, not, I hasten to say, between a man and an animal, but between a man and a rock or a stump or anything else of the kind? No, we must turn a deaf ear to those who insist that virtue is something hard and steely, so to speak. On the contrary, in many respects, and especially in friendship, it is soft and malleable, so that when our friends are blessed, it expands, and when they suffer misfortune, it contracts. No, indeed! That pain which we frequently must suffer on our friends' behalf is not an adequate reason for banishing friendship from our lives, any more than the cares and troubles which accompany virtue are reason for rejecting it.

XIV.   Now then, a compact of friendship is formed, as I said earlier, when some indication of virtue shines forth; the heart fastens and yokes itself to this as to something like itself, and when this happens, love is bound to arise.

49   For what is so ridiculous as to take delight in a host of unsubstantial things, such as honor, glory, a house, the clothing and care of the body, and not to take as much delight in a living soul endowed with virtue—a soul that has the power to love, or—so to speak—to return love? For there is nothing more productive of joy than the repayment of kindness, or the sharing of interests and exchange of favors.

50   But if we add this further point—and we shall be quite right in so doing—that there is nothing that so attracts and draws anything to itself as likeness of character does friendship, we shall surely be granted the truth of the assertion that good men are attracted to other good men, and league themselves with them as if they were related by blood and by nature. Now nothing is so eager, so greedy for its like as is nature, and for this reason, Fannius and Scaevola, men generally agree, as I think, that goodwill is bound to arise between good men, and goodwill is the very fount, established by nature, from which friendship springs. But this same goodness is found among ordinary people, too. Virtue is not cold-blooded or selfish or proud; she very commonly extends her protecting arm over whole nations and gives them the benefit of her loving admonition, and she most certainly would not do this if she felt repelled by the affection of the common people.

51   And, you know, I surely think that those who form friendships for the sake of advantage destroy the link in friendship that is most productive of affection. It is not so much what we gain from our friend as the very love of the friend itself that gives us joy, and what we get from a friend gives us joy since it comes to us

with love. And it is far from the truth to say that friendship is sought because of our poverty and weakness. This is proven by the fact those very individuals who have wealth and power, and being most richly endowed with virtue, man's strongest bulwark, have least need of any other man, who are the most generous and kindhearted among us. Of course, as a matter of fact, I am inclined to think that it may not be quite right for friends never to have any needs at all. For how could my interest in Scipio have retained its vigor if he had never needed my advice or my help, either in civil or in military matters? No, truly: friendship does not follow upon advantage, but advantage upon friendship.

We must not, then, listen to men weakened by luxurious living xv.52 if they shall seek to discourse on the subject of friendship, for they have never learned anything about it, either by experience or by dialectic. Why! What man on earth—in the name of all that's holy!—would agree to care for no one, and be himself cared for by no one, if on those terms he might abound in all manner of wealth and live in the lap of luxury? This is how tyrants live—a life in which, as you well know, there can be no charity, no lasting assurance of the goodwill of men; always and everywhere there is suspicion and insecurity. No place for friendship here!

Think! Who could love the man he fears, or the man who, he 53 thinks, fears him? Tyrants are, to be sure, the objects of men's devotion, but it is all show and expediency. For if they should chance to fall, as frequently happens, it then becomes clear how poor in friends they are. This is the point of the remark ascribed to Tarquin when he was on his way into exile: he had discovered which of his friends were loyal and which disloyal only after he had lost the power of rendering to either their just deserts.

I do wonder, of course, if Tarquin, what with his arrogance 54 and insolence, could have had any friends at all. And certainly if it is true that a character like his lacked the power to make friends, it is equally true that the wealth and power of many a man in high station have cut him off from lasting friendships. For not only is Fortune herself blind; often, too, she makes blind men of those whom she has taken to her bosom. In the end they are virtually driven out of their minds by pride and arrogance— and nothing in creation is more unbearable than an imbecile blessed by Fortune. More than that: it is perfectly possible to observe that men who to begin with were charming persons suffer strange alteration under the influence of military command, civil power, or just plain prosperity. They scorn their old friends and spoil their new ones.

55   How could they be more foolish? Here they are, overflowing with influence, power, and wealth. They get hold of everything that can be bought for money: horses, slaves, fine clothes, expensive furnishings, but they fail to get hold of friends, although these are the best and the finest of the furnishings, so to speak, of life. When they purchase these other things, they have no way of knowing for whom they are purchasing them or for whose benefit they are going to all this trouble, for things of that kind, every last one of them, belong always to the strongest. But friendships are a man's own possession, permanent, stable, and reliable, so much so that even if he should be able to keep those things which we call the gifts of fortune, still his life could not possibly be happy if it were devoid and empty of friends. So much for this aspect of our problem.

xvi.56   Our task now is to determine what limits, what boundaries, so to speak, should be set to friendship. On this general subject I find three opinions expressed, none of which meets my approval. The first is that we should feel toward our friends exactly as we do toward ourselves; the second, that our affection and kindness toward our friends should find an exact and precise balance in their affection and kindness toward us; the third, that as a man values himself so should he be valued by his friends.

57   I cannot agree at all with any of these three views. The first one, for example, is simply not true—that a man should show toward his friend the same affection that he shows toward himself. How many things are there which we would not do for our own sake, but which we are constantly doing for the sake of our friends: asking favors of those beneath us, humbling ourselves before them, making truly violent attacks on others, pursuing them relentlessly. Such things we cannot do on our own behalf without loss of honor, but on behalf of our friends they may be done without the slightest stigma. And there are many circumstances in which good men give up many an advantage quite properly their own, or even allow such advantage to be wrested from them, in order that their friends rather than they themselves may have the good of it.

58   The second view was that which limits friendship to an exact exchange of duties and kindnesses. This, of course, demands a

far too nice and narrow calculation of friendship, to make sure
that there is a precise balance between income and outgo. In my
opinion true friendship is too rich, yes, too affluent, for this sort
of thing, and does not keep a sharp eye out for fear it may give
more than it has received. It does not need to worry for fear
something may be lost or drop on the ground, or that a friend
may receive more than is coming to him.

However, the third view is much the worst of all, that as a   59
man values himself, so should he be valued by his friends. Many
times it happens that some friend may be very low in his spirit,
or become deeply discouraged about bettering his lot in life. Now
it is not the part of a friend to be toward his friend as the friend
is toward himself, but rather to put forth every effort to spur on
his friend's lagging spirits, to give him hope and a more optimis-
tic attitude. No, indeed; we must establish some other limits
for friendship—but first let me tell you what it was that Scipio
invariably and most emphatically condemned. He always insisted that it would be impossible to find any idea more out of
harmony with friendship than the one expressed by someone
who had declared that one ought to love in the expectation of
someday hating. Scipio said he could not be induced to believe
that this saying, as was generally held, should be ascribed to
Bias, who was accounted one of the Seven Wise Men; it must
have been some foul or unscrupulous or completely self-centered
man who said such a thing. For how in the world can anybody
be a friend to a man whose enemy he thinks he may become?
Why, no! It follows that he will hope and pray that his friend
may go astray as often as possible, so that he may have the more
handles, as it were, for hauling him up short; and again it follows
that if his friends do anything good, or gain any advantage, he
will feel pain, regret, and envy.

This concept, therefore, said he, whose ever it was, was good   60
only for destroying friendship. The proper principle to follow
was this: we should exercise such care in making friends that we
would never offer affection to anyone whom we might someday
come to hate. More than that: if we had been unfortunate in our
choice of friends, Scipio thought that we should accept and put
up with this rather than seek occasion for disagreement.

In my opinion, then, these are the limits we must place on   XVII.61
friendship: first, that the character of friends be without blemish;
second, that they share with each other, without reservation, all

their concerns, their plans, their aims. Then, if friends should perhaps feel obliged to assist each other in aims that were not entirely commendable—aims that involved life and death or good reputation—they would feel that they could leave the straight and narrow provided that they avoided complete disgrace; for to a certain degree concessions of this kind must be made to friendship. At the same time reputation must not be forgotten, and we must realize that the goodwill of the people is no mean weapon for the accomplishment of our ends. To acquire that goodwill by demagoguery and flattery is wrong, but a virtue which arouses popularity is by no means to be brushed aside.

62   But—for here I go back to Scipio again, who was always talking about friendship—he constantly objected to the fact that in all other matters men were extremely careful; they could tell you how many goats and sheep they had, but not how many friends; in acquiring the former they took great pains, but in choosing friends they were careless, and did not even have signs, so to speak, or marks by which to judge which individuals were likely to make good friends. Obviously it is the reliable, the well-adjusted, and the loyal who should be chosen, but of this kind of people there is a great shortage, and in any case it is hard to pick them out unless one has had experience. But where is the experience to be gained except in friendship itself? Friendship comes before the ability to judge people, and thus precludes the opportunity to gain experience.

63   If a man is wise, then, he will keep a close check both on the direction which his feelings of friendship are taking and on the speed with which they are developing, so that he may, so to speak, drive them like a tried and tested team, watching the development of his friendships by putting his friends' characters to the test now here, now there. Often when men are asked for small loans they make it abundantly evident how little we may rely on them; others, who find it unthinkable to get excited about small loans, show their true colors when a larger request is made of them. But if we do find some individuals who would think it shameful to put money ahead of friendship, where shall we find those who would not put honors, public office, military command, civil authority, or wealth ahead of friendship—the sort who, if these things were placed on one side of the scales and the laws of friendship on the other, would show a definite

leaning toward the latter? The fact is that human nature finds it hard to make light of power, and if men have cast aside friendship in order to attain power, they think that this defection from duty will scarcely be open to criticism, since men will assume that some really important reason must have led them to cast friendship aside.

Thus it is very hard to discover true friendships among men who are engaged in politics and affairs of state. Where indeed may one find the man who would put his friend's chance for public office ahead of his own? Why! I had best say nothing of the reluctance, the unwillingness, with which most men view the prospect of association in disaster. It is not easy to find anyone who would let himself be involved in that. Ennius may be right when he says "A friend in need is a friend indeed." Still, the fact remains that the two things which most commonly prove men to be unreliable and weak are these: if, when they are prospering, they drop their friends, or if when their friends are in trouble, they desert them. And so, when anyone in either of these circumstances has shown himself a man of conviction, reliable, and loyal, we are bound to adjudge him one of a very rare species of men—a species virtually divine.

64

Now the foundation of that steadfastness and loyalty for which we are looking in friendship is trust, for nothing endures that cannot be trusted. The man we choose should be honest too, and unpretentious and congenial—with interests and concerns like our own. All of these qualities are related to trust, for we can have no trust in a devious and deceitful character, and the man whose interests are not like ours and who is not by nature sympathetic to us, cannot be either a trustworthy or reliable friend. We should add as a further point that he should not take delight in bringing charges against us nor believe them when they are brought; these qualities are related to that loyalty which I have already discussed. And so what I said in the beginning is true, that friendship cannot exist except between truly good men. Now it is the plain duty of a good man—and we may well call this "good man" our true philosopher—to keep two principles ever before him in the matter of friendship: first, that there be no element of deception or hypocrisy, for it is more characteristic of a gentleman to hate quite openly than to conceal his true opinion behind a front; second, not only to refuse to listen to

xviii.65

accusations made by anybody against his friend, but to be himself above suspecting him—not be always thinking that his friend has done something wrong.

66   A man ought in addition to have a certain graciousness of speech and manners, for this adds no mean zest to friendship. People speak of rectitude, too, and of an all-pervading seriousness; the latter, to be sure, does impart solidity, but friendship must be more relaxed and less constricting and more pleasurable, and more inclined to affability and congeniality in all aspects.

XIX.67   At this point a question of some difficulty arises: are there any circumstances in which new friends, found worthy of friendship, should be put ahead of old friends, as, for example, we commonly put fresh young horses ahead of old, worn-out ones. No man worthy of the name will feel any hesitation here, for we have no right to get tired of friendships as we do of other things. It is always true that the old and familiar, like wines which can stand aging, is bound to have the best savor, and there is real truth in the familiar saying that people must eat many a peck of salt together if they are to know the full meaning of friendship.

68   Now if our new acquaintances arouse in us the hope that—as in the case of a healthy stand of grain—the fruits are bound to appear, we must of course not slough them off; still old friendships must always have their proper place reserved for them, for nothing carries the weight of the old and familiar. Why, no! Even in the case of the horse that I just mentioned, if there is nothing wrong with him there is no one who would not prefer to ride the one he was used to rather than one that was new and untried. And this holds good not only in the case of living things, but in the inanimate as well: we like best what we are used to. Even in the matter of places—even mountains and wild forests—we like best those where we have lived the longest.

69   But the most important thing in friendship is the preservation of a right attitude toward our inferiors. So many times there are among us men of extraordinary distinction, as Scipio was, for example, in our little group. Yet he never set himself above Philus or Rupilius or Mummius, or above those of his friends who were of inferior station. His brother, Quintus Maximus, was, all things considered, a very fine man, but by no means Scipio's equal; still, he was the older of the two, and for this reason Scipio always showed him deference. His wish for all his

friends and relatives was that they might rise in life because of
him.

This is what we should all do; this is the lead we all should 70
follow. If we attain to any distinction through moral character,
native endowment, or good fortune, we should pass this on to
our friends and relatives, and share it with those who are closest
to us. If, for example, they come of humble parents, if they
have brothers and sisters who have not been well-blessed with
intelligence or luck, we should help them in material ways and
lend them honor and respect. You know how it is on the stage.
There are characters who, because their origin and birth are
unknown, have passed years in the position of slaves. Then,
when their true station is discovered, when they are found to be
the children of gods or kings, they still keep their love and respect
for the peasants whom for many years they had thought to be
their parents. It is certainly all the more obligatory on us to do
this in the case of our real parents, whom we have always known
to be ours. And of course we reap the highest rewards from our
native endowment, our moral character, and everything else that
tends to give us distinction, when we share those rewards with
those who are nearest and dearest to us.

It is incumbent, then, upon those who are the superiors among xx.71
friends or relatives to avoid making any invidious distinctions
between themselves and their inferiors. Similarly, it is incumbent
upon the inferiors not to take umbrage at the fact that others
surpass them in natural endowments, fortune, or rank. As a
matter of fact, however, most such men are constantly complain-
ing about this, or are even reproachful about it, especially if they
think they have got hold of something which they may say they
did through a sense of duty, or for love, or at some trouble to
themselves. What an unpleasant kind of people these are! They
reproach us with the favors they have done us—favors which
ought to be remembered by the one upon whom they were
conferred, but never mentioned by the one who conferred them.

We see, then, that those who are the superiors in a relation of 72
friendship must avoid all invidious distinctions and similarly that
those who are the inferiors must, in a way, rise above themselves.
There are, you know, people who turn friendship into something
quite distasteful, the minute they get the idea that someone
thinks them inferior. This rarely happens except with individuals

who really think that they are inferior. Such people need to be disabused of this idea, either by persuasion, or—if that is not enough—by more tangible assistance.

73   How far, then, should we go in aiding our friends? First of all, we must give them only such aid as is within our powers; second, only as much as the man we love and wish to help can himself sustain. For you can't—no, not even you, for all your excellent qualities—you can't possibly see every friend you possess placed in positions of the highest honor. Scipio was able to get Publius Rupilius elected consul, but not his brother, Lucius. And even if you could confer anything you wished upon your friend, still you must carefully consider exactly how much he is capable of sustaining.

74   Speaking in general terms, we must sit in judgment on our friendships after we have reached physical and intellectual maturity. There may be some individuals who in their earlier years were enthusiastic about hunting or ball-games; we are under no obligation to keep them in a relation of intimacy because we liked them at a time when we shared their enthusiasms. By any such principle as that, we shall be bound to reserve the greatest share of our affection for our nurses and tutors, just for old time's sake. We must not forget them, of course, but our relations with them must be judged by some other standard. Under any other rule, stable and lasting friendships cannot exist. For men's ways of acting and thinking change, and with them their interests, and when interests become different, friends begin to grow away from each other. This, in fact, is the very reason why the good cannot be friends with the wicked, nor the wicked with the good: there lies between them the widest imaginable gap in character and in interests.

75   Another good rule in friendship is this: we must not let an excess of affectionate concern—something very common—interfere with things that may mean a great deal to our friends. For— to go back once more to the stage—Neoptolemus could not have captured Troy if he had not turned a deaf ear to Lycomedes, his old foster-father, when he burst into tears and tried to keep him from leaving home. It happens many times in life that important considerations compel us to part from our friends. Anyone who tries to keep us from doing what we must and should in such cases, simply because he cannot bear the thought of losing us,

is weak and self-indulgent, and for that very reason no true friend.

Yes, indeed, in every case we must watch carefully what we demand of our friends and what we allow them to demand of us.   76

To continue: in the matter of the breaking up of friendships, disasters, so to speak, do occur, and they sometimes leave us no choice—for now I shall turn my discourse away from the friendships of the wise toward those of the common sort. Many times people's vices explode in the very faces of their friends, and sometimes in the faces of others, but the hurt that they cause then falls back upon their friends. Well, friendships like these must be washed out by discontinuance of intimacy, and, as I once heard Cato say, must be unlearned rather than cut sharply off. Sometimes, of course, wrongdoing that is completely intolerable flares up, and in such instances it is neither right nor honorable—in fact it is simply impossible—to refrain from an immediate act of divorce and separation.   XXI.

Most commonly, however, a gradual change in character or in interests takes place, or people fall into disagreement about politics—for I am speaking now, as I said a moment ago, not about the friendships of the wise, but about those of ordinary folk—and if this happens, we shall have to take care lest people think that we are not just terminating a friendship, but rather becoming active enemies. For there is nothing more unseemly than openly to enter the lists against someone with whom you have lived on terms of intimacy. Scipio was a friend of Quintus Pompeius, but, as you know, he broke that friendship off for my sake. Metellus had been my friend and colleague in office, yet Scipio broke with him over a disagreement in matters of public policy. He did this in both cases with dignity and restraint and without the kind of clash that causes hard feelings.   77

Our first task, then, must be to see that no break in our friendships occurs, or, if it does, that our friendships should seem to fade away rather than to be stamped out. We must be extremely careful not to let friendship turn into serious personal enmity, for this is what causes hard feelings, harsh words, even insult and abuse. Sometimes we can put up even with these, and if we can, we must. There is a degree of respect which we must pay to a friendship that has been: we must see that the wrong lies   78 always on the side of the one who has done the injury, and not on the side of the one who has suffered it. In general, there is only one way to foresee and guard against all faults and hurts of this kind: we must not be too quick to bestow our affections, and we must not bestow them on men unworthy of them.

79   Now the men who are worthy of friendship are those who possess within themselves something that causes men to love them. They are a rare species—but of course the really fine is always rare, and there is nothing harder than to find something which in all respects is perfect of its kind. But the vast majority of mankind recognize nothing as good in the human sphere unless it be something profitable. In the matter of friends, as if they were so many domestic animals, they lavish their affections chiefly on those from whom they expect to derive the highest profit.

80   As a result, they know nothing of friendship in its finest and most natural guise—the friendship that is desirable for its own sake—and they set before themselves no image of the true nature and significance of friendship. For a man loves himself not in order to exact from himself some pay for his affection, but simply because every man is by his very nature dear to himself. Unless this same principle is transferred to friendship, a man will never find a true friend, for the true friend is, so to speak, a second self.

81   Is this not apparent among animals, birds, and fish, the creatures of the field, the farmyard, the forest? Do they not love themselves? Is not self-love born into them, as it is into all animate creation? And do they not also need and search for creatures of their own kind to whom they may attach themselves? And is their action in this case not accompanied by yearning and by something like our human love? How much the more natural is this, then, in the case of man, who does indeed love himself, and in addition is ever on the search for that companion, whose heart's blood he may so mingle with his own that they become virtually one person instead of two!

XXII.82   But a great many men act quite wrongly, not to say shamelessly. They want their friends to be the kind of man they cannot themselves possibly be, and they demand from their friends services they are unwilling to render to them. But it is only right that a man should first of all be a good man himself, and should then seek out another man like himself. It is under conditions like these that those lasting friendships of which we spoke awhile ago can be built up. Men find themselves thrown together by a feeling of sympathy and goodwill; they learn first of all to govern those passions to which most men are enslaved; then they learn to take delight in decency and justice. Finally, the one learns to stand by the other in his every need, and never under any circumstances to demand of him anything but what is honorable and right. Then they will not only love and cherish each other, but will also know mutual respect. Yes indeed: take respect out of friendship and you deprive it of its noblest crown.

Believe me, people fall into very dangerous error when they   83 think that in friendship the gates are down for all kinds of wilfulness and waywardness. Nature gave us friendship as an aid to virtue, not as an assistant to vice. It was her hope that since virtue when solitary cannot arrive at the highest kind of life, it might do so when joined and shared with a companion. If between any individuals such a partnership either now exists, or ever has existed, or shall exist, this will be the kind of companionship which we shall be bound to adjudge the best and the richest in terms of the highest good which nature has to offer.

This, I declare, is the partnership which contains within itself   84 everything men deem desirable: honor, glory, peace of mind, and joy. When men have these, life is happy; without them, it cannot be. This is the best and finest thing in life. If we wish to obtain it, we must strive ever for virtue, for without virtue we cannot gain possession either of friendship or of anything else desirable. If men pass virtue by, they may think they have friends, but in the end they discover their error: some serious misfortune will compel them to put those supposed friends to the test.

And so—and this we cannot say too often—we must test and   85 observe first, and then bestow our affections, and not first bestow our affections, and then test and observe. But there are so many instances in which we are plagued by carelessness, and above all in the matter of choosing and making friends. We do things upside down, "put the cart before the horse," a thing which the old proverb tells us not to do. We get wrapped up, both our friends and ourselves, in the daily round and even in our friendly obligation; then all at once, in the very middle of things, something happens that offends us, and we break off our friendships.

For this reason we must pass even severer censure on care-   XXIII.86 lessness in a matter so extremely vital. Friendship, as you know, is the one thing in human life which all men with one voice agree is worthwhile—this in spite of the fact that many men have no use for virtue itself, and call it mere window dressing and empty show. Many men scorn wealth; they are content with little and really enjoy a very modest standard of living. Public office, again, is a thing that some men burn with longing to possess, yet how many have no interest in it at all, and consider it the most meaningless and ephemeral of all things. One could make up a long list of things that seem wonderful to some people, but which many, many others deem completely valueless. But all men, to the last man, are in agreement on the subject of friendship, whether they devote themselves to the public service, or choose a life of study and learning, or spend their lives in leisure, wholly wrapped up in their private concerns—yes, even those who totally surrender themselves to pleasure and amusement. All of them agree that without friendship life is not worth living—that is, if they have any interest at all in living the life of a decent human being.

87   Friendship, you know, somehow threads its way through the life of every man; no matter how he chooses to live, he cannot divorce himself from it. Yes, even if a man is so antisocial and so abnormal in his nature that he shuns and loathes any meeting with his fellows—even if he is a man like that Timon of Athens we have heard about (whoever he was!), still he would be completely unable to refrain from searching out someone in whose presence he might pour out the vials of his wrath. There is one way in which we may most accurately determine the truth of our proposition: suppose it should happen, somehow, that a god should lift us up out of human society here and set us down in some uninhabited spot, where he would see that we had an abundance of everything that nature requires, but would take away from us every single chance of seeing any other human being. What man would be so steel-hard as to be able to stand a life like that? What man, alone like that, would not feel that every delight had lost its savor?

88   No, indeed! There is real truth in the sentiment voiced so many times—I think it was by Archytas of Tarentum. At any rate I have heard it repeated by men much older than myself, and they said they had heard it from other men, older than they: "If someone should climb heaven's height and behold the magnificence of the earth and the heavenly bodies, he would find all

that wonder quite tasteless; yet it would have been a supreme joy if he had had someone to whom he could have told all about it." Yes, nature abhors solitude. She always pushes her way toward some prop, so to speak, and when men are very close friends, this is a wonderful source of joy.

Nature, again makes quite clear, by sign after sign, what it is that she wants—what goal she passionately seeks; and yet somehow we turn a deaf ear and fail to hear her admonitions. Yes, friendship is a kaleidoscopic and complicated thing; it affords many possible grounds for suspicion and offense, but a truly wise man always finds it possible to avoid them or smooth them over or put up with them. One thing however must be shunned, and that is hypersensitivity, if we are to preserve the mutual confidence and practical value of friendship. For it often happens that friends must be admonished and even reprimanded, and this we must take in good part when it is offered in a spirit of charity. xxiv.

But somehow what my good friend (Terence) says in *The Woman of Andros* has the ring of truth: 89

"Flattery wins friends, but frankness earns ill will."

A sorry thing, frankness, if it is a source of ill will, for ill will can be the death of friendship! But flattery is far sorrier, for by failing to call wrongdoing to account, it lets a friend fall to his ruin. And the greatest blame of all attaches to the man who finds the truth distasteful and is driven to falsehood by his desire to flatter. In this whole matter, then, we must be reasonable and cautious. We may admonish, but we must not scold; we may reprimand, but we must not humiliate; and if—since I like Terence's word—we do "flatter," let it be in a spirit of good humor, without any trace of the servility that encourages men in their faults, for this is unworthy of a friend—unworthy, in fact, of anyone who calls himself a man. Life with a friend is different from life with a tyrant.

Now some men's ears are closed to the truth, with the result that they simply cannot hear the friend who speaks frankly to them. For such people, there is no hope. As in many instances, what Cato said here is very much to the point: "In some respects our worst enemies do us greater favors than those we think of as agreeable friends. The former often tell us the truth; the latter, never." And the ridiculous part of it is that the people who have 90 been admonished do not take offense when they should, but do take it when they shouldn't. The fact that they have done wrong causes them no pain, but they are upset at being reprimanded; whereas they really ought to be grieved at their wrongdoing and glad when someone sets them straight.

xxv.91   It is an essential part of true friendship, then, to offer and to receive admonition; but it must be offered courteously, not peremptorily, and received with forbearance, not with resentment. By the same sign, we must maintain that there is no danger more deadly to friendship than servility, sycophancy, flattery— put as many names as you like upon it, but let it be branded as the vicious practice of disloyal, untruthful men, who measure everything they say by what people want to hear, and never anything by the truth.

92   Now in all matters, hypocrisy is vicious (for it distorts and destroys our judgment), but it is particularly inimical to friendship, for it makes honesty impossible, and without honesty the word "friendship" has no meaning. For the essence of friendship consists in the fact that many souls, so to speak, become one, and how can that take place if even in the one individual the soul is not single and forever the same, but various, changeable, kaleidoscopic?

93   For what could be so pliable, so devious, as the soul of the man who bends not only to the wish and will of his neighbor, but to his merest gesture or change of expression?

> "He says no, I say no; he says yes, I say yes. In the end, I give myself this order: 'Agree with him, no matter what!' "

Those are Terence's words again, but he is speaking in the person of Gnatho, the kind of friend no one but a fool would want.

94   There are lots of people like the Gnathos, too, who are our superiors in station, wealth, and reputation; flattery on their part is particularly dangerous, for in them dishonesty and personal influence are combined.

95   Now by the exercise of caution the sycophant can be set apart and distinguished from the true friend just as well as any other counterfeit or sham can be told from the genuine and the real. The Popular Assembly is made up of unsophisticated people,

but even so it commonly judges the difference between the dema-
gogue, that is, the dishonest politician and the honest, solid, and
patriotic citizen.

What a flood of demagoguery Gaius Papierius poured into the   96
ears of the Assembly not so long ago, when he was proposing
to legalize the reelection of incumbents in the tribunate! We two
argued against him—but never mind about me: I'd prefer to
speak of Scipio. How weighty and impressive was the speech he
made! One might easily have styled him Chief of State, not just
fellow-citizen of Rome. But you were present, and his speech is
available to us. The result was that a popular piece of legislation
was defeated by popular vote. To return to my own case, you
recall the consulship of Scipio's brother, Quintus Maximus, and
Lucius Mancinus, and how much popular support Gaius Licinius
Crassus seemed to be gaining in that year for his law on priestly
offices. He had moved to transfer the election of new members
of the sacerdotal colleges to the vote of the people; he was the
first man, too, to turn around toward the forum and address his
plea directly to the people. He made a very plausible speech, but
with Scipio and me as defenders, religion easily won the day.
This took place, you remember, when I was praetor, five years
before I was elected consul, so the case was won on its merits
and not because of any vast personal influence I might have
exerted.

But if on the public platform, that is, in the Assembly, where   xxvi.97
there is ample room for lies and subterfuge, the truth still pre-
vails, if only it is unveiled and brought out into the light of day,
what ought to be the case with friendship, which must ever and
always be weighed in the scales of truth and honesty? For in
friendship unless, as we say, you see the naked heart and let your
own be seen, there is nothing that you can deem trustworthy or
reliable, not even the mere fact of loving and being loved, since
you cannot know how genuine the sentiment is. To be sure, that
flattery of which we have been speaking, dangerous though it
may be, still can harm no one unless he listens to it and finds it
pleasant. In point of fact, the man who tends to flatter himself
and to find himself a thoroughly charming fellow is the one who
most readily lends an ear to the sycophant.

In general, to be sure, virtue is self-appreciative, for it knows   98
itself best, and realizes how estimable it is. However, I am not

now speaking of virtue properly so-called, but rather of the outward appearance of virtue: not nearly so many people want actually to be possessed of virtue as want to appear to be possessed of it. It is these latter who enjoy flattery; it is they who, when they hear remarks composed for the purpose of pleasing them, think that such talk is proof of their own excellence. This, then, is no friendship, when the one party is unwilling to hear the truth, and the other is ever ready to tell lies. Why! We wouldn't think the sycophancy engaged in by parasites in the comedy amusing, if there were no braggart soldiers!

> Thais is very grateful to me, is she?

It would have been enough to reply, "Very"; but the parasite says "Enormously"! Yes, when a man wants to hear something said that will flatter his vanity, the sycophant always goes him one better.

99   For this reason, although the honeyed hypocrisy of which we have been speaking is most effective with people who encourage and invite it, yet we must warn the more substantial and genuine among us to be on their guard against capture by cleverly phrased flattery. None but the abnormally dull can fail to detect the obvious sycophant; it is the clever and subtle individual against whom men must be on their guard, lest he worm his way in. It is not at all easy to identify him, for he often flatters people by disagreeing with them, and pretends to be quarreling with them when in fact he is catering to their weaknesses; he concludes then by throwing up his hands and letting himself be defeated, thus leaving his dupes with the impression that they had possessed the greater wisdom. Is there anything more unseemly than being duped? We must take particular care that this does not happen.

> "You've tricked me worse than all the graybeard fools that walk the stage—oh, neatly, neatly done!"

100   Yes, indeed; the silliest character in the comedy is the unintelligent and credulous old man. But somehow our discourse has drifted away from the friendships of perfect men, that is, of the wise (I am referring to the kind of "wisdom" that may reasonably be thought to occur among men) to unsubstantial friendships. Let us return then to those with which we began and try at long last to bring our discussion of them to a conclusion.

I tell you, Gaius Fannius, and you, Quintus Mucius: it is virtue, yes virtue, that initiates and preserves friendship. For it is virtue that is the source of the rational, the stable, the consistent element in life. When virtue raises herself up and displays her light, and sees and recognizes the same light in another, she moves toward it and shares reciprocally in that which the other possesses; from this a flame bursts forth, whether of love or of friendship. Both terms after all are derived from the verb "to love" (*amor, amicitia, amare*), and "to love" means nothing but to cherish the person for whom one feels affection, without any special need and without any thought of advantage—although advantage in fact does grow out of friendship, even if one does not seek it.

It was this kind of goodwill that characterized the affection 101 that I felt in my younger days for older men like Lucius Paulus, Marcus Cato, Gaius Galus, Publius Nasica, and Tiberius Gracchus, father-in-law of my dear friend Scipio; it was this, too, that shone forth even more brightly between those of us who were of the same age, for example between myself and Scipio, Lucius Furius, Publius Rupilius, and Spurius Mummius. Then again, now that I have grown old, I find comfort in the affection of young men, in yours, for instance, and in Quintus Tubero's. I even take real joy in my friendships with the very young—with Publius Rutilius, and Aulus Verginius. And since human life and the human creature have been so organized that a new generation is forever arising out of the old, it is very much to be desired that one may arrive at the finish-line, so to speak, in the company of the same people with whom one leaped from the mark.

But since human life is a fragile and unstable thing, we have 102 no choice but to be ever on the search for people whom we may love, and by whom we may be loved in turn, for if charity and goodwill are removed from life, all the joy is gone out of it. As far as I am concerned, although Scipio was taken away from me unexpectedly, he is still living and will live forever, for it was the man's virtue that I loved, and this has not been destroyed; it is still as bright as day to me—and not only to me, who had it always before me: it will shine in all its glory and splendor for generations to come. No man will ever see greater visions or dreams without feeling that he must set Scipio before him as a record to know and a pattern to follow.

103   For my own part, of all the good things I have had, whether they were special blessings or the normal events of life, I know of nothing that I could compare with the friendship of Scipio. Here I found sympathy for my political opinions, here, advice and assistance in private affairs, here, joy to fill my hours of ease. As far as I know, I never offended him even in the most insignificant way, and I myself never heard a word from him that I would not have wished to hear. One home served us both, one table, too—and that a plain and simple one; we shared not only the life of the soldier but also our travels and our days of rest and retirement.

104   What should I say, too, of our perennial enthusiasm for study and learning? (This is how we spent all our time when we were out of the public eye.) If I had lost along with Scipio himself my memories of all these things, and could not recall them, I would be completely incapable of supporting my sorrow for a man who was so very close and very dear to me. But those memories have not been blotted out; rather, they are strengthened and made more vivid by my thinking about them and recalling them; and even if I had been totally stripped of them, I still have one solace: time itself. My sorrow, you see, cannot be with me for any great length of time, and the brief is always bearable, even if it is severe.

    This concludes my remarks on friendship. I earnestly urge the two of you, then, to raise virtue—without which friendship cannot exist—to such position that only friendship will be second to it in your thoughts.

Seneca

ON PHILOSOPHY AND FRIENDSHIP ON GRIEF FOR LOST FRIENDS

Introduction

Aristotle had raised the difficulty in *Ethics* IX.9 of whether a happy person needs friends, if in fact he has the characteristic, which belongs to happiness, of being self-sufficient (see *Ethics* 1097b8–16). Aristotle resolved the difficulty by holding, in effect, that the self-sufficiency of the happy person *includes* his having friends. But this resolution was not available to Cicero, who understands self-sufficiency in the Stoic manner as a way of living *prior* to acquiring any friends. Hence, in *De Amicitia*, the difficulty arises in a sharp form. On the one hand, Cicero holds that self-sufficiency is a precondition of forming true friendships and that friends each remain self-sufficient even as they are friends. (Recall his "Now what need did Africanus have of me? By Hercules! None at all." at IX.30.) On the other hand, he does not wish to deny that we become truly attached to friends (XIII.45), and he speaks, surely correctly, of our needing their advice and counsel (XIV.51).

In "On Philosophy and Friendship," Seneca attempts to show that there is no contradiction in the Stoic view. He does this by making three points. First, he says that self-sufficiency means that the virtuous person *can* do without friends, not that he *wishes* to be without them. Second, he says that our attachment to friends is based not on need but on a kind of excess: a virtuous person forms friendships so that "his noble qualities may not lie dormant." Third, he claims that, if friendship is sought for its own sake and not for advantage, then it shares with virtue an insulation from changes of fortune, and this is not incompatible with self-sufficiency.

His view generally is that the virtuous person's activity towards his friends should be controlled neither by the necessity of want nor by the randomness of fortune. Rather, it should be controlled by his own will—an expression of a rational self-possession.

In his "On Grief for Lost Friends," Seneca is intent on showing that grief arises only from some defect in how we have loved the deceased friend or in how we love others who are alive. We grieve to prove to others or to ourselves that we in fact loved the deceased—but such proof ought to be unnecessary. Or we grieve because we cannot be consoled by friends who are alive, either because we have not made other friends (which would be a sign that we did not practice genuine friendship in the first place) or because we have other friends but their presence does not comfort us (which would imply that we do not love them sufficiently).

Seneca

ON PHILOSOPHY AND FRIENDSHIP
EPISTLE IX

You desire to know whether Epicurus is right when, in one of his letters,[1] he rebukes those who hold that the wise man is self-sufficient and for that reason does not stand in need of friendships. This is the objection raised by Epicurus against Stilbo and those who believe[2] that the Supreme Good is a soul which is insensible to feeling.

We are bound to meet with a double meaning if we try to express the Greek term "lack of feeling" summarily, in a single word, rendering it by the Latin word *impatientia*. For it may be understood in the meaning the opposite to that which we wish it to have. What we mean to express is, a soul which rejects any sensation of evil; but people will interpret the idea as that of a soul which can endure no evil. Consider, therefore, whether it is not better to say "a soul that cannot be harmed," or "a soul entirely beyond the realm of suffering." There is this difference between ourselves and the other school[3]: our ideal wise man feels his troubles, but overcomes them; their wise man does not even feel them. But we and they alike hold this idea,—that the wise man is self-sufficient. Nevertheless, he desires friends, neighbours, and associates, no matter how much he is sufficient unto himself. And mark how self-sufficient he is; for on occasion he can be content with a part of himself. If he lose a hand through

1. Frag. 174 Usener.
2. *i.e.*, the Cynics.
3. *i.e.*, the Cynics.

disease or war, or if some accident puts out one or both of his eyes, he will be satisfied with what is left, taking as much pleasure in his impaired and maimed body as he took when it was sound. But while he does not pine for these parts if they are missing, he prefers not to lose them. In this sense the wise man is self-sufficient, that he can do without friends, not that he desires to do without them. When I say "can," I mean this: he endures the loss of a friend with equanimity.

But he need never lack friends, for it lies in his own control how soon he shall make good a loss. Just as Phidias, if he lose a statue, can straightway carve another, even so our master in the art of making friendships can fill the place of a friend he has lost. If you ask how one can make oneself a friend quickly, I will tell you, provided we are agreed that I may pay my debt[4] at once and square the account, so far as this letter is concerned. Hecato[5] says: "I can show you a philtre, compounded without drugs, herbs, or any witch's incantation: 'If you would be loved, love.' " Now there is great pleasure, not only in maintaining old and established friendships, but also in beginning and acquiring new ones. There is the same difference between winning a new friend and having already won him, as there is between the farmer who sows and the farmer who reaps. The philosopher Attalus used to say: "It is more pleasant to make than to keep a friend, as it is more pleasant to the artist to paint than to have finished painting." When one is busy and absorbed in one's work, the very absorption affords great delight; but when one has withdrawn one's hand from the completed masterpiece, the pleasure is not so keen. Henceforth it is the fruits of his art that he enjoys; it was the art itself that he enjoyed while he was painting. In the case of our children, their young manhood yields the more abundant fruits, but their infancy was sweeter.

Let us now return to the question. The wise man, I say, self-sufficient though he be, nevertheless desires friends if only for the purpose of practising friendship, in order that his noble qualities may not lie dormant. Not, however, for the purpose mentioned by Epicurus[6] in the letter quoted above: "That there may be someone to sit by him when he is ill, to help him when

---

4. *i.e.*, the *diurna mercedula;* see *Ep.* vi. 7.

5. Frag. 27 Fowler.

6. Frag. 175 Usener.

he is in prison or in want;" but that he may have someone by whose sick-bed he himself may sit, someone a prisoner in hostile hands whom he himself may set free. He who regards himself only, and enters upon friendships for this reason, reckons wrongly. The end will be like the beginning: he has made friends with one who might assist him out of bondage; at the first rattle of the chain such a friend will desert him. These are the so-called "fair-weather" friendships; one who is chosen for the sake of utility will be satisfactory only so long as he is useful. Hence prosperous men are blockaded by troops of friends; but those who have failed stand amid vast loneliness, their friends fleeing from the very crisis which is to test their worth. Hence, also, we notice those many shameful cases of persons who, through fear, desert or betray. The beginning and the end cannot but harmonize. He who begins to be your friend because it pays will also cease because it pays. A man will be attracted by some reward offered in exchange for his friendship, if he be attracted by aught in friendship other than friendship itself.

For what purpose, then, do I make a man my friend? In order to have someone for whom I may die, whom I may follow into exile, against whose death I may stake my own life, and pay the pledge, too. The friendship which you portray is a bargain and not a friendship; it regards convenience only, and looks to the results. Beyond question the feeling of a lover has in it something akin to friendship; one might call it friendship run mad. But, though this is true, does anyone love for the sake of gain, or promotion, or renown? Pure[7] love, careless of all other things, kindles the soul with desire for the beautiful object, not without the hope of a return of the affection. What then? Can a cause which is more honourable produce a passion that is base? You may retort: "We are not now discussing the question whether friendship is to be cultivated for its own sake." On the contrary, nothing more urgently requires demonstration; for if friendship is to be sought for its own sake, he may seek it who is self-sufficient. "How, then," you ask, "does he seek it?" Precisely as he seeks an object of great beauty, not attracted to it by desire for gain, nor yet frightened by the instability of Fortune. One who seeks friendship for favourable occasions, strips it of all its nobility.

---

7. "Pure love," *i.e.*, love in its essence, unalloyed with other emotions.

"The wise man is self-sufficient." This phrase, my dear Lucilius, is incorrectly explained by many; for they withdraw the
wise man from the world, and force him to dwell within his own
skin. But we must mark with care what this sentence signifies
and how far it applies; the wise man is sufficient unto himself
for a happy existence, but not for mere existence. For he needs
many helps towards mere existence; but for a happy existence he
needs only a sound and upright soul, one that despises Fortune.

I should like also to state to you one of the distinctions of
Chrysippus,[8] who declares that the wise man is in want of nothing, and yet needs many things.[9] "On the other hand," he says,
"nothing is needed by the fool, for he does not understand how
to use anything, but he is in want of everything." The wise man
needs hands, eyes, and many things that are necessary for his
daily use; but he is in want of nothing. For want implies a
necessity, and nothing is necessary to the wise man. Therefore,
although he is self-sufficient, yet he has need of friends. He
craves as many friends as possible, not, however, that he may
live happily; for he will live happily even without friends. The
Supreme Good calls for no practical aids from outside; it is developed at home, and arises entirely within itself. If the good seeks
any portion of itself from without, it begins to be subject to the
play of Fortune.

People may say: "But what sort of existence will the wise man
have, if he be left friendless when thrown into prison, or when
stranded in some foreign nation, or when delayed on a long
voyage, or when cast upon a lonely shore? "His life will be like
that of Jupiter, who, amid the dissolution of the world, when
the gods are confounded together and Nature rests for a space
from her work, can retire into himself and give himself over to
his own thoughts.[10] In some such way as this the sage will act;
he will retreat into himself, and live with himself. As long as he
is allowed to order his affairs according to his judgment, he

---

8. *Cf.* his *Frag. moral.* 674 von Arnim.

9. The distinction is based upon the meaning of *egere*, "to be in want of" something indispensable, and *opus esse*, "to have need of" something which one can
do without.

10. This refers to the Stoic conflagration; after certain cycles their world was
destroyed by fire. *Cf.* E. V. Arnold, *Roman Stoicism*, pp. 192 f.; *cf.* also Chrysippus,
Frag. phys. 1065 von Arnim.

is self-sufficient—and marries a wife; he is self-sufficient—and brings up children; he is self-sufficient—and yet could not live if he had to live without the society of man. Natural promptings, and not his own selfish needs, draw him into friendships. For just as other things have for us an inherent attractiveness, so has friendship. As we hate solitude and crave society, as nature draws men to each other, so in this matter also there is an attraction which makes us desirous of friendship. Nevertheless, though the sage may love his friends dearly, often comparing them with himself, and putting them ahead of himself, yet all the good will be limited to his own being, and he will speak the words which were spoken by the very Stilbo[11] whom Epicurus criticizes in his letter. For Stilbo, after his country was captured and his children and his wife lost, as he emerged from the general desolation alone and yet happy, spoke as follows to Demetrius, called Sacker of Cities because of the destruction he brought upon them, in answer to the question whether he had lost anything: "I have all my goods with me!" There is a brave and stout-hearted man for you! The enemy conquered, but Stilbo conquered his conqueror. "I have lost nothing!" Aye, he forced Demetrius to wonder whether he himself had conquered after all. "My goods are all with me!" In other words, he deemed nothing that might be taken from him to be a good.

We marvel at certain animals because they can pass through fire and suffer no bodily harm; but how much more marvellous is a man who has marched forth unhurt and unscathed through fire and sword and devastation! Do you understand now how much easier it is to conquer a whole tribe than to conquer one *man*? This saying of Stilbo makes common ground with Stoicism; the Stoic also can carry his goods unimpaired through cities that have been burned to ashes; for he is self-sufficient. Such are the bounds which he sets to his own happiness.

But you must not think that our school alone can utter noble words; Epicurus himself, the reviler of Stilbo, spoke similar language[12]; put it down to my credit, though I have already wiped out my debt for the present day.[13] He says: "Whoever does not regard what he has as most ample wealth, is unhappy, though

11. *Gnomologici Vaticani* 515ᵃ Sternberg.
12. Frag. 474 Usener.
13. *Cf.* above, § 6.

he be master of the whole world." Or, if the following seems to you a more suitable phrase,—for we must try to render the meaning and not the mere words: "A man may rule the world and still be unhappy, if he does not feel that he is supremely happy." In order, however, that you may know that these sentiments are universal,[14] suggested, of course, by Nature, you will find in one of the comic poets this verse:

Unblest is he who thinks himself unblest.[15]

For what does your condition matter, if it is bad in your own eyes? You may say: "What then? If yonder man, rich by base means, and yonder man, lord of many but slave of more, shall call themselves happy, will their own opinion make them happy?" It matters not what one says, but what one feels; also, not how one feels on one particular day, but how one feels at all times. There is no reason, however, why you should fear that this great privilege will fall into unworthy hands; only the wise man is pleased with his own. Folly is ever troubled with weariness of itself. Farewell.

14. *i.e.*, not confined to the Stoics, etc.
15. Author unknown; perhaps, as Buecheler thinks, adapted from the Greek.

Seneca

ON GRIEF FOR LOST FRIENDS
EPISTLE LXIII

I am grieved to hear that your friend Flaccus is dead, but I would not have you sorrow more than is fitting. That you should not mourn at all I shall hardly dare to insist; and yet I know that it is the better way. But what man will ever be so blessed with that ideal steadfastness of soul, unless he has already risen far above the reach of Fortune? Even such a man will be stung by an event like this, but it will be only a sting. We, however, may be forgiven for bursting into tears, if only our tears have not flowed to excess, and if we have checked them by our own efforts. Let not the eyes be dry when we have lost a friend, nor let them overflow. We may weep, but we must not wail.

Do you think that the law which I lay down for you is harsh, when the greatest of Greek poets has extended the privilege of weeping to one day only, in the lines where he tells us that even Niobe took thought of food?[1] Do you wish to know the reason for lamentations and excessive weeping? It is because we seek the proofs of our bereavement in our tears, and do not give way to sorrow, but merely parade it. No man goes into mourning for his own sake. Shame on our ill-timed folly! There is an element of self-seeking even in our sorrow.

"What," you say, "am I to forget my friend?" It is surely a short-lived memory that you vouchsafe to him, if it is to endure only as long as your grief; presently that brow of yours will be smoothed out in laughter by some circumstance, however casual.

1. Homer, *Iliad*, xix. 229 and xxiv. 602.

It is to a time no more distant than this that I put off the soothing of every regret, the quieting of even the bitterest grief. As soon as you cease to observe yourself, the picture of sorrow which you have contemplated will fade away; at present you are keeping watch over your own suffering. But even while you keep watch it slips away from you, and the sharper it is, the more speedily it comes to an end.

Let us see to it that the recollection of those whom we have lost becomes a pleasant memory to us. No man reverts with pleasure to any subject which he will not be able to reflect upon without pain. So too it cannot but be that the names of those whom we have loved and lost come back to us with a sort of sting; but there is a pleasure even in this sting. For, as my friend Attalus[2] used to say: "The remembrance of lost friends is pleasant in the same way that certain fruits have an agreeably acid taste, or as in extremely old wines it is their very bitterness that pleases us. Indeed, after a certain lapse of time, every thought that gave pain is quenched, and the pleasure comes to us unalloyed." If we take the word of Attalus for it, "to think of friends who are alive and well is like enjoying a meal of cakes and honey; the recollection of friends who have passed away gives a pleasure that is not without a touch of bitterness. Yet who will deny that even these things, which are bitter and contain an element of sourness, do serve to arouse the stomach?" For my part, I do not agree with him. To me, the thought of my dead friends is sweet and appealing. For I have had them as if I should one day lose them; I have lost them as if I have them still.

Therefore, Lucilius, act as befits your own serenity of mind, and cease to put a wrong interpretation on the gifts of Fortune. Fortune has taken away, but Fortune has given. Let us greedily enjoy our friends, because we do not know how long this privilege will be ours. Let us think how often we shall leave them when we go upon distant journeys, and how often we shall fail to see them when we tarry together in the same place; we shall thus understand that we have lost too much of their time while they were alive. But will you tolerate men who are most careless of their friends, and then mourn them most abjectly, and do not love anyone unless they have lost him? The reason why they lament too unrestrainedly at such times is that they are afraid

2. The teacher of Seneca, often mentioned by him.

lest men doubt whether they really have loved; all too late they seek for proofs of their emotions. If we have other friends, we surely deserve ill at their hands and think ill of them, if they are of so little account that they fail to console us for the loss of one. If, on the other hand, we have no other friends, we have injured ourselves more than Fortune has injured us; since Fortune has robbed us of one friend, but we have robbed ourselves of every friend whom we have failed to make. Again, he who has been unable to love more than one, has had none too much love even for that one.[3] If a man who has lost his one and only tunic through robbery chooses to bewail his plight rather than look about him for some way to escape the cold, or for something with which to cover his shoulders, would you not think him an utter fool?

You have buried one whom you loved; look about for someone to love. It is better to replace your friend than to weep for him. What I am about to add is, I know, a very hackneyed remark, but I shall not omit it simply because it is a common phrase: A man ends his grief by the mere passing of time, even if he has not ended it of his own accord. But the most shameful cure for sorrow, in the case of a sensible man, is to grow weary of sorrowing. I should prefer you to abandon grief, rather than have grief abandon you; and you should stop grieving as soon as possible, since, even if you wish to do so, it is impossible to keep it up for a long time. Our forefathers[4] have enacted that, in the case of women, a year should be the limit for mourning; not that they needed to mourn for so long, but that they should mourn no longer. In the case of men, no rules are laid down, because to mourn at all is not regarded as honourable. For all that, what woman can you show me, of all the pathetic females that could scarcely be dragged away from the funeral-pile or torn from the corpse, whose tears have lasted a whole month? Nothing becomes offensive so quickly as grief; when fresh, it finds someone to console it and attracts one or another to itself; but after becoming chronic, it is ridiculed, and rightly. For it is either assumed or foolish.

---

3. The reason is, as Lipsius observed, that friendship is essentially a social virtue, and is not confined to one object. The pretended friendship for one and only one is a form of self-love, and is not unselfish love.

4. According to tradition, from the time of Numa Pompilius.

He who writes these words to you is no other than I, who wept so excessively for my dear friend Annaeus Serenus[5] that, in spite of my wishes, I must be included among the examples of men who have been overcome by grief. To-day, however, I condemn this act of mine, and I understand that the reason why I lamented so greatly was chiefly that I had never imagined it possible for his death to precede mine. The only thought which occurred to my mind was that he was the younger, and much younger, too,—as if the Fates kept to the order of our ages!

Therefore let us continually think as much about our own mortality as about that of all those we love. In former days I ought to have said: "My friend Serenus is younger than I; but what does that matter? He would naturally die after me, but he may precede me." It was just because I did not do this that I was unprepared when Fortune dealt me the sudden blow. Now is the time for you to reflect, not only that all things are mortal, but also that their mortality is subject to no fixed law. Whatever can happen at any time can happen to-day. Let us therefore reflect, my beloved Lucilius, that we shall soon come to the goal which this friend, to our own sorrow, has reached. And perhaps, if only the tale told by wise men is true[6] and there is a bourne to welcome us, then he whom we think we have lost has only been sent on ahead. Farewell.

5. An intimate friend of Seneca, probably a relative, who died in the year 63 from eating poisoned mushrooms (Pliny, *N. H.* xxii. 96). Seneca dedicated to Serenus several of his philosophical essays.

6. *Cf.* the closing chapter of the *Agricola* of Tacitus: *si, ut sapientibus placet, non cum corpore exstinguuntur magnae animae,* etc.

Aelred of Rievaulx

SPIRITUAL FRIENDSHIP (*DE SPIRITALI AMICITIA*)

Introduction

Aelred, abbot of the Cistercian monastery of Rievaulx in York-shire, England, from 1147 until his death in 1167, was deeply impressed by Cicero's *De Amicitia* when he read it in his youth. In his *De Spiritali Amicitia*, or *Spiritual Friendship*, he attempts to write an analogous work, for a Christian rather than Roman society. The various innovations that Aelred introduces, which are substantial and which underlie many modern ideas about friendship, are consequences of his Christian worldview.

There are at least three important innovations to be found in Book I, which concerns the definition and origin of friendship. The first is that, because he takes Christ to be the model and inspiration for friendship, Aelred holds that any true friendship should display the following characteristics: each friend should be willing to die for the other (30); the love between them should be unconditional and hence eternal (23); and their possessions should be in common (28). But to hold this is, in effect, to make friendship an ideal, a standard for anyone who aims to be a friend—in the way that the Sermon on the Mount presents an ideal. A paradoxical consequence of this view is that true friendship then becomes both unattainable and widely accessible: unattainable because the ideal is in practice fully realized by no one (except the model of this ideal, Christ), yet widely accessible, because every friendship is measured by and can aspire to this ideal (26).

A second innovation is that Aelred denies that there can be secondary friendships, like Aristotle's "friendship for utility" or "friendship for pleasure," which are good but of lesser value. His view on this matter seems to stem from the doctrine of original sin. For Aelred, a person enters either into a true friendship—which is spiritual friendship—or into a corrupted, sinful friendship. The two sorts of corrupted friendship are carnal friendship, in which pleasures are sought, and worldly friendship, in which material advantages are sought. According to Aelred, there can be no innocent seeking of pleasures or advantage apart from some orientation to spiritual goods.

A third innovation is that *intimacy* rather than love becomes the distinctive mark of friendship. The reason for this is that Aelred distinguishes between friendship and the theological virtue of charity. In principle, he says, friendship ought to bind all members of the human race together, but it cannot in fact do so, because of the consequences of original sin (58). Charity now plays this role originally intended for friendship: out of love for God, Christians are to love everyone unconditionally, even enemies and wicked persons (59). But since the love we show for those close to us is also the work of charity, the distinguishing feature of friendship must be something in addition to love, which Aelred identifies as a certain intimacy. A friend is a "guardian of love," a "guardian of the spirit" (20); a friend is above all one to whom you reveal the secrets of your heart (1, 32, 45).

Aelred ends Book I with the striking suggestion that "God is friendship." This claim is, on its face, inconsistent with the cosmological view he expressed in 51–58, according to which friendship arises in creatures precisely because they are not self-sufficient, as is God. Aelred's reasons for holding that "God is friendship" are probably to be located in the doctrine of the Trinity—God as a communion of Divine Persons—rather than in the views he states in *Spiritual Friendship*.

Aelred of Rievaulx

SPIRITUAL FRIENDSHIP
BOOK I
THE ORIGIN OF FRIENDSHIP

Aelred. Here we are, you and I, and I hope a third, Christ, is in our midst.[1] There is no one now to disturb us; there is no one to break in upon our friendly chat, no man's prattle or noise of any kind will creep into this pleasant solitude. Come now, beloved, open your heart, and pour into these friendly ears whatsoever you will, and let us accept gracefully the boon of this place, time, and leisure.

2. Just a little while ago as I was sitting with the brethren, while all around were talking noisily, one questioning, another arguing—one advancing some point on Sacred Scripture, another information on vices, and yet another on virtue—you alone were silent. At times you would raise your head and make ready to say something, but just as quickly, as though your voice had been trapped in your throat, you would drop your head again and continue your silence. Then you would leave us for a while, and later return looking rather disheartened. I concluded from all this that you wanted to talk to me, but that you dreaded the crowd, and hoped to be alone with me.

3. *Ivo.*[2] That's it exactly, and I deeply appreciate your solicitude

1. In the opening sentence of the dialogue Aelred expresses succinctly the essence of Christian friendship, two persons together with Christ as their bond.

2. Ivo is usually identified as a monk of Wardon in Bedforshire. He might have been sent there from Rievaulx sometime after 1135. Since Wardon was a foundation of Rievaulx, Aelred would have gone there at least once a year to make the regular visitation. It was at the request of Ivo (presumably the same person) that Aelred wrote his *Jesus at the Age of Twelve*. See *The Works of Aelred of Rievaulx*, vol. I (Cistercian Fathers Series 2); also *Ailred of Rievaulx, Christian*

for your son. His state of mind and his desire have been disclosed to you by none other than the Spirit of Love. And would that your Lordship would grant me this favor, that, as often as you visit your sons here, I may be permitted, at least once, to have you all to myself and to disclose to you the deep feelings of my heart without disturbance.

4. *Aelred.* Indeed, I shall do that, and gladly. For I am greatly pleased to see that you are not bent on empty and idle pursuits, but that you are always speaking of things useful and necessary for your progress. Speak freely, therefore, and entrust to your friend all your cares and thoughts, that you may both learn and teach, give and receive, pour out and drink in.

5. *Ivo.* I am certainly ready to learn, not to teach; not to give, but to receive; to drink in, not to pour out; as indeed my youth demands of me, inexperience compels, and my religious profession exhorts. But that I may not foolishly squander on these considerations the time that I need for other matters, I wish that you would teach me something about spiritual friendship, namely, its nature and value, its source and end, whether it can be cultivated among all, and, if not among all, then by whom; how it can be preserved unbroken, and without any disturbance of misunderstanding be brought to a holy end.

6. *Aelred.* I wonder why you think it proper to seek this information from me, since it is evident that there has been enough, and more, discussion on matters of this kind by ancient and excellent teachers; particularly since you spent your youth in studies of this sort, and have read Cicero's treatise, *On Friendship*, in which in a delightful style he treats at length all those matters which appear to pertain to friendship, and there he sets forth certain laws and precepts, so to speak, for friendship.

7. *Ivo.* That treatise is not altogether unknown to me. In fact, at one time I took great delight in it. But since I began to taste some of the sweetness from the honey comb of Holy Scripture, and since the sweet name of Christ claimed my affection for itself, whatever I henceforth read or hear, though it be treated ever so subtly and eloquently, will have no relish or enlightenment for me, if it lacks the salt of the heavenly books and the flavoring of that most sweet name.[3] 8. Therefore, those things

---

Friendship, trans. H. Talbot (London: Catholic Book Club, 1942) p. 9: Dubois, *op. cit.* p. lxxiii.

3. See Prologue to *Spiritual Friendship*.

which have already been said, even though they are in harmony with reason, and other things which the utility of this discussion demands that we treat, I should like proved to me with the authority of the Scriptures. I should like also to be instructed more fully as to how the friendship which ought to exist among us begins in Christ, is preserved according to the Spirit of Christ, and how its end and fruition are referred to Christ. For it is evident that Tullius was unacquainted with the virtue of true friendship, since he was completely unaware of its beginning and end, Christ.

9. *Aelred.* I confess I have been won over, but, not knowing myself or the extent of my own ability, I am not going to teach you anything about these matters but rather to discuss them with you. For you yourself have opened the way for both of us, and have enkindled that brilliant light on the very threshold of our inquiry, which will not allow us to wander along unknown paths, but will lead us along the sure path to the certain goal of our proposed quest. 10. For what more sublime can be said of friendship, what more true, what more profitable, than that it ought to, and is proved to, begin in Christ, continue in Christ, and be perfected in Christ? Come now, tell me, what do you think ought to be our first consideration in this matter of friendship?

Ivo. In the first place, I think we should discuss the nature of friendship so as not to appear to be painting in emptiness, as we would, indeed, if we were unaware of the precise identity of that about which an ordered discussion on our part should proceed.

11. *Aelred.* But surely you are satisfied, as a starting point, with what Tullius says, are you not? "Friendship is mutual harmony in affairs human and divine coupled with benevolence and charity."[4]

12. *Ivo.* If that definition satisfies you, I agree that it satisfies me.

13. *Aelred.* In that case, those who have the same opinion, the same will, in matters human and divine, along with mutual benevolence and charity, have, we shall admit, reached the perfection of friendship.

14. *Ivo.* Why not? But still, I do not see what the pagan Cicero meant by the word "charity" and "benevolence."

15. *Aelred.* Perhaps for him the word "charity" expresses an

4. Amic 20.

affection of the heart, and the word "benevolence," carrying it out in deed. For mutual harmony itself in matters human and divine ought to be dear to the hearts of both, that is, attractive and precious;[5] and the carrying out of these works in actual practice ought to be both benevolent and pleasant.

16. *Ivo.* I grant that this definition pleases me adequately, except that I should think it applied equally to pagans and Jews, and even to bad Christians. However, I confess that I am convinced that true friendship cannot exist among those who live without Christ.

17. *Aelred.* What follows will make it sufficiently clear to us whether the definition contains too much or too little, so that it may either be rejected, or if, so to say sufficient and not over inclusive, be admitted. You can, however, get some idea of the nature of friendship from the definition, even though it should seem somewhat imperfect.

18. *Ivo.* Please, will I annoy you if I say that this definition does not satisfy me unless you unravel for me the meaning of the word itself?

19. *Aelred.* I shall be glad to comply with your wishes if only you will pardon my lack of knowledge and not force me to teach what I do not know. Now I think the word *amicus* [friend] comes from the word *amor* [love], and *amicitia* [friendship] from *amicus*.[6] For love is a certain "affection" of the rational soul whereby it seeks and eagerly strives after some object to possess it and enjoy it. Having attained its object through love, it enjoys it with a certain interior sweetness, embraces it, and preserves it. We have explained the affections and movements of love as clearly and carefully as we could in our *Mirror*[7] with which you are already familiar.

20. Furthermore, a friend is called a guardian of love or, as some would have it, a guardian of the spirit itself.[8] Since it is fitting that my friend be a guardian of our mutual love or the

---

5. In Latin a connection is seen between the words *caritas* (charity) and *carus* (precious).

6. Amic 26.

7. The *Speculum Caritatis, Mirror of Charity* (Cistercian Fathers Series 17), written by Aelred while he was still novice master of Rievaulx at the command of his Father Immediate (as Cistercians are accustomed to call the abbot of the motherhouse of their abbey), Bernard of Clairvaux. The third book especially of this work treats of friendship.

8. Isidore, *Etymologiae*, 10–5.

guardian of my own spirit so as to preserve all its secrets in faithful silence, let him, as far as he can, cure and endure such defects as he may observe in it; let him rejoice with his friend in his joys, and weep with him in his sorrows,[9] and feel as his own all that his friend experiences.

21. Friendship, therefore, is that virtue by which spirits are bound by ties of love and sweetness, and out of many are made one.[10] Even the philosophers of this world have ranked friendship not with things casual or transitory but with the virtues which are eternal.[11] Solomon in the *Book of Proverbs* appears to agree with them when he says: "He that is a friend loves at all times,"[12] manifestly declaring that friendship is eternal if it is true friendship; but, if it should ever cease to be, then it was not true friendship, even though it seemed to be so.

22. *Ivo.* Why is it, then, that we read about bitter enmities arising between the most devoted friends?[13]

23. *Aelred.* God-willing, we shall discuss that matter more amply in its own place.[14] Meantime remember this: he was never a friend who could offend him whom he at one time received into his friendship; on the other hand, that other has not tasted the delights of true friendship who even when offended has ceased to love him whom he once cherished. For "he that is a friend loves at all times."[15] 24. Although he be accused unjustly, though he be injured, though he be cast in the flames, though he be crucified, "he that is a friend loves at all times."[16] Our Jerome speaks similarly: "A friendship which can cease to be was never true friendship."[17]

25. *Ivo.* Since such perfection is expected of true friendship, it

---

9. Rom 12:15.

10. Amic 81, 92. Cf. Spec car 3:39. Bernard of Clairvaux, Letter 53 (PL 182:160); tr. B. S. James, *The Letters of Bernard of Clairvaux* (London: Burns Oates, 1953) Letter 56, p. 84.

11. See Amic 32.

12. Prov 17:17. Aelred quotes this verse from Proverbs again in the Third Book, n. 63, where he teaches that the fidelity of a person should be tested before he is accepted into full friendship. There he includes the second portion of the text: "He that is a friend loves at all times and a brother is proved in distress."

13. Amic 34.

14. See *Spiritual Friendship*, 3:39ff.

15. Prov 17:17.

16. *Ibid.*

17. St Jerome, *Letters*, 3:6; PL 22:335.

is not surprising that those were so rare whom the ancients commended as true friends. As Tullius says: "In so many past ages, tradition extols scarcely three or four pairs of friends."[18] But if in our day, that is, in this age of Christianity, friends are so few, it seems to me that I am exerting myself uselessly in striving after this virtue which I, terrified by its admirable sublimity, now almost despair of ever acquiring.

26. *Aelred.* "Effort in great things," as someone has said, "is itself great."[19] Hence it is the mark of a virtuous mind to reflect continually upon sublime and noble thoughts, that it may either attain the desired object or understand more clearly and gain knowledge of what ought to be desired. Thus, too, he must be supposed to have advanced not a little who has learned, by a knowledge of virtue, how far he is from virtue itself. 27. Indeed, the Christian ought not to despair of acquiring any virtue since daily the divine voice from the Gospel reechoes: "Ask, and you shall receive. . . . "[20] It is no wonder, then, that pursuers of true virtue were rare among the pagans since they did not know the Lord, the Dispenser of virtue,[21] of whom it is written: "The Lord of hosts, he is the King of glory."[22] 28. Indeed, through faith in him they were prepared to die for one another—I do not say three or four, but I offer you thousands of pairs of friends— although the ancients declared or imagined the devotion of Pylades and Orestes a great marvel.[23] Were they not, according to the definition of Tullius, strong in the virtue of true friendship,

---

18. Amic 15.

19. Cf. Julius Pomerius, *De vita contemplativa*, I, Prologue, 2 (PL 59:416), taken from the Pseudo-Seneca, *Monita*, 97.

20. Mt 7:7; Jn 16:24.

21. Cf. *Leonine Sacramentary*, 1229; ed. Mohlberg, p. 156, 17.

22. Ps 23:10.

23. Orestes, the son of Agamemnon, after the murder of his father was secretly taken to the home of his uncle Strophius. Here he was raised along with his cousin Pylades and a very deep bond of union and love grew up between these two cousins. Pylades helped Orestes to avenge the murder of his father and the two fled together. However, Orestes was condemned to death in the land of his exile. At this point Pylades proved the depth of his friendship by seeking to take the place of Orestes and die in his stead. Their friendship became proverbial, and they were even worshiped by the Scythians. It was Pacuvius who brought their legend into Latin literature. However Aelred probably knew it from Cicero (Amic 24) and Augustine (*Confessions* 4:6).

of whom it is written: "And the multitude of believers had but one heart and one soul; neither did anyone say that aught was his own, but all things were common unto them"?[24] 29. How could they fail to have complete agreement on all things divine and human with charity and benevolence,[25] seeing that they had but one heart and one soul? How many martyrs gave their lives for their brethren! How many spared neither cost, nor even physical torments! I am sure you have often read—and that not dry-eyed—about the girl of Antioch rescued from a house of ill-repute by a fine bit of strategy on the part of a certain soldier.[26] Sometime later he whom she had discovered as a guardian of her chastity in that house of ill-repute became her companion in martyrdom. 30. I might go on citing many examples of this kind, did not the danger of verboseness forbid, and their very abundance enjoin us to be silent. For Christ Jesus announced their coming. He spoke, and they were multiplied above number.[27] "Greater love than this," he says, "no man has, that a man lay down his life for his friends."[28]

31. *Ivo.* Are we then to believe that there is no difference between charity and friendship?

32. *Aelred.* On the contrary, there is a vast difference; for divine authority approves that more are to be received into the bosom of charity than into the embrace of friendship. For we are compelled by the law of charity to receive in the embrace of love not only our friends but also our enemies.[29] But only those do we call friends to whom we can fearlessly entrust our heart and all its secrets; those, too, who, in turn, are bound to us by the same law of faith and security.

33. *Ivo.* How many persons leading a worldly existence and

---

24. Acts 4:32.

25. Aelred is here repeating the definition of Cicero, adding however the significant adjective "complete."

26. St Ambrose, *On Virgins*, 2:4 (PL 16:224f.). Aelred repeats here what is evidently an error on the part of Ambrose. The reference seems undoubtedly to be to Theodora of Alexandria rather than of Antioch, whose story is related in the Martyrology (April 28th). Didyme is the "certain soldier." Actually he simply disguised himself as a soldier in order to save Theodora and for this paid the price of being beheaded.

27. Ps 39:6.

28. Jn 15:13.

29. Mt 5:44; Lk 6:27f.

acting as partners in some form of vice, are united by a similar pact and find the bond of even that sort of friendship to be more pleasant and sweet than all the delights of this world!

34. I hope that you will not find it burdensome to isolate, as it were, from the company of so many types of friendship that one which we think should be called "spiritual" to distinguish it from the others with which it is to some extent bound up and confused and which accost and clamor for the attention of those who seek and long for it. For by contrasting them you would make spiritual friendship better known to us and consequently more desirable, and thus more actively rouse and fire us to its acquisition.

35. *Aelred*. Falsely do they claim the illustrious name of friends among whom there exists a harmony of vices; since he who does not love is not a friend, but he does not love his fellow-man who loves iniquity. "For he that loves iniquity" does not love, but "hates his own soul."[30] Truly, he who does not love his own soul will not be able to love the soul of another.[31] 36. Thus it follows that they glory only in the name of friendship and are deceived by a distorted image and are not supported by truth. Yet, since such great joy is experienced in friendship which either lust defiles, avarice dishonors, or luxury pollutes, we may infer how much sweetness that friendship possesses which, in proportion as it is nobler, is the more secure; purer, it is the more pleasing; freer, it is the more happy. 37. Let us allow that, because of some similarity in feelings, those friendships which are not true, be, nevertheless, called friendships, provided, however, they are judiciously distinguished from that friendship which is spiritual and therefore true. 38. Hence let one kind of friendship be called carnal, another worldly, and another spiritual. The carnal springs from mutual harmony in vice; the worldly is enkindled by the hope of gain; and the spiritual is cemented by similarity of life, morals, and pursuits among the just.[32]

39. The real beginning of carnal friendship proceeds from an affection which like a harlot directs its step after every passer-by,[33] following its own lustful ears and eyes in every direction.[34] By

30. Ps 10:6.

31. Cf. Spec car 3:2.

32. Cf. Cassian, *Conferences*, 16:2 (Cistercian Studies Series 31).

33. Cf. Ezek 16:25 and Jerome's commentary on this: *Commentary on Ezekiel*, 4:16 (PL 25:138).

34. Num 15:39.

means of the avenues of these senses it brings into the mind itself
images of beautiful bodies or voluptuous objects. To enjoy these
as he pleases the carnal man thinks is blessedness, but to enjoy
them without an associate he considers less delightful. 40. Then
by gesture, nod, words, compliance, spirit is captivated by spirit,
and one is inflamed by the other, and they are kindled to form
a sinful bond, so that, after they have entered upon such a deplor-
able pact, the one will do or suffer any crime or sacrilege whatsoever for the sake of the other. They consider nothing sweeter than
this type of friendship, they judge nothing more equable, be-
lieving community of like and dislike[35] to be imposed upon them
by the laws of friendship. 41. And so, this sort of friendship is
undertaken without deliberation, is tested by no act of judgment,
is in no wise governed by reason; but through the violence of
affection is carried away through divers paths, observing no limit,
caring naught for uprightness, foreseeing neither gains nor
losses, but advancing toward everything heedlessly, indiscrimi-
nately, lightly and immoderately. For that reason, goaded on, as
if by furies, it is consumed by its own self, or is dissolved with
the same levity with which it was originally fashioned.

42. But worldly friendship, which is born of a desire for temporal advantage or possessions, is always full of deceit and intrigue;
it contains nothing certain, nothing constant, nothing secure;
for, to be sure, it ever changes with fortune and follows the
purse.[36] 43. Hence it is written: "He is a fair-weather friend, and
he will not abide in the day of your trouble."[37] Take away his
hope of profit, and immediately he will cease to be a friend. This
type of friendship the following lines very aptly deride:

> A friend, not of the man, but of his purse is he,
> Held fast by fortune fair, by evil made to flee.[38]

44. And yet, the beginning of this vicious friendship leads
many individuals to a certain degree of true friendship: those,

---

35. *Idem velle et idem nolle*—this is a proverbial saying which Sallust places in the
mouth of Cataline as he urges his fellow conspirators in the name of friendship
to join him in revolt; *Cataline* 20:4; tr. J. Watson, *Sallust, Flores and Vellius Paterculus*
(New York: Harper, 1885) p. 25.

36. Cf. Jerome, *Adv. Rufinum*, 1:17 (PL 23:430).

37. Sir 6:8.

38. No one seems to have been able yet to trace the source of this verse. Hoste
(Spir amic, p. 176), Dubois (p. 29), Talbot (p. 135) all confess their ignorance as
to the source.

namely, who at first enter into a compact of friendship in the hope of common profit while they cherish in themselves faith in baneful riches, and who, in so far as human affairs are concerned, reach an acme of pleasing mutual agreement. But a friendship ought in no wise be called true which is begun and preserved for the sake of some temporal advantage.

45. For spiritual friendship, which we call true, should be desired, not for consideration of any worldly advantage or for any extrinsic cause, but from the dignity of its own nature and the feelings of the human heart, so that its fruition and reward is nothing other than itself.[39] 46. Whence the Lord in the Gospel says: "I have appointed you that you should go, and should bring forth fruit,"[40] that is, that you should love one another. For true friendship advances by perfecting itself, and the fruit is derived from feeling the sweetness of that perfection. And so spiritual friendship among the just is born of a similarity in life, morals, and pursuits, that is, it is a mutual conformity in matters human and divine united with benevolence and charity.[41]

47. Indeed, this definition seems to me to be adequate for representing friendship. If, however, "charity" is, according to our way of thinking, named in the sense that friendship excludes every vice, then "benevolence" expresses the feeling to love which is pleasantly roused interiorly. 48. Where such friendship exists, there, indeed, is a community of likes and dislikes,[42] the more pleasant in proportion as it is more sincere, the more agreeable as it is more sacred; those who love in this way can will nothing that is unbecoming, and reject nothing that is expedient. 49. Surely, such friendship prudence directs, justice rules, fortitude guards, and temperance moderates.[43] But of these mat-

---

39. Amic 31. Cf. Bernard of Clairvaux, *On the Song of Songs*, Sermon 83:4, OB 2:301; CF 40: "Love requires no other cause but itself, nor does it command a reward. Its reward is its enjoyment."

40. Jn 15:16f.

41. Amic 8,65. Cf. Conf. 16:3: "There is friendship which is constant and indissoluble, which is formed neither . . . in gifts received, nor in partnership in business, nor by instinct of nature, but which is cemented by likeness of manners or by the possession of the same virtues." SCh 54:224, CS 31. See also Chapter 5, *ibid*.

42. See above, note 35.

43. In his treatise on *Jesus at the Age of Twelve*, 20 (CF 2:27), Aelred brings out that the four cardinal virtues which he mentions here are nothing more than charity exercised in different circumstances. Therefore true friendship is simply friendship which is animated by charity.

ters we shall speak in their place. Now, then, tell me whether you think enough has been said about the matter you first brought up, namely, the nature of friendship.

50. *Ivo.* Your explanation is certainly sufficient, and nothing else suggests itself to me for further inquiry. But before we go on to other things, I should like to know how friendship first originated among men. Was it by nature, by chance or by necessity of some kind? Or did it come into practice by some statute or law imposed upon the human race, and did practice then commend it to man?

51. *Aelred.* At first, as I see it, nature itself impressed upon the human soul a desire for friendship, then experience increased that desire, and finally the sanction of the law confirmed it.[44] For God, supremely powerful and supremely good, is sufficient good unto himself, since his good, his joy, his glory, his happiness, is himself.[45] 52. Nor is there anything outside himself which he needs, neither man, nor angel, nor heaven, nor earth, nor anything which these contain. To him every creature proclaims: "You are my God, for you have no need of my goods."[46] Not only is he sufficient unto himself, but he is himself the sufficiency of all things: giving simple being to some, sensation to other, and wisdom over and above these to still others, himself the Cause of all being, the Life of all sensation, the Wisdom of all intelligence. 53. And thus Sovereign Nature has established all natures, has arranged all things in their places, and has discreetly distributed all things in their own times. He has willed, moreover, for so his eternal reason has directed, that peace encompass all his creatures and society unite them; and thus all creatures obtain from him, who is supremely and purely one, some trace of that unity. For that reason he has left no type of beings alone, but out of many has drawn them together by means of a certain society.

54. Suppose we begin with inanimate creation—what soil or what river produces one single stone of one kind? Or what forest bears but a single tree of a single kind? And so even in inanimate nature a certain love of companionship, so to speak, is apparent, since none of these exists alone but everything is created and thrives in a certain society with its own kind.

44. Amic 27.
45. Spec car 1:2.
46. Ps 15:2.

And surely in animate life who can easily describe how clear the picture of friendship is, and the image of society and love?[47] 55. And though in all other respects animals are rated irrational, yet they imitate man in this regard to such an extent that we almost believe they act with reason. How they run after one another, play with one another, so express and betray their love by sound and movement, so eagerly and happily do they enjoy their mutual company, that they seem to prize nothing else so much as they do whatever pertains to friendship.[48]

56. For the angels too divine Wisdom provided, in that he created not one but many. Among them pleasant companionship and delightful love created the same will, the same desire. Assuredly, since one seemed to be superior, the other inferior, there would have been occasion for envy,[49] had not the charity of friendship prevented it. Their multitude thus excluded solitude, and the bond of charity among many increased their mutual happiness.

57. Finally, when God created man, in order to commend more highly the good of society, he said: "It is not good for man to be alone: let us make him a helper like unto himself."[50] It was from no similar, nor even from the same, material that divine Might formed this help mate, but as a clearer inspiration to charity and friendship he produced the woman from the very substance of the man.[51] How beautiful it is that the second human being was taken from the side of the first, so that nature might teach that human beings are equal and, as it were, collateral, and that there is in human affairs neither a superior nor an inferior, a characteristic of true friendship. 58. Hence, nature from the very beginning implanted the desire for friendship and charity in the heart of man, a desire which an inner sense of affection soon increased with a taste of sweetness. But after the fall of the first man, when with the cooling of charity concupiscence made secret inroads and caused private good to take precedence over the common weal, it corrupted the splendor of friendship and charity

---

47. Amic 81.

48. Amic 81. Cf. Conf. 16:2.

49. Amic 69, 71. Cf. Bernard of Clairvaux, *On the Song of Songs*, Sermon 59:2 (CF 31). See below, no. 57.

50. Gen 2:18.

51. Gen 2:21f.

through avarice and envy, introducing contentions, emulations, hates and suspicions because the morals of men had been corrupted. 59. From that time the good distinguished between charity and friendship, observing that love ought to be extended even to the hostile and perverse, while no union of will and ideas can exist between the good and wicked. And so friendship which, like charity, was first preserved among all by all, remained according to the natural law among the few good. They saw the sacred laws of faith and society violated by many and bound themselves together by a closer bond of love and friendship. In the midst of the evils which they saw and felt, they rested in the joy of mutual charity. 60. But in those in whom wickedness obliterated every feeling for virtue, reason, which could not be extinguished in them, left the inclination toward friendship and society, so that without companionship riches could hold no charm for the greedy, nor glory for the ambitious, nor pleasure for the sensuous man. There are compacts—even sworn bonds—of union among the wicked which ought to be abhorred. These, clothed with the beautiful name of friendship, ought to have been distinguished from true friendship by law and precept, so that when true friendship was sought, one might not incautiously be ensnared among those other friendships because of some slight resemblance. 61. Thus friendship, which nature has brought into being and practice has strengthened, has by the power of law been regulated. It is evident, then, that friendship is natural, like virtue, wisdom, and the like, which should be sought after and preserved for their own sake as natural goods. Everyone that possesses them makes good use of them, and no one entirely abuses them.[52]

62. *Ivo.* May I ask, do not many people abuse wisdom? Those, I mean, who desire to please men through it, or take pride in themselves by reason of the wisdom placed in them or certainly those who consider it a thing that can be sold, just as they imagine there is a source of revenue in piety.[53]

63. *Aelred.* Our Augustine should satisfy you on that point. Here are his words: "He who pleases himself, pleases a foolish man, because, to be sure, he is foolish who pleases himself."[54]

---

52. St Augustine, *On Free Will*, 2:19.
53. St Augustine, Sermon 47:9ff. (PL 38:303).
54. Cf. St Bernard, SC 36:3; OB 2:5–6, CF 7.

But the man who is foolish is not wise; and he who is not wise is not wise because he does not possess wisdom. How then does he abuse wisdom who does not even possess it? And so proud chastity is no virtue, because pride itself, which is a vice, makes conformable to itself that which was considered a virtue. Therefore, it is not a virtue, but a vice.

64. *Ivo.* But I tell you, with your forbearance, that it does not seem consistent to me to join wisdom to friendship, since there is no comparison between the two.

65. *Aelred.* In spite of the fact that they are not coequal, very often lesser things are linked with greater, good with better, weaker with stronger. This is particularly true in the case of virtues. Although they vary by reason of a difference in degree, still they are close to one another by reason of similarity. Thus widowhood is near to virginity, conjugal chastity to widowhood. Although there is a great difference between these individual virtues, there is, nevertheless, a conformity in this, that they are virtues. 66. Now, then, conjugal chastity does not fail to be a virtue for the reason that widowhood is superior in continency. And whereas holy virginity is preferred to both, it does not thereby take away the excellence of the others. And yet, if you consider carefully what has been said about friendship, you will find it so close to, even replete with, wisdom, that I might almost say friendship is nothing else but wisdom.

67. *Ivo.* I am amazed, I admit, but I do not think that I can easily be convinced of your view.

68. *Aelred.* Have you forgotten that Scripture says: "He that is a friend loves at all times"?[55] Our Jerome also, as you recall, says: "Friendship which can end was never true friendship."[56] That friendship cannot even endure without charity has been more than adequately established. Since then in friendship eternity blossoms, truth shines forth, and charity grows sweet, consider whether you ought to separate the name of wisdom from these three.

69. *Ivo.* What does this all add up to? Shall I say of friendship what John, the friend of Jesus, says of charity: "God is friendship"?[57]

55. Prov 17:17.
56. Jerome, Letter 3:6; PL 22:335.
57. Cf. 1 Jn 4:16.

70. *Aelred*. That would be unusual, to be sure, nor does it have the sanction of the Scriptures. But still what is true of charity, I surely do not hesitate to grant to friendship, since "he that abides in friendship, abides in God, and God in him."[58] That we shall see more clearly when we begin to discuss its fruition and utility. Now if we have said enough on the nature of friendship in view of the simplicity of our poor wit, let us reserve for another time the other points you proposed for solution.

71. *Ivo*. I admit that my eagerness finds such a delay quite annoying, but it is necessary since not only is it time for the evening meal, from which no one may be absent, but, in addition, there are the burdensome demands of the other religious who have a right to your care.

58. *Ibid.*

Aquinas

SUMMA THEOLOGIAE QUESTIONS ON LOVE AND CHARITY

Introduction

Thomas Aquinas discusses friendship twice in his *Summa Theologiae*. The first discussion is part of an extended treatment of love, occupying qq. 26–28 of the "first part of the second part" (I-II) of the *Summa*. Here Aquinas treats love as a 'passion' or emotion, along with hatred, hope, despair, fear, daring, and anger. The second is found in his detailed investigation of the theological virtue of charity, in qq. 23–46 of the "second part of the second part" (II-II). Here he construes charity as friendship with God and with neighbor for God's sake; hence, in explaining charity, he discusses the nature and characteristics of friendship.

For Aquinas, it would be his discussion of love that would more closely correspond to the accounts of friendship proposed by non-Christian philosophers before him. He understands charity to be a new and supernatural friendship, unique to Christianity. Strictly speaking, then, his discussion of charity is a work in theology, rather than philosophy, because it presupposes the truth of revealed theological doctrines, such as the Incarnation. Nevertheless, like many of Aquinas's theological writings, the work has great philosophical interest, because of the philosophical arguments and insights that Aquinas articulates in the course of the discussion. Moreover, since Aquinas holds that charity assists and perfects natural affection, rather than replacing or destroying it

146

(see, for example, I-II, q. 28, a. 2, *sed contra*, and II-II, q. 26, a. 6, *corpus*), there must be various analogies between charity and friendship, so that much of what Aquinas says about charity can be used to draw analogous conclusions, which Aquinas would presumably admit, about friendship in the ordinary sense.

Just as Aelred's *Spiritual Friendship* is the great medieval work on friendship on the Ciceronian model, so the questions on love and charity constitute the great medieval work on friendship which builds upon Aristotle. After the Bible, the *Nicomachean Ethics* is the work most frequently cited by Aquinas. He refers to every book of the *Ethics* except IV and VII and to fifteen of the twenty-six chapters of books VIII and IX on friendship. Consequently, much of Aquinas's discussion of love can be located within the context provided by the *Nicomachean Ethics*. But certain innovations are quite striking: for example, he isolates a certain kind of love, 'dilection', which he understands as love that is consequent solely upon a free choice of the will, and he insists that love is a power that extends beyond knowledge (q. 27, a. 2, ad 2; q. 28, a. 1, ad 3).

Perhaps the most important distinction drawn by Aquinas is that between *love of friendship* and *love of concupiscence*, and the corresponding distinction in relationships based on these loves (q. 26, a. 4). This is his reworking of Aristotle's distinction between complete friendship and friendships for pleasure or utility. The question of whether goodwill is a constituent of the latter types of friendship is answered negatively by Aquinas: he considers the love characteristic of such friendships to be basically the same as the desires we have to consume food or acquire possessions (see also II-II, q. 23, a. 1). The modern distinction between altruistic and egoistic love may have had its origin in this distinction.

Aquinas uses the distinction suggestively in his investigation of the "effects" of love in q. 28, in which he tries to provide philosophical accounts of various metaphorical descriptions of love—that lover and beloved each 'dwell' in the other; that they 'go out of themselves' in ecstasy; that love 'wounds' the soul. Aquinas claims that each of these descriptions also applies to love of concupiscence, but in a very different sense, since that sort of love is essentially possessive.

Every human action without exception is done out of love,

according to Aquinas (q. 28, a. 6). Hence, if that love is charity—a kind of friendship—then friendship of a certain kind becomes the overarching and organizing virtue of one's entire moral life. This is indeed what we find in Aquinas's discussion of charity (II-II, q. 26). Moral action becomes nothing other than action that observes the proper order of charity, and this order depends upon two relations: the closeness of a person to oneself and the nearness of a person to God.

Thomas Aquinas

SUMMA THEOLOGIAE QUESTIONS ON LOVE AND CHARITY

ST I-II Question 26
Of the Passions of the Soul in Particular:
And First, of Love

(IN FOUR ARTICLES)

We have now to consider the soul's passions in particular, and (1) the passions of the concupiscible faculty; (2) the passions of the irascible faculty.

The first of these considerations will be threefold: since we shall consider (1) Love and hatred; (2) Desire and aversion; (3) Pleasure and sadness.

Concerning love, three points must be considered: (1) Love itself; (2) The cause of love; (3) The effects of love. Under the first head there are four points of inquiry: (1) Whether love is in the concupiscible power? (2) Whether love is a passion? (3) Whether love is the same as dilection? (4) Whether love is properly divided into love of friendship, and love of concupiscence?

FIRST ARTICLE
WHETHER LOVE IS IN THE CONCUPISCIBLE POWER?

We proceed thus to the First Article:—

Objection 1. It would seem that love is not in the concupiscible power. For it is written (Wis. viii. 2): *Her,* namely, wisdom, *have*

I loved, and have sought her out from my youth. But the concupiscible power, being a part of the sensitive appetite, cannot tend to wisdom, which is not apprehended by the senses. Therefore love is not in the concupiscible power.

Obj. 2. Further, love seems to be identified with every passion: for Augustine says (*De Civ. Dei* xiv. 7): *Love, yearning for the object beloved, is desire; having and enjoying it, is joy; fleeing what is contrary to it, is fear; and feeling what is contrary to it, is sadness.* But not every passion is in the concupiscible power; indeed, fear, which is mentioned in this passage, is in the irascible power. Therefore we must not say absolutely that love is in the concupiscible power.

Obj. 3. Further, Dionysius (*Div. Nom.* iv) mentions a *natural love.* But natural love seems to pertain rather to the natural powers, which belong to the vegetal soul. Therefore love is not simply in the concupiscible power.

On the contrary, The Philosopher says (*Topic.* ii. 7) that *love is in the concupiscible power.*

I answer that, Love is something pertaining to the appetite; since good is the object of both. Wherefore love differs according to the difference of appetites. For there is an appetite which arises from an apprehension existing, not in the subject of the appetite, but in some other: and this is called the *natural appetite.* Because natural things seek what is suitable to them according to their nature, by reason of an apprehension which is not in them, but in the Author of their nature, as stated in the First Part (Q. 6, A. 1 *ad* 2; Q. 103, A. 1 *ad* 1, 3).—And there is another appetite arising from an apprehension in the subject of the appetite, but from necessity and not from free-will. Such is, in irrational animals, the *sensitive appetite,* which, however, in man, has a certain share of liberty, in so far as it obeys reason.—Again, there is another appetite following freely from an apprehension in the subject of the appetite. And this is the rational or intellectual appetite, which is called the *will.*

Now in each of these appetites, the name *love* is given to the principle of movement towards the end loved. In the natural appetite the principle of this movement is the appetitive subject's connaturalness with the thing to which it tends, and may be called *natural love:* thus the connaturalness of a heavy body for the centre, is by reason of its weight and may be called *natural love.* In like manner the aptitude of the sensitive appetite or of the will to some good, that is to say, its very complacency in good, is called *sensitive love*, or *intellectual* or *rational love*. So that sensitive love is in the sensitive appetite, just as intellectual love is in the intellectual appetite. And it belongs to the concupiscible power, because it regards good absolutely, and not under the aspect of difficulty, which is the object of the irascible faculty.

Reply Obj. 1. The words quoted refer to intellectual or rational love.

Reply Obj. 2. Love is spoken of as being fear, joy, desire and sadness, not essentially but causally.

Reply Obj. 3. Natural love is not only in the powers of the vegetal soul, but in all the soul's powers, and also in all the parts of the body, and universally in all things: because, as Dionysius says (*Div. Nom.* iv), *Beauty and goodness are beloved by all things;* since each single thing has a connaturalness with that which is naturally suitable to it.

SECOND ARTICLE
WHETHER LOVE IS A PASSION?

We proceed thus to the Second Article:—

Objection 1. It would seem that love is not a passion. For no power is a passion. But every love is a power, as Dionysius says (*Div. Nom.* iv). Therefore love is not a passion.

Obj. 2. Further, love is a kind of union or bond, as Augustine says (*De Trin.* viii. 10). But a union or bond is not a passion, but rather a relation. Therefore love is not a passion.

Obj. 3. Further, Damascene says (*De Fide Orthod.* ii. 22) that passion is a movement. But love does not imply the movement of the appetite; for this is desire, of which movement love is the principle. Therefore love is not a passion.

On the contrary, The Philosopher says (*Ethic.* viii. 5) that *love is a passion.*

I answer that, Passion is the effect of the agent on the patient. Now a natural agent produces a twofold effect on the patient: for in the first place it gives it the form; and secondly it gives it the movement that results from the form. Thus the generator gives the generated body both weight and the movement resulting from weight: so that weight, from being the principle of movement to the place, which is connatural to that body by reason of its weight, can, in a way, be called *natural love*. In the same way the appetible object gives the appetite, first, a certain adaptation to itself, which consists in complacency in that object; and from this follows movement towards the appetible object. For *the appetitive movement is circular*, as stated in *De Anima* iii. 10; because the appetible object moves the appetite, introducing itself, as it were, into its intention; while the appetite moves towards the realization of the appetible object, so that the movement ends where it began. Accordingly, the first change wrought in the appetite by the appetible object is called *love*, and is nothing else than complacency in that object; and from this complacency results a movement towards that same object, and this movement is *desire*; and lastly, there is rest which is *joy*. Since, therefore, love consists in a change wrought in the appetite by the appetible object, it is evident that love is a passion: properly so called, according as it is in the concupiscible faculty; in a wider and extended sense, according as it is in the will.

Reply Obj. 1. Since power denotes a principle of movement or action, Dionysius calls love a power, in so far as it is a principle of movement in the appetite.

Reply Obj. 2. Union belongs to love in so far as by reason of the complacency of the appetite, the lover stands in relation to that which he loves, as though it were himself or part of himself. Hence it is clear that love is not the very relation of union, but that union is a result of love. Hence, too, Dionysius says that *love is a unitive force* (*Div. Nom.* iv), and the Philosopher says (*Polit.* ii. 1) that union is the work of love.

Reply Obj. 3. Although love does not denote the movement of the appetite in tending towards the appetible object, yet it denotes that movement whereby the appetite is changed by the appetible object, so as to have complacency therein.

THIRD ARTICLE
WHETHER LOVE IS THE SAME AS DILECTION?

We proceed thus to the Third Article:—

Objection 1. It would seem that love is the same as dilection. For Dionysius says (*Div. Nom.* iv) that love is to dilection, *as four is to twice two, and as a rectilinear figure is to one composed of straight lines.* But these have the same meaning. Therefore love and dilection denote the same thing.

Obj. 2. Further, the movements of the appetite differ by reason of their objects. But the objects of dilection and love are the same. Therefore these are the same.

Obj. 3. Further, if dilection and love differ, it seems that it is chiefly in the fact that *dilection refers to good things, love to evil things, as some have maintained,* according to Augustine (*De Civ. Dei* xiv. 7). But they do not differ thus; because as Augustine says (*ibid.*) the holy Scripture uses both words in reference to either good or bad things. Therefore love and dilection do not differ: thus indeed Augustine concludes (*ibid.*) that *it is not one thing to speak of love, and another to speak of dilection.*

On the contrary, Dionysius says (*Div. Nom.* iv) that *some holy men have held that love means something more Godlike than dilection does.*

I answer that, We find four words referring in a way, to the same thing: viz., love, dilection, charity and friendship. They differ, however, in this, that *friendship,* according to the Philosopher (*Ethic.* viii. 5), *is like a habit,* whereas *love* and *dilection* are expressed by way of act or passion; and *charity* can be taken either way.

Moreover these three express act in different ways. For love has a wider signification than the others, since every dilection or charity is love, but not vice versa. Because dilection implies, in addition to love, a choice (*electionem*) made beforehand, as the very word denotes: and therefore dilection is not in the concupiscible power, but only in the will, and only in the rational nature.—Charity denotes, in addition to love, a certain perfection of love, in so far as that which is loved is held to be of great price, as the word itself implies.[1]

Reply Obj. 1. Dionysius is speaking of love and dilection, in so far as they are in the intellectual appetite; for thus love is the same as dilection.

Reply Obj. 2. The object of love is more general than the object of dilection: because love extends to more than dilection does, as stated above.

Reply Obj. 3. Love and dilection differ, not in respect of good and evil, but as stated. Yet in the intellectual faculty love is the same as dilection. And it is in this sense that Augustine speaks of love in the passage quoted: hence a little further on he adds

1. Referring to the Latin *carus* (*dear*).

that *a right will is well-directed love, and a wrong will is ill-directed love*. However, the fact that love, which is a concupiscible passion, inclines many to evil, is the reason why some assigned the difference spoken of.

Reply Obj. 4. The reason why some held that, even when applied to the will itself, the word *love* signifies something more Godlike than *dilection,* was because love denotes a passion, especially in so far as it is in the sensitive appetite; whereas dilection presupposes the judgment of reason. But it is possible for man to tend to God by love, being as it were passively drawn by Him, more than he can possibly be drawn thereto by his reason, which pertains to the nature of dilection, as stated above. And consequently love is more Godlike than dilection.

FOURTH ARTICLE
WHETHER LOVE IS PROPERLY DIVIDED INTO LOVE OF FRIENDSHIP AND LOVE OF CONCUPISCENCE?

We proceed thus to the Fourth Article:—

Objection 1. It would seem that love is not properly divided into love of friendship and love of concupiscence. For *love is a passion, while friendship is a habit,* according to the Philosopher (Ethic. viii. 5). But habit cannot be the member of a division of passions. Therefore love is not properly divided into love of concupiscence and love of friendship.

Obj. 2. Further, a thing cannot be divided by another member of the same division; for man is not a member of the same division as *animal.* But concupiscence is a member of the same division as love, as a passion distinct from love. Therefore concupiscence is not a division of love.

Obj. 3. Further, according to the Philosopher (*Ethic.* viii. 3) friendship is threefold, that which is founded on *usefulness,* that which is founded on *pleasure,* and that which is founded on *goodness.* But useful and pleasant friendship are not without concupiscence. Therefore concupiscence should not be contrasted with friendship.

On the contrary, We are said to love certain things, because we desire them: thus *a man is said to love wine, on account of its sweetness which he desires;* as stated in *Topic.* ii. 3. But we have no friendship for wine and suchlike things, as stated in *Ethic.* viii. 2. Therefore love of concupiscence is distinct from love of friendship.

I answer that, As the Philosopher says (*Rhet.* ii. 4), *to love is to wish good to someone.* Hence the movement of love has a twofold tendency: towards the good which a man wishes to someone,— to himself or to another, and towards that to which he wishes some good. Accordingly, man has love of concupiscence towards the good that he wishes to another, and love of friendship, towards him to whom he wishes good.

Now the members of this division are related as primary and secondary: since that which is loved with the love of friendship is loved simply and for itself; whereas that which is loved with the love of concupiscence, is loved, not simply and for itself, but for something else. For just as that which has existence, is a being simply, while that which exists in another is a relative being; so, because good is convertible with being, the good, which itself has goodness, is good simply; but that which is another's good, is a relative good. Consequently the love with which a thing is loved, that it may have some good, is love simply; while the love, with which a thing is loved, that it may be another's good, is relative love.

Reply Obj. 1. Love is not divided into friendship and concupiscence, but into love of friendship, and love of concupiscence. For a friend is, properly speaking, one to whom we wish good: while we are said to desire, what we wish for ourselves.

Hence the Reply to the Second Objection is evident.

Reply Obj. 3. When friendship is based on usefulness or pleasure, a man does indeed wish his friend some good: and in this respect the character of friendship is preserved. But since he refers this good further to his own pleasure or use, the result is that friendship of the useful or pleasant, in so far as it is connected with love of concupiscence, loses the character of true friendship.

ST I-II Question 27
Of the Cause of Love

(IN FOUR ARTICLES)

We must now consider the cause of love: and under this head there are four points of inquiry: (1) Whether good is the only cause of love? (2) Whether knowledge is a cause of love? (3)

Whether likeness is a cause of love? (4) Whether any other passion of the soul is a cause of love?

FIRST ARTICLE
Whether Good Is the Only Cause of Love?

We proceed thus to the First Article:—

Objection 1. It would seem that good is not the only cause of love. For good does not cause love, except because it is loved. But it happens that evil also is loved, according to Ps. x. 6: *He that loveth iniquity, hateth his own soul:* else, every love would be good. Therefore good is not the only cause of love.

Obj. 2. Further, the Philosopher says (*Rhet.* ii. 4) that *we love those who acknowledge their evils.* Therefore it seems that evil is the cause of love.

Obj. 3. Further, Dionysius says (*Div. Nom.* iv) that not *the good* only but also *the beautiful is beloved by all.*

On the contrary, Augustine says (*De Trin.* viii. 3): *Assuredly, the good alone is beloved.* Therefore good alone is the cause of love.

I answer that, As stated above (Q. 26, A. 1), Love belongs to the appetitive power which is a passive faculty. Wherefore its object stands in relation to it as the cause of its movement or act. Therefore the cause of love must needs be love's object. Now the proper object of love is the good; because, as stated above (Q. 26, AA. 1, 2), love implies a certain connaturalness or complacency of the lover for the thing beloved, and to everything, that thing is a good, which is akin and proportionate to it. It follows, therefore, that good is the proper cause of love.

Reply Obj. 1. Evil is never loved except under the aspect of good, that is to say, in so far as it is good in some respect, and is considered as being good simply. And thus a certain love is evil, in so far as it tends to that which is not simply a true good. It is in this way that man *loves iniquity,* inasmuch as, by means of iniquity, some good is gained; pleasure, for instance, or money, or such like.

Reply Obj. 2. Those who acknowledge their evils, are beloved, not for their evils, but because they acknowledge them, for it is a good thing to acknowledge one's faults, in so far as it excludes insincerity or hypocrisy.

Reply Obj. 3. The beautiful is the same as the good, and they differ in aspect only. For since good is what all seek, the notion of good is that which calms the desire; while the notion of the beautiful is that which calms the desire, by being seen or known. Consequently those senses chiefly regard the beautiful, which are the most cognitive, viz., sight and hearing, as ministering to reason; for we speak of beautiful sights and beautiful sounds. But in reference to the other objects of the other senses, we do not use the expression *beautiful*, for we do not speak of beautiful tastes, and beautiful odors. Thus it is evident that beauty adds to goodness a relation to the cognitive faculty: so that *good* means that which simply pleases the appetite; while the *beautiful* is something pleasant to apprehend.

SECOND ARTICLE
WHETHER KNOWLEDGE IS A CAUSE OF LOVE?

We proceed thus to the Second Article:—

Objection 1. It would seem that knowledge is not a cause of love. For it is due to love that a thing is sought. But some things are sought without being known, for instance, the sciences; for since *to have them is the same as to know them*, as Augustine says (QQ. 83, qu. 35), if we knew them we should have them, and should not seek them. Therefore knowledge is not the cause of love.

Obj. 2. Further, to love what we know not seems like loving something more than we know it. But some things are loved more than they are known: thus in this life God can be loved in Himself, but cannot be known in Himself. Therefore knowledge is not the cause of love.

Obj. 3. Further, if knowledge were the cause of love, there would be no love, where there is no knowledge. But in all things there is love, as Dionysius says (*Div. Nom.* iv); whereas there is not knowledge in all things. Therefore knowledge is not the cause of love.

On the contrary, Augustine proves (*De Trin.* x. 1, 2) that *none can love what he does not know.*

I answer that, As stated above (A. 1), good is the cause of love, as being its object. But good is not the object of the appetite, except as apprehended. And therefore love demands some apprehension of the good that is loved. For this reason the Philosopher (*Ethic.* ix. 5, 12) says that bodily sight is the beginning of sensitive love: and in like manner the contemplation of spiritual beauty or goodness is the beginning of spiritual love. Accordingly knowledge is the cause of love for the same reason as good is, which can be loved only if known.

Reply Obj. 1. He who seeks science, is not entirely without knowledge thereof: but knows something about it already in some respect, either in a general way, or in some one of its effects, or from having heard it commended, as Augustine says (*De Trin.* x. 1, 2). But to have it is not to know it thus, but to know it perfectly.

Reply Obj. 2. Something is required for the perfection of knowledge, that is not requisite for the perfection of love. For knowledge belongs to the reason, whose function it is to distinguish things which in reality are united, and to unite together, after a fashion, things that are distinct, by comparing one with another. Consequently the perfection of knowledge requires that man should know distinctly all that is in a thing, such as its parts, powers, and properties. On the other hand, love is in the appetitive power, which regards a thing as it is in itself: wherefore it suffices, for the perfection of love, that a thing be loved according as it is known in itself. Hence it is, therefore, that a thing is loved more than it is known; since it can be loved perfectly, even without being perfectly known. This is most evident in regard to the sciences, which some love through having a certain general knowledge of them: for instance, they know that rhetoric is a science that enables man to persuade others; and this is what they love in rhetoric. The same applies to the love of God.

Reply Obj. 3. Even natural love, which is in all things, is caused by a kind of knowledge, not indeed existing in natural things themselves, but in Him Who created their nature, as stated above (Q. 26, A. 1; *cf.* P. 1, Q. 6, A. 1 *ad* 2).

THIRD ARTICLE
WHETHER LIKENESS IS A CAUSE OF LOVE?

We proceed thus to the Third Article:—

Objection 1. It would seem that likeness is not a cause of love. For the same thing is not the cause of contraries. But likeness is the cause of hatred; for it is written (Prov. xiii. 10) that *among the proud there are always contentions;* and the Philosopher says (*Ethic.* viii. 1) that *potters quarrel with one another.* Therefore likeness is not a cause of love.

Obj. 2. Further, Augustine says (*Confess.* iv. 14) that *a man loves in another that which he would not be himself: thus he loves an actor, but would not himself be an actor.* But it would not be so, if likeness were the proper cause of love; for in that case a man would love in another, that which he possesses himself, or would like to possess. Therefore likeness is not a cause of love.

Obj. 3. Further, everyone loves that which he needs, even if he have it not: thus a sick man loves health, and a poor man loves riches. But in so far as he needs them and lacks them, he is unlike them. Therefore not only likeness but also unlikeness is a cause of love.

Obj. 4. Further, the Philosopher says (*Rhet.* ii. 4) that *we love those who bestow money and health on us; and also those who retain their friendship for the dead.* But all are not such. Therefore likeness is not a cause of love.

On the contrary, It is written (Ecclus. xiii. 19): *Every beast loveth its like.*

I answer that, Likeness, properly speaking, is a cause of love. But it must be observed that likeness between things is twofold. One kind of likeness arises from each thing having the same quality actually: for example, two things possessing the quality of whiteness are said to be alike. Another kind of likeness arises from one thing having potentially and by way of inclination, a quality which the other has actually: thus we may say that a heavy body existing outside its proper place is like another heavy body that exists in its proper place: or again, according as potentiality bears a resemblance to its act; since act is contained, in a manner, in the potentiality itself.

Accordingly the first kind of likeness causes love of friendship or well-being. For the very fact that two men are alike, having, as it were, one form, makes them to be, in a manner, one in that form: thus two men are one thing in the species of humanity, and two white men are one thing in whiteness. Hence the affections of one tend to the other, as being one with him; and he wishes good to him as to himself. But the second kind of likeness causes love of concupiscence, or friendship founded on usefulness or pleasure: because whatever is in potentiality, as such, has the desire for its act; and it takes pleasure in its realization, if it be a sentient and cognitive being.

Now it has been stated above (Q. 26, A. 4), that in the love of concupiscence, the lover, properly speaking, loves himself, in willing the good that he desires. But a man loves himself more than another: because he is one with himself substantially, whereas with another he is one only in the likeness of some form. Consequently, if this other's likeness to him arising from the participation of a form, hinders him from gaining the good that he loves, he becomes hateful to him, not for being like him, but for hindering him from gaining his own good. This is why *potters quarrel among themselves*, because they hinder one another's gain: and why *there are contentions among the proud*, because they hinder one another in attaining the position they covet.

Hence the Reply to the First Objection is evident.

Reply Obj. 2. Even when a man loves in another what he loves not in himself, there is a certain likeness of proportion: because as the latter is to that which is loved in him, so is the former to that which he loves in himself: for instance, if a good singer love a good writer, we can see a likeness of proportion, inasmuch as each one has that which is becoming to him in respect of his art.

Reply Obj. 3. He that loves what he needs, bears a likeness to what he loves, as potentiality bears a likeness to its act, as stated above.

Reply Obj. 4. According to the same likeness of potentiality to its act, the illiberal man loves the man who is liberal, in so far as he expects from him something which he desires. The same applies to the man who is constant in his friendship as compared to one who is inconstant. For in either case friendship seems to be based on usefulness. We might also say that although not all men have these virtues in the complete habit, yet they have them according to certain seminal principles in the reason, in force of which principles the man who is not virtuous loves the virtuous man, as being in conformity with his own natural reason.

FOURTH ARTICLE
WHETHER ANY OTHER PASSION OF THE SOUL
IS A CAUSE OF LOVE?

We proceed thus to the Fourth Article:—

Objection 1. It would seem that some other passion can be the cause of love. For the Philosopher (*Ethic.* viii. 3) says that some are loved for the sake of the pleasure they give. But pleasure is a passion. Therefore another passion is a cause of love.

Obj. 2. Further, desire is a passion. But we love some because we desire to receive something from them: as happens in every friendship based on usefulness. Therefore another passion is a cause of love.

Obj. 3. Further, Augustine says (*De Trin.* x. 1): *When we have no hope of getting a thing, we love it but half-heartedly or not at all, even if we see how beautiful it is.* Therefore hope too is a cause of love.

On the contrary, All the other emotions of the soul are caused by love, as Augustine says (*De Civ. Dei* xiv. 7, 9).

I answer that, There is no other passion of the soul that does not presuppose love of some kind. The reason is that every other passion of the soul implies either movement towards something, or rest in something. Now every movement towards something, or rest in something, arises from some kinship or aptness to that thing; and in this does love consist. Therefore it is not possible for any other passion of the soul to be universally the cause of every love. But it may happen that some other passion is the cause of some particular love: just as one good is the cause of another.

Reply Obj. 1. When a man loves a thing for the pleasure it affords, his love is indeed caused by pleasure; but that very pleasure is caused, in its turn, by another preceding love; for none takes pleasure save in that which is loved in some way.

Reply Obj. 2. Desire for a thing always presupposes love for that thing. But desire of one thing can be the cause of another thing's being loved; thus he that desires money, for this reason loves him from whom he receives it.

Reply Obj. 3. Hope causes or increases love; both by reason of pleasure, because it causes pleasure; and by reason of desire, because hope strengthens desire, since we do not desire so intensely that which we have no hope of receiving. Nevertheless hope itself is of a good that is loved.

ST I-II Question 28
Of the Effects of Love

(IN SIX ARTICLES)

We now have to consider the effects of love: under which head there are six points of inquiry: (1) Whether union is an effect of love? (2) Whether mutual indwelling is an effect of love? (3) Whether ecstasy is an effect of love? (4) Whether zeal is an effect

of love? (5) Whether love is a passion that is hurtful to the lover?
(6) Whether love is cause of all that the lover does?

FIRST ARTICLE
WHETHER UNION IS AN EFFECT OF LOVE?

We proceed thus to the First Article:—

Objection 1. It would seem that union is not an effect of love.
For absence is incompatible with union. But love is compatible
with absence; for the Apostle says (Gal. iv. 18): *Be zealous for that
which is good in a good thing always* (speaking of himself, according
to a gloss), *and not only when I am present with you.* Therefore
union is not an effect of love.

Obj. 2. Further, every union is either according to essence,—
thus form is united to matter, accident to subject, and a part to
the whole, or to another part in order to make up the whole: or
according to likeness, in genus, species, or accident. But love
does not cause union of essence; else love could not be between
things essentially distinct. On the other hand, love does not
cause union of likeness, but rather is caused by it, as stated above
(Q. 27, A. 3). Therefore union is not an effect of love.

Obj. 3. Further, the sense in act is the sensible in act, and the
intellect in act is the thing actually understood. But the lover in
act is not the beloved in act. Therefore union is the effect of
knowledge rather than of love.

On the contrary, Dionysius says (*Div. Nom.* iv) that every love
is a *unitive force.*

I answer that, The union of lover and beloved is twofold. The
first is real union; for instance, when the beloved is present with
the lover.—The second is union of affection: and this union must
be considered in relation to the preceding apprehension; since
movement of the appetite follows apprehension. Now love being
twofold, viz., love of concupiscence, and love of friendship; each
of these arises from a kind of apprehension of the oneness of the
thing loved with the lover. For when we love a thing, by desiring
it, we apprehend it as belonging to our well-being. In like manner
when a man loves another with the love of friendship, he wills
good to him, just as he wills good to himself: wherefore he
apprehends him as his other self, in so far, to wit, as he wills
good to him as to himself. Hence a friend is called a man's *other
self* (*Ethic.* ix. 4), and Augustine says (*Confess.* iv. 6), *Well did one
say to his friend: Thou half of my soul.*

The first of these unions is caused *effectively* by love; because love moves man to desire and seek the presence of the beloved, as of something suitable and belonging to him. The second union is caused *formally* by love; because love itself is this union or bond. In this sense Augustine says (*De Trin.* viii. 10) that *love is a vital principle uniting, or seeking to unite two together, the lover, to wit, and the beloved.* For in describing it as *uniting* he refers to the union of affection, without which there is no love: and in saying that *it seeks to unite,* he refers to real union.

Reply Obj. 1. This argument is true of real union. That is necessary to pleasure as being its cause; desire implies the real absence of the beloved: but love remains whether the beloved be absent or present.

Reply Obj. 2. Union has a threefold relation to love. There is a union which causes love; and this is substantial union, as regards the love with which one loves oneself; while as regards the love wherewith one loves other things, it is the union of likeness, as stated above (Q. 27, A. 3). There is also a union which is essentially love itself. This union is according to a bond of affection, and is likened to substantial union, inasmuch as the lover stands to the object of his love, as to himself, if it be love of friendship; as to something belonging to himself, if it be love of concupiscence. Again there is a union, which is the effect of love. This is real union, which the lover seeks with the object of his love. Moreover this union is in keeping with the demands of love: for as the Philosopher relates (*Polit.* ii. 1), *Aristophanes stated that lovers would wish to be united both into one,* but since *this would result in either one or both being destroyed,* they seek a suitable and becoming union;—to live together, speak together, and be united together in other like things.

Reply Obj. 3. Knowledge is perfected by the thing known being united, through its likeness, to the knower. But the effect of love is that the thing itself which is loved, is, in a way, united to the lover, as stated above. Consequently the union caused by love is closer than that which is caused by knowledge.

SECOND ARTICLE
WHETHER MUTUAL INDWELLING IS AN EFFECT OF LOVE?

We proceed thus to the Second Article:—

Objection 1. It would seem that love does not cause mutual indwelling, so that the lover be in the beloved and vice versa. For that which is in another is contained in it. But the same cannot be container and contents. Therefore love cannot cause mutual indwelling, so that the lover be in the beloved and vice versa.

Obj. 2. Further, nothing can penetrate within a whole, except by means of a division of the whole. But it is the function of the reason, not of the appetite where love resides, to divide things that are really united. Therefore mutual indwelling is not an effect of love.

Obj. 3. Further, if love involves the lover being in the beloved and vice versa, it follows that the beloved is united to the lover, in the same way as the lover is united to the beloved. But the union itself is love, as stated above (A. 1). Therefore it follows that the lover is always loved by the object of his love; which is evidently false. Therefore mutual indwelling is not an effect of love.

On the contrary, It is written (1 Jo. iv. 16): *He that abideth in charity abideth in God, and God in him.* Now charity is the love of God. Therefore, for the same reason, every love makes the beloved to be in the lover, and vice versa.

I answer that, This effect of mutual indwelling may be understood as referring both to the apprehensive and to the appetitive power. Because, as to the apprehensive power, the beloved is said to be in the lover, inasmuch as the beloved abides in the apprehension of the lover, according to Phil. i. 7, *For that I have you in my heart:* while the lover is said to be in the beloved, according to apprehension, inasmuch as the lover is not satisfied with a superficial apprehension of the beloved, but strives to gain an intimate knowledge of everything pertaining to the beloved, so as to penetrate into his very soul. Thus it is written concerning the Holy Ghost, Who is God's Love, that He *searcheth all things, yea the deep things of God* (1 Cor. ii. 10).

As the appetitive power, the object loved is said to be in the lover, inasmuch as it is in his affections, by a kind of complacency: causing him either to take pleasure in it, or in its good, when present; or, in the absence of the object loved, by his longing, to tend towards it with the love of concupiscence, or towards the good that he wills to the beloved, with the love of friendship: not indeed from any extrinsic cause (as when we desire one thing on account of another, or wish good to another on account of something else), but because the complacency in the beloved is rooted in the lover's heart. For this reason we speak of love as being *intimate;* and of *the bowels of charity.* On the other hand, the lover is in the beloved, by the love of concupiscence and by the love of friendship, but not in the same way. For the love of concupiscence is not satisfied with any external or superficial possession or enjoyment of the beloved; but seeks to possess the beloved perfectly, by penetrating into his heart, as it were. Whereas, in the love of friendship, the lover is in the beloved, inasmuch as he reckons what is good or evil to his friend, as being so to himself; and his friend's will as his own, so that it seems as though he felt the good or suffered the evil in the person of his friend. Hence it is proper to friends *to desire the same things, and to grieve and rejoice at the same,* as the Philosopher says (*Ethic.* ix. 3 and *Rhet.* ii. 4). Consequently in so far as he reckons what affects his friend as affecting himself, the lover seems to be in the beloved, as though he were become one with him: but in so far as, on the other hand, he wills and acts for his friend's sake as for his own sake, looking on his friend as identified with himself, thus the beloved is in the lover.

In yet a third way, mutual indwelling in the love of friendship can be understood in regard to reciprocal love: inasmuch as friends return love for love, and both desire and do good things for one another.

Reply Obj. 1. The beloved is contained in the lover, by being impressed on his heart and thus becoming the object of his complacency. On the other hand, the lover is contained in the beloved, inasmuch as the lover penetrates, so to speak, into the beloved. For nothing hinders a thing from being both container and contents in different ways: just as a genus is contained in its species, and vice versa.

Reply Obj. 2. The apprehension of the reason precedes the movement of love. Consequently, just as the reason divides, so does the movement of love penetrate into the beloved, as was explained above.

Reply Obj. 3. This argument is true of the third kind of mutual indwelling, which is not to be found in every kind of love.

THIRD ARTICLE
WHETHER ECSTASY IS AN EFFECT OF LOVE?

We proceed thus to the Third Article:—

Objection 1. It would seem that ecstasy is not an effect of love.

For ecstasy seems to imply loss of reason. But love does not always result in loss of reason: for lovers are masters of themselves at times. Therefore love does not cause ecstasy.

Obj. 2. Further, the lover desires the beloved to be united to him. Therefore he draws the beloved to himself, rather than betakes himself into the beloved, going forth out from himself as it were.

Obj. 3. Further, love unites the beloved to the lover, as stated above (A. 1). If, therefore, the lover goes out from himself, in order to betake himself into the beloved, it follows that the lover always loves the beloved more than himself: which is evidently false. Therefore ecstasy is not an effect of love.

On the contrary, Dionysius says (*Div. Nom.* iv) that *the Divine love produces ecstasy,* and that *God Himself suffered ecstasy through love.* Since therefore according to the same author (*ibid.*), every love is a participated likeness of the Divine Love, it seems that every love causes ecstasy.

I answer that, To suffer ecstasy means to be placed outside oneself. This happens as to the apprehensive power and as to the appetitive power. As to the apprehensive power, a man is said to be placed outside himself, when he is placed outside the knowledge proper to him. This may be due to his being raised to a higher knowledge; thus, a man is said to suffer ecstasy, inasmuch as he is placed outside the connatural apprehension of his sense and reason, when he is raised up so as to comprehend things that surpass sense and reason: or it may be due to his being cast down into a state of debasement; thus a man may be said to suffer ecstasy, when he is overcome by violent passion or madness.—As to the appetitive power, a man is said to suffer ecstasy, when that power is borne towards something else, so that it goes forth out from itself, as it were.

The first of these ecstasies is caused by love dispositively, in so far, namely, as love makes the lover dwell on the beloved, as stated above (A. 2), and to dwell intently on one thing draws the mind from other things.—The second ecstasy is caused by love directly; by love of friendship, simply; by love of concupiscence, not simply but in a restricted sense. Because in love of concupiscence, the lover is carried out of himself, in a certain sense; in so far, namely, as not being satisfied with enjoying the good that he has, he seeks to enjoy something outside himself. But since he seeks to have this extrinsic good for himself, he does not go out from himself simply, and this movement remains finally within him. On the other hand, in the love of friendship, a man's affection goes out from itself simply; because he wishes and does good to his friend, by caring and providing for him, for his sake.

Reply Obj. 1. This argument is true of the first kind of ecstasy.

Reply Obj. 2. This argument applies to love of concupiscence, which, as stated above, does not cause ecstasy simply.

Reply Obj. 3. He who loves, goes out from himself, in so far as he wills the good of his friend and works for it. Yet he does not will the good of his friend more than his own good: and so it does not follow that he loves another more than himself.

FOURTH ARTICLE
WHETHER ZEAL IS AN EFFECT OF LOVE?

We proceed thus to the Fourth Article:—

Objection 1. It would seem that zeal is not an effect of love. For zeal is a beginning of contention; wherefore it is written (1 Cor. iii. 3): *Whereas there is among you zeal* (Douay,—*envying*) *and contention,* etc. But contention is incompatible with love. Therefore zeal is not an effect of love.

Obj. 2. Further, the object of love is the good, which communicates itself to others. But zeal is opposed to communication; since it seems an effect of zeal, that a man refuses to share the object of his love with another: thus husbands are said to be jealous of (*zelare*) their wives, because they will not share them with others. Therefore zeal is not an effect of love.

Obj. 3. Further, there is no zeal without hatred, as neither is there without love: for it is written (Ps. lxxii. 3): *I had a zeal on occasion of the wicked.* Therefore it should not be set down as an effect of love any more than of hatred.

On the contrary, Dionysius says (*Div. Nom.* iv): *God is said to be a zealot, on account of his great love for all things.*

I answer that, Zeal, whatever way we take it, arises from the intensity of love. For it is evident that the more intensely a power tends to anything, the more vigorously it withstands opposition or resistance. Since therefore love is *a movement towards the object loved,* as *Augustine says* (QQ. 83, qu. 35), an intense love seeks to remove everything that opposes it.

But this happens in different ways according to love of concupiscence, and love of friendship. For in love of concupiscence he who desires something intensely, is moved against all that hinders his gaining or quietly enjoying the object of his love. It is thus that husbands are said to be jealous of their wives, lest association with others prove a hindrance to their exclusive individual rights. In like manner those who seek to excel, are moved against those who seem to excel, as though these were a hindrance to their excelling. And this is the zeal of envy, of which it is written (Ps. xxxvi. 1): *Be not emulous of evil doers, nor envy* (*zelaveris*) *them that work iniquity.*

On the other hand, love of friendship seeks the friend's good: wherefore, when it is intense, it causes a man to be moved against everything that opposes the friend's good. In this respect, a man is said to be zealous on behalf of his friend, when he makes a point of repelling whatever may be said or done against the friend's good. In this way, too, a man is said to be zealous on God's behalf, when he endeavors, to the best of his means, to repel whatever is contrary to the honor or will of God; according to 3 Kings xix. 14: *With zeal I have been zealous for the Lord of hosts.* Again on the words of Jo. ii. 17: *The zeal of Thy house hath eaten me up,* a gloss says that *a man is eaten up with a good zeal, who strives to remedy whatever evil he perceives; and if he cannot, bears with it and laments it.*

Reply Obj. 1. The Apostle is speaking in this passage of the zeal of envy; which is indeed the cause of contention, not against the object of love, but for it, and against that which is opposed to it.

Reply Obj. 2. Good is loved inasmuch as it can be communicated to the lover. Consequently whatever hinders the perfection of this communication, becomes hateful. Thus zeal arises from love of good.—But through defect of goodness, it happens that certain small goods cannot, in their entirety, be possessed by many at the same time: and from the love of such things arises the zeal of envy. But it does not arise, properly speaking, in the case of those things which, in their entirety, can be possessed by many: for no one envies another the knowledge of truth, which can be known entirely by many; except perhaps one may envy another his superiority in the knowledge of it.

Reply Obj. 3. The very fact that a man hates whatever is opposed to the object of his love, is the effect of love. Hence zeal is set down as an effect of love rather than of hatred.

FIFTH ARTICLE
WHETHER LOVE IS A PASSION THAT WOUNDS THE LOVER?

We proceed thus to the Fifth Article:—

Objection 1. It would seem that love wounds the lover. For languor denotes a hurt in the one that languishes. But love causes languor: for it is written (Cant. ii. 5): *Stay me up with flowers, compass me about with apples; because I languish with love.* Therefore love is a wounding passion.

Obj. 2. Further, melting is a kind of dissolution. But love melts that in which it is: for it is written (Cant. v. 6): *My soul melted when my beloved spoke.* Therefore love is a dissolvent: therefore it is a corruptive and a wounding passion.

Obj. 3. Further, fervor denotes a certain excess of heat; which excess has a corruptive effect. But love causes fervor: for Dionysius (*Cael. Hier.* vii) in reckoning the properties belonging to the Seraphim's love, includes *hot* and *piercing* and *most fervent.* Moreover it is said of love (Cant. viii. 6) that *its lamps are fire and flames.* Therefore love is a wounding and corruptive passion.

On the contrary, Dionysius says (*Div.* iv) that *everything loves itself with a love that holds it together,* i.e., that preserves it. Therefore love is not a wounding passion, but rather one that preserves and perfects.

I answer that, As stated above (Q. 26, AA. 1, 2; Q. 27, A. 1), love denotes a certain adapting of the appetitive power to some good. Now nothing is hurt by being adapted to that which is suitable to it; rather, if possible, it is perfected and bettered. But if a thing be adapted to that which is not suitable to it, it is hurt and made worse thereby. Consequently love of a suitable good perfects and betters the lover; but love of a good which is unsuitable to the lover, wounds and worsens him. Wherefore man is perfected and bettered chiefly by the love of God: but is wounded and worsened by the love of sin, according to Osee ix. 10: *They became abominable, as those things which they loved.*

And let this be understood as applying to love in respect of its formal element, *i.e.,* in regard to the appetite. But in respect of the material element in the passion of love, *i.e.,* a certain bodily change, it happens that love is hurtful, by reason of this change being excessive: just as it happens in the senses, and in every act of a power of the soul that is exercised through the change of some bodily organ.

In reply to the objections, it is to be observed that four proximate effects may be ascribed to love: viz., melting, enjoyment, languor, and fervor. Of these the first is *melting*, which is opposed to freezing. For things that are frozen, are closely bound together, so as to be hard to pierce. But it belongs to love that the appetite is fitted to receive the good which is loved, inasmuch as the object loved is in the lover, as stated above (A. 2). Consequently the freezing or hardening of the heart is a disposition incompatible with love: while melting denotes a softening of the heart, whereby the heart shows itself to be ready for the entrance of the beloved.—If, then, the beloved is present and possessed, pleasure or enjoyment ensues. But if the beloved be absent, two passions arise; viz., sadness at its absence, which is denoted by *languor* (hence Cicero in *De Tuscul. Quaest.* iii. 11 applies the term *ailment* chiefly to sadness); and an intense desire to possess the beloved, which is signified by *fervor*.—And these are the effects of love considered formally, according to the relation of the appetitive power to its object. But in the passion of love, other effects ensue, proportionate to the above, in respect of a change in the organ.

SIXTH ARTICLE
Whether Love Is Cause of All That the Lover Does?

We proceed thus to the Sixth Article:—

Objection 1. It would seem that the lover does not do everything from love. For love is a passion, as stated above (Q. 26, A. 2). But man does not do everything from passion: but some things he does from choice, and some things from ignorance, as stated in *Ethic.* v. 8. Therefore not everything that a man does, is done from love.

Obj. 2. Further, the appetite is a principle of movement and action in all animals, as stated in *De Anima* iii. 10. If, therefore, whatever a man does is done from love, the other passions of the appetitive faculty are superfluous.

Obj. 3. Further, nothing is produced at one and the same time by contrary causes. But some things are done from hatred. Therefore all things are not done from love.

On the contrary, Dionysius says (*Div. Nom.* iv.) that *all things, whatever they do, they do for the love of good.*

I answer that, Every agent acts for an end, as stated above (Q. 1, A. 2). Now the end is the good desired and loved by each one.

Wherefore it is evident that every agent, whatever it be, does every action from love of some kind.

Reply Obj. 1. This objection takes love as a passion existing in the sensitive appetite. But here we are speaking of love in a general sense, inasmuch as it includes intellectual, rational, animal, and natural love: for it is in this sense that Dionysius speaks of love in chap. iv. of *De Divinis Nominibus*.

Reply Obj. 2. As stated above (A. 5; Q. 27, A. 4) desire, sadness and pleasure, and consequently all the other passions of the soul, result from love. Wherefore every act that proceeds from any passion, proceeds also from love as from a first cause: and so the other passions, which are proximate causes, are not superfluous.

Reply Obj. 3. Hatred also is a result of love, as we shall state further on (Q. 29, A. 2).

ST II-II Question 23
Of Charity, Considered in Itself

(IN EIGHT ARTICLES)

FIRST ARTICLE
WHETHER CHARITY IS FRIENDSHIP?

We proceed thus to the First Article:—

Objection 1. It would seem that charity is not friendship. For nothing is so appropriate to friendship as to dwell with one's friend, according to the Philosopher (*Ethic.* viii. 5). Now charity is of man towards God and the angels, *whose dwelling* (Douay,—*conversation*) *is not with men* (Dan. ii. 11). Therefore charity is not friendship.

Obj. 2. Further, there is no friendship without return of love (*Ethic.* viii. 2). But charity extends even to one's enemies, according to Matth. v. 44: *Love your enemies.* Therefore charity is not friendship.

Obj. 3. Further, according to the Philosopher (*Ethic.* viii. 3) there are three kinds of friendship, directed respectively towards the delightful, the useful, or the virtuous. Now charity is not friendship for the useful or delightful; for Jerome says in his letter to Paulinus which is to be found at the beginning of the Bible: *True friendship cemented by Christ, is where men are drawn together, not by household interests, not by mere bodily presence, not by crafty and cajoling flattery, but by the fear of God, and the study of the Divine Scriptures.* No more is it friendship for the virtuous, since by charity we love even sinners, whereas friendship based on the virtuous is only for virtuous men (*Ethic.* viii). Therefore charity is not friendship.

On the contrary, It is written (Jo. xv. 15): *I will not now call you servants . . . but My friends.* Now this was said to them by reason of nothing else than charity. Therefore charity is friendship.

I answer that, According to the Philosopher (*Ethic.* viii. 2, 3), not every love has the character of friendship, but that love which is together with benevolence, when, to wit, we love someone so as to wish good to him. If, however, we do not wish good to what we love, but wish its good for ourselves, (thus we are said to love wine, or a horse, or the like) it is love not of friendship, but of a kind of concupiscence. For it would be absurd to speak of having friendship for wine or for a horse.

Yet neither does well-wishing suffice for friendship, for a certain mutual love is requisite, since friendship is between friend and friend: and this well-wishing is founded on some kind of communication.

Accordingly, since there is a communication between man and God, inasmuch as He communicates His happiness to us, some kind of friendship must needs be based on this same communication, of which it is written (1 Cor. i. 9): *God is faithful: by Whom you are called unto the fellowship of His Son.* The love which is based on this communication, is charity: wherefore it is evident that charity is the friendship of man for God.

Reply Obj. 1. Man's life is twofold. There is his outward life in respect of his sensitive and corporeal nature: and with regard to this life there is no communication or fellowship between us and God or the angels. The other is man's spiritual life in respect of his mind, and with regard to this life there is fellowship between us and both God and the angels, imperfectly indeed in this present state of life, wherefore it is written (Phil. iii. 20): *Our conversation is in heaven.* But this *conversation* will be perfected in heaven, when *His servants shall serve Him, and they shall see His face* (Apoc. xxii. 3, 4). Therefore charity is imperfect here, but will be perfected in heaven.

Reply Obj. 2. Friendship extends to a person in two ways: first in respect of himself, and in this way friendship never extends but to one's friends: secondly, it extends to someone in respect of another, as, when a man has friendship for a certain person, for his sake he loves all belonging to him, be they children, servants, or connected with him in any way. Indeed, so much do we love our friends, that for their sake we love all who belong to them, even if they hurt or hate us; so that, in this way, the friendship of charity extends even to our enemies, whom we love out of charity in relation to God, to Whom the friendship of charity is chiefly directed.

Reply Obj. 3. The friendship that is based on the virtuous is directed to none but a virtuous man as the principal person, but for his sake we love those who belong to him, even though they be not virtuous: in this way charity, which above all is friendship based on the virtuous, extends to sinners, whom, out of charity, we love for God's sake.

FIFTH ARTICLE
WHETHER CHARITY IS ONE VIRTUE?

We proceed thus to the Fifth Article:—

Objection 1: It would seem that charity is not one virtue. For habits are distinct according to their objects. Now there are two objects of charity,—God and our neighbor, which are infinitely distant from one another. Therefore charity is not one virtue.

Obj. 2. Further, different aspects of the object diversify a habit, even though that object be one in reality, as shown above (Q. 17, A. 6: I–II, Q. 54, A. 2, *ad* 1). Now there are many aspects under which God is an object of love, because we are debtors to His love by reason of each one of His favors. Therefore charity is not one virtue.

Obj. 3. Further, charity comprises friendship for our neighbor. But the Philosopher reckons several species of friendship (*Ethic.* viii. 3, 11, 12). Therefore charity is not one virtue, but is divided into a number of various species.

On the contrary, Just as God is the object of faith, so is He the object of charity. Now faith is one virtue by reason of the unity of the Divine truth, according to Eph. iv. 5: *One faith.* Therefore charity also is one virtue by reason of the unity of the Divine goodness.

I answer that, Charity, as stated above (A. 1) is a kind of friendship of man for God. Now the different species of friendship are differentiated, first of all, in respect of a diversity of end, and in this way there are three species of friendship, namely friendship for the useful, for the delightful, and for the virtuous; secondly, in respect of the different kinds of communion on which friendships are based; thus there is one species of friendship between kinsmen, and another between fellow citizens or fellow travellers, the former being based on natural communion, the latter on civil communion or on the comradeship of the road, as the Philosopher explains (*Ethic.* viii. 12).

Now charity cannot be differentiated in either of these ways: for its end is one, namely the goodness of God; and the fellowship of everlasting happiness, on which this friendship is based, is also one. Hence it follows that charity is simply one virtue, and not divided into several species.

Reply Obj. 1. This argument would hold, if God and our neighbor were equally objects of charity. But this is not true: for God is the principal object of charity, while our neighbor is loved out of charity for God's sake.

Reply Obj. 2. God is loved by charity for His own sake: wherefore charity regards principally but one aspect of lovableness, namely God's goodness, which is His substance, according to Ps. cv. 1: *Give glory to the Lord for He is good.* Other reasons that inspire us with love for Him, or which make it our duty to love Him, are secondary and result from the first.

Reply Obj. 3. Human friendship of which the Philosopher treats has various ends and various forms of fellowship. This does not apply to charity, as stated above: wherefore the comparison fails.

ST II-II Question 25
Of the Object of Charity

(IN TWELVE ARTICLES)

FIRST ARTICLE
WHETHER THE LOVE OF CHARITY STOPS AT GOD, OR EXTENDS TO OUR NEIGHBOR?

We proceed thus to the First Article:—

Objection 1. It would seem that the love of charity stops at God and does not extend to our neighbor. For as we owe God love, so do we owe Him fear, according Deut. x. 12: *And now Israel, what doth the Lord thy God require of thee, but that thou fear . . . and love Him?* Now the fear with which we fear man, and which is called human fear, is distinct from the fear with which we fear God, and which is either servile or filial, as is evident from what has been stated above (Q. 10, A. 2). Therefore also the love with which we love God, is distinct from the love with which we love our neighbor.

Obj. 2. Further, the Philosopher says (*Ethic.* viii. 8) that *to be loved is to be honored.* Now the honor due to God, which is known as *latria,* is distinct from the honor due to a creature, and known as *dulia.* Therefore again the love wherewith we love God, is distinct from that with which we love our neighbor.

Obj. 3. Further, hope begets charity, as a gloss states on Matth. i. 2. Now hope is so due to God that it is reprehensible to hope in man, according to Jerem. xvii. 5: *Cursed be the man that trusteth in man.* Therefore charity is so due to God, as not to extend to our neighbor.

On the contrary, It is written (1 Jo. iv. 21): *This commandment we have from God, that he, who loveth God, love also his brother.*

I answer that, As stated above (Q. 17, A. 6: Q. 19, A. 3: I–II, Q. 54, A. 3) habits are not differentiated except their acts be of different species. For every act of the one species belongs to the same habit. Now since the species of an act is derived from its object, considered under its formal aspect, it follows of necessity that it is specifically the same act that tends to an aspect of the object, and that tends to the object under that aspect: thus it is specifically the same visual act whereby we see the light, and whereby we see the color under the aspect of light.

Now the aspect under which our neighbor is to be loved, is God, since what we ought to love in our neighbor is that he may be in God. Hence it is clear that it is specifically the same act whereby we love God, and whereby we love our neighbor. Consequently the habit of charity extends not only to the love of God, but also to the love of our neighbor.

Reply Obj. 1. We may fear our neighbor, even as we may love him, in two ways: first, on account of something that is proper to him, as when a man fears a tyrant on account of his cruelty, or loves him by reason of his own desire to get something from him. Such like human fear is distinct from the fear of God, and the same applies to love. Secondly, we fear a man, or love him on account of what he has of God; as when we fear the secular power by reason of its exercising the ministry of God for the punishment of evildoers, and love it for its justice: such like fear of man is not distinct from fear of God, as neither is such like love.

Reply Obj. 2. Love regards good in general, whereas honor regards the honored person's own good, for it is given to a person in recognition of his own virtue. Hence love is not differentiated specifically on account of the various degrees of goodness in various persons, so long as it is referred to one good common to all, whereas honor is distinguished according to the good belonging to individuals. Consequently we love all our neighbors with the same love of charity, in so far as they are referred to one good common to them all, which is God; whereas we give various honors to various people, according to each one's own virtue, and likewise to God we give the singular honor of latria on account of His singular virtue.

Reply Obj. 3. It is wrong to hope in man as though he were the principal author of salvation, but not, to hope in man as helping us ministerially under God. In like manner it would be wrong if a man loved his neighbor as though he were his last end, but not, if he loved him for God's sake; and this is what charity does.

THIRD ARTICLE
WHETHER IRRATIONAL CREATURES ALSO OUGHT TO BE LOVED OUT OF CHARITY?

We proceed thus to the Third Article:—

Objection 1. It would seem that irrational creatures also ought to be loved out of charity. For it is chiefly by charity that we are conformed to God. Now God loves irrational creatures out of charity, for He loves *all things that are* (Wis. xi. 25), and whatever He loves, He loves by Himself Who is charity. Therefore we also should love irrational creatures out of charity.

Obj. 2. Further, charity is referred to God principally, and extends to other things as referable to God. Now just as the rational creature is referable to God, in as much as it bears the resemblance of image, so too, are the irrational creatures, in as much as they bear the resemblance of a trace.[1] Therefore charity extends also to irrational creatures.

1. *Cf.* P. 1, Q. 45, A. 7.

Obj. 3. Further, just as the object of charity is God, so is the object of faith. Now faith extends to irrational creatures, since we believe that heaven and earth were created by God, that the fishes and birds were brought forth out of the waters, and animals that walk, and plants, out of the earth. Therefore charity extends also to irrational creatures.

On the contrary, The love of charity extends to none but God and our neighbor. But the word neighbor cannot be extended to irrational creatures, since they have no fellowship with man in the rational life. Therefore charity does not extend to irrational creatures.

I answer that, According to what has been stated above (Q. 13, A. 1) charity is a kind of friendship. Now the love of friendship is twofold: first, there is the love for the friend to whom our friendship is given, secondly, the love for those good things which we desire for our friend. With regard to the first, no irrational creature can be loved out of charity; and for three reasons. Two of these reasons refer in a general way to friendship, which cannot have an irrational creature for its object: first because friendship is towards one to whom we wish good things, while, properly speaking, we cannot wish good things to an irrational creature, because it is not competent, properly speaking, to possess good, this being proper to the rational creature which, through its free-will, is the master of its disposal of the good it possesses. Hence the Philosopher says (*Phys.* ii. 6) that we do not speak of good or evil befalling such like things, except metaphorically. Secondly, because all friendship is based on some fellowship in life; since *nothing is so proper to friendship as to live together*, as the Philosopher proves (*Ethic.* viii. 5). Now irrational creatures can have no fellowship in human life which is regulated by reason. Hence friendship with irrational creatures is impossible, except metaphorically speaking. The third reason is proper to charity, for charity is based on the fellowship of everlasting happiness, to which the irrational creature cannot attain. Therefore we cannot have the friendship of charity towards an irrational creature.

Nevertheless we can love irrational creatures out of charity, if we regard them as the good things that we desire for others, in so far, to wit, as we wish for their preservation, to God's honor and man's use; thus too does God love them out of charity.

Wherefore the *Reply* to the *First Objection* is evident.

Reply Obj. 2. The likeness by way of trace does not confer the capacity for everlasting life, whereas the likeness of image does: and so the comparison fails.

Reply Obj. 3. Faith can extend to all that is in any way true, whereas the friendship of charity extends only to such things as have a natural capacity for everlasting life; wherefore the comparison fails.

FOURTH ARTICLE
WHETHER A MAN OUGHT TO LOVE HIMSELF OUT OF CHARITY?

We proceed thus to the Fourth Article:—

Objection 1. It would seem that a man is not bound to love himself out of charity. For Gregory says in a homily (*In Evang.* xvii) that there *can be no charity between less than two.* Therefore no man has charity towards himself.

Obj. 2. Further, friendship, by its very nature, implies mutual love and equality (*Ethic.* viii. 2, 7), which cannot be of one man towards himself. But charity is a kind of friendship, as stated above (Q. 23, A. 1). Therefore a man cannot have charity towards himself.

Obj. 3. Further, anything relating to charity cannot be blameworthy, since charity *dealeth not perversely* (1 Cor. xiii. 4). Now a man deserves to be blamed for loving himself, since it is written (2 Tim. iii. 1, 2): *In the last days shall come dangerous times, men shall be lovers of themselves.* Therefore a man cannot love himself out of charity.

On the contrary, It is written (Levit. xix. 18): *Thou shalt love thy friend as thyself.* Now we love our friends out of charity. Therefore we should love ourselves too out of charity.

I answer that, Since charity is a kind of friendship, as stated above (Q. 23, A. 1), we may consider charity from two standpoints: first, under the general notion of friendship, and in this way we must hold that, properly speaking, a man is not a friend to himself, but something more than a friend, since friendship implies union, for Dionysius says (*Div. Nom.* iv) that *love is a unitive force,* whereas a man is one with himself which is more than being united to another. Hence, just as unity is the principle of union, so the love with which a man loves himself is the form and root of friendship. For if we have friendship with others it is because we do unto them as we do unto ourselves, hence we read in *Ethic.* ix. 4, 8, that *the origin of friendly relations with others lies in our relations to ourselves.* Thus too with regard to principles we have something greater than science, namely understanding.

Secondly, we may speak of charity in respect of its specific nature, namely as denoting man's friendship with God in the first place, and, consequently, with the things of God, among which things is man himself who has charity. Hence, among these other things which he loves out of charity because they pertain to God, he loves also himself out of charity.

Reply Obj. 1. Gregory speaks there of charity under the general notion of friendship: and the *Second Objection* is to be taken in the same sense.

Reply Obj. 3. Those who love themselves are to be blamed, in so far as they love themselves as regards their sensitive nature, which they humor. This is not to love oneself truly according to one's rational nature, so as to desire for oneself the good things which pertain to the perfection of reason: and in this way chiefly it is through charity that a man loves himself.

SEVENTH ARTICLE
WHETHER SINNERS LOVE THEMSELVES?

We proceed thus to the Seventh Article:—

Objection 1. It would seem that sinners love themselves. For that which is the principle of sin, is most of all in the sinner. Now love of self is the principle of sin, since Augustine says (*De Civ. Dei* xiv. 28) that it *builds up the city of Babylon.* Therefore sinners most of all love themselves.

Obj. 2. Further, sin does not destroy nature. Now it is in keeping with nature that every man should love himself: wherefore even irrational creatures naturally desire their own good, for instance, the preservation of their being, and so forth. Therefore sinners love themselves.

Obj. 3. Further, good is beloved by all, as Dionysius states (*Div. Nom.* iv). Now many sinners reckon themselves to be good. Therefore many sinners love themselves.

On the contrary, It is written (Ps. x. 6): *He that loveth iniquity, hateth his own soul.*

I answer that, Love of self is common to all, in one way; in another way it is proper to the good; in a third way, it is proper to the wicked. For it is common to all for each one to love what he thinks himself to be. Now a man is said to be a thing, in two ways: first, in respect of his substance and nature, and, this way all think themselves to be what they are, that is, composed of a soul and body. In this way too, all men, both good and wicked, love themselves, in so far as they love their own preservation.

Secondly, a man is said to be something in respect of some predominance, as the sovereign of a state is spoken of as being the state, and so, what the sovereign does, the state is said to do. In this way, all do not think themselves to be what they are. For the reasoning mind is the predominant part of man, while the sensitive and corporeal nature takes the second place, the former of which the Apostle calls the *inward man*, and the latter, the *outward man* (2 Cor. iv. 16). Now the good look upon their rational nature or the inward man as being the chief thing in them, wherefore in this way they think themselves to be what they are. On the other hand, the wicked reckon their sensitive and corporeal nature, or the outward man, to hold the first place. Wherefore, since they know not themselves aright, they do not love themselves aright, but love what they think themselves to be. But the good know themselves truly, and therefore truly love themselves.

The Philosopher proves this from five things that are proper to friendship. For in the first place, every friend wishes his friend to be and to live; secondly, he desires good things for him; thirdly, he does good things to him; fourthly, he takes pleasure in his company; fifthly, he is of one mind with him, rejoicing and sorrowing in almost the same things. In this way the good love themselves, as to the inward man, because they wish the preservation thereof in its integrity, they desire good things for him, namely spiritual goods, indeed they do their best to obtain them, and they take pleasure in entering into their own hearts, because they find there good thoughts in the present, the memory of past good, and the hope of future good, all of which are sources of pleasure. Likewise they experience no clashing of wills, since their whole soul tends to one thing.

On the other hand, the wicked have no wish to be preserved in the integrity of the inward man, nor do they desire spiritual goods for him, nor do they work for that end, nor do they take pleasure in their own company by entering into their own hearts, because whatever they find there, present, past and future, is evil and horrible; nor do they agree with themselves, on account of the gnawings of conscience, according to Ps. xlix. 21: *I will reprove thee and set before thy face.*

In the same manner it may be shown that the wicked love themselves, as regards the corruption of the outward man, whereas the good do not love themselves thus.

Reply Obj. 1. The love of self which is the principle of sin is that which is proper to the wicked, and reaches *to the contempt of God*, as stated in the passage quoted, because the wicked so desire external goods as to despise spiritual goods.

Reply Obj. 2. Although natural love is not altogether forfeited by wicked men, yet it is perverted in them, as explained above.

Reply Obj. 3. The wicked have some share of self-love, in so far as they think themselves good. Yet such love of self is not true but apparent: and even this is not possible in those who are very wicked.

ST II-II Question 26
Of the Order of Charity

(IN THIRTEEN ARTICLES)

FOURTH ARTICLE
WHETHER OUT OF CHARITY, MAN OUGHT TO LOVE HIMSELF MORE THAN HIS NEIGHBOR?

We proceed thus to the Fourth Article:—

Objection 1. It would seem that a man ought not, out of charity, to love himself more than his neighbor. For the principal object of charity is God, as stated above (A. 2: Q. 25, AA. 1, 12). Now sometimes our neighbor is more closely united to God than we are ourselves. Therefore we ought to love such a one more than ourselves.

Obj. 2. Further, the more we love a person, the more we avoid injuring him. Now a man, out of charity, submits to injury for his neighbor's sake, according to Prov. xii. 26: *He that neglecteth a loss for the sake of a friend, is just.* Therefore a man ought, out of charity, to love his neighbor more than himself.

Obj. 3. Further, it is written (1 Cor. xiii. 5) that *charity seeketh not its own.* Now the thing we love most is the one whose good we seek most. Therefore a man does not, out of charity, love himself more than his neighbor.

On the contrary, It is written (Lev. xix. 18, Matth. xxii. 39): *Thou shalt love thy neighbor* (Lev. *loc. cit.,—friend*) *as thyself.* Whence it seems to follow that man's love for himself is the model of his love for another. But the model exceeds the copy. Therefore, out of charity, a man ought to love himself more than his neighbor.

I answer that, There are two things in man, his spiritual nature and his corporeal nature. And a man is said to love himself by reason of his loving himself with regard to his spiritual nature, as stated above (Q. 25, A. 7): so that accordingly, a man ought, out of charity, to love himself more than he loves any other person.

This is evident from the very reason for loving: since, as stated above (Q. 25, AA. 1, 12), God is loved as the principle of good, on which the love of charity is founded; while man, out of charity, loves himself by reason of his being a partaker of the aforesaid good, and loves his neighbor by reason of his fellowship in that good. Now fellowship is a reason for love according to a certain union in relation to God. Wherefore just as unity surpasses union, the fact that a man himself has a share of the Divine good, is a more potent reason for loving than that another should be a partner with him in that share. Therefore a man, out of charity, ought to love himself more than his neighbor: in sign whereof, a man ought not to give way to any evil of sin, which counteracts his share of happiness, not even that he may free his neighbor from sin.

Reply Obj. 1. The love of charity takes its quantity not only from its object which is God, but also from the lover, who is the man that has charity, even as the quantity of any action depends in some way on the subject. Wherefore, though a better neighbor is nearer to God, yet because he is not as near to the man who has charity, as this man is to himself, it does not follow that a man is bound to love his neighbor more than himself.

Reply Obj. 2. A man ought to bear bodily injury for his friend's sake, and precisely in so doing he loves himself more as regards his spiritual mind, because it pertains to the perfection of virtue, which is a good of the mind. In spiritual matters, however, man ought not to suffer injury by sinning, in order to free his neighbor from sin, as stated above.

Reply Obj. 3. As Augustine says in his Rule (*Ep.* ccxi), the saying, *"charity seeks not her own,"* means that it prefers the common *to the private good.* Now the common good is always more lovable to the individual than his private good, even as the good of the whole is more lovable to the part, than the latter's own partial good, as stated above (A. 3).

SIXTH ARTICLE
WHETHER WE OUGHT TO LOVE ONE NEIGHBOR MORE THAN ANOTHER?

We proceed thus to the Sixth Article:—

Objection 1. It would seem that we ought not to love one neighbor more than another. For Augustine says (*De Doctr. Christ.* i. 28): *One ought to love all men equally. Since, however, one cannot do good to all, we ought to consider those chiefly who by reason of place, time or any other circumstance, by a kind of chance, are more closely united to us.* Therefore one neighbor ought not to be loved more than another.

Obj. 2. Further, where there is one and the same reason for loving several, there should be no inequality of love. Now there is one and the same reason for loving all one's neighbors, which reason is God, as Augustine states (*De Doctr. Christ.* i. 27). Therefore we ought to love all our neighbors equally.

Obj. 3. Further, to love a man is to wish him good things, as the Philosopher states (*Rhet.* ii. 4). Now to all our neighbors we wish an equal good, viz. everlasting life. Therefore we ought to love all our neighbors equally.

On the contrary, One's obligation to love a person is proportionate to the gravity of the sin one commits in acting against that love. Now it is a more grievous sin to act against the love of certain neighbors, than against the love of others. Hence the commandment (Lev. xx. 9),—*He that curseth his father or mother, dying let him die,* which does not apply to those who cursed others than the above. Therefore we ought to love some neighbors more than others.

I answer that, There have been two opinions on this question: for some have said that we ought, out of charity, to love all our neighbors equally, as regards our affection, but not as regards the outward effect. They held that the order of love is to be understood as applying to outward favors, which we ought to confer on those who are connected with us in preference to those who are unconnected, and not to the inward affection, which ought to be given equally to all including our enemies.

But this is unreasonable. For the affection of charity, which is the inclination of grace, is not less orderly than the natural appetite, which is the inclination of nature, for both inclinations flow from Divine wisdom. Now we observe in the physical order that the natural inclination in each thing is proportionate to the act or movement that is becoming to the nature of that thing: thus in earth the inclination of gravity is greater than in water, because it is becoming to earth to be beneath water. Consequently the inclination also of grace which is the effect of charity, must needs be proportionate to those actions which have to be performed outwardly, so that, to wit, the affection of our charity be more intense towards those to whom we ought to behave with greater kindness.

We must, therefore, say that, even as regards the affection we ought to love one neighbor more than another. The reason is that, since the principle of love is God, and the person who loves, it must needs be that the affection of love increases in proportion to the nearness to one or the other of those principles. For as we stated above (A. 1), wherever we find a principle, order depends on relation to that principle.

Reply Obj. 1. Love can be unequal in two ways: first on the part of the good we wish our friend. In this respect we love all men equally out of charity: because we wish them all one same generic good, namely everlasting happiness. Secondly love is said to be greater through its action being more intense: and in this way we ought not to love all equally.

Or we may reply that we have unequal love for certain persons in two ways: first, through our loving some and not loving others. As regards beneficence we are bound to observe this inequality, because we cannot do good to all: but as regards benevolence, love ought not to be thus unequal. The other inequality arises from our loving some more than others: and Augustine does not mean to exclude the latter inequality, but the former, as is evident from what he says of beneficence.

Reply Obj. 2. Our neighbors are not all equally related to God; some are nearer to Him, by reason of their greater goodness, and those we ought, out of charity, to love more than those who are not so near to Him.

Reply Obj. 3. This argument considers the quantity of love on the part of the good which we wish our friends.

Montaigne

OF FRIENDSHIP

Introduction

Cicero intended that his reader recognize himself when reading the dialogue on friendship; Montaigne intends his *Essays* to be a self-portrait, in which we might discern Montaigne. "I am myself the matter of the book," Montaigne declares in the preface to the first volume of essays. He writes them, he tells us, "for his friends and relatives," so that "they may recover here some features of my habits and temperament, and by this means keep the knowledge they have had of me more complete and alive."

The twenty-eighth essay is on friendship. As he implies at the opening of the essay, Montaigne has placed it almost exactly in the middle of the complete group of fifty-seven essays, so that "best spot" in the collection might be used to exhibit the work of his deceased friend, Etienne de La Boétie. Thus Montaigne seems to act on the maxim that a friend is another self, by featuring his friend in the central position of what is meant to be a portrait of himself.

The essay describes the "sovereign and masterful" type of friendship Montaigne had with La Boétie. Montaigne knows Aristotle, Cicero, and Seneca thoroughly, but he complains that "the very discourses that antiquity has left us on this subject seem to me weak compared with the feeling I have." He goes on to describe instead a kind of friendship in which friends are not merely united but rather become one. Aware that such assertions will be taken as exaggerations and metaphors by his readers, Montaigne warns that only those "who have experienced what I tell" are fit judges.

The essay on friendship is written in Montaigne's "Stoic" period, and one finds in it, as in Seneca, the notion that friendship should be an unconstrained product of the will: "our free will has no product more properly its own than affection and friendship." But his notion of the will is modern and anticipates Romanticism. There is no foundation for the love of true friends, just as there is no foundation for self-love: "If you press me to tell why I love him, I feel that this cannot be expressed, except by answering: Because it was he, because it was I." Moreover, each friendship produced by the will is a new creation, spontaneous and not conventional: "Our friendship has no other model than itself, and can be compared only with itself."

For Montaigne, any sort of constraint or necessity is incompatible with such a friendship, whether this arise from precaution, prudence, calculation, duty, or obligation. Indeed, true friendship is prior to and transcends every other commitment or obligation. What, then, guarantees its moral character? At this point Montaigne relies on the Stoic view of reason infusing all of nature: such friends, he assures us, are necessarily "guided by the strength and leadership of reason."

Montaigne argues neatly that it is because friendship excludes obligations or duties that it is impossible truly to be friends with more than one person at a time: if a person had more than one friend, then he would have to regulate his affection toward each with a view to the other, but this would imply introducing rules having the character of necessity, which cannot exist in a true friendship.

Montaigne

OF FRIENDSHIP
ESSAY 28

As I was considering the way a painter I employ went about his work, I had a mind to imitate him. He chooses the best spot, the middle of each wall, to put a picture labored over with all his skill, and the empty space all around it he fills with grotesques, which are fantastic paintings whose only charm lies in their variety and strangeness. And what are these things of mine, in truth, but grotesques and monstrous bodies, pieced together of divers members, without definite shape, having no order, sequence, or proportion other than accidental?

A lovely woman tapers off into a fish.

HORACE

I do indeed go along with my painter in this second point, but I fall short in the first and better part; for my ability does not go far enough for me to dare to undertake a rich, polished picture, formed according to art. It has occurred to me to borrow one from Etienne de La Boétie, which will do honor to all the rest of this work. It is a discourse to which he gave the name *La Servitude Volontaire*; but those who did not know this have since very fitly rebaptized it *Le Contre Un*.[1] He wrote it by way of essay in his early youth, in honor of liberty against tyrants. It has long been circulating in the hands of men of understanding, not without great and well-merited commendation; for it is a fine thing, and as full as can be. Still, it is far from being the best he could do; and if at the more mature age when I knew him, he had adopted a plan such as mine, of putting his ideas in writing, we should

1. *La Servitude Volontaire*, "Voluntary Servitude." *Le Contre Un*, "Against One Man."

see many rare things which would bring us very close to the glory of antiquity; for particularly in the matter of natural gifts, I know no one who can be compared with him. But nothing of his has remained except this treatise—and that by chance, and I think he never saw it after it left his hands—and some observations on that Edict of January, made famous by our civil wars, which will perhaps yet find their place elsewhere. That was all I could recover of what he left—I, to whom in his will, with such loving recommendation, with death in his throat, he bequeathed his library and his papers—except for the little volume of his works which I have had published.

And yet I am particularly obliged to this work, since it served as the medium of our first acquaintance. For it was shown to me long before I had seen him, and gave me my first knowledge of his name, thus starting on its way this friendship which together we fostered, as long as God willed, so entire and so perfect that certainly you will hardly read of the like, and among men of today you see no trace of it in practice. So many coincidences are needed to build up such a friendship that it is a lot if fortune can do it once in three centuries.

There is nothing to which nature seems to have inclined us more than to society. And Aristotle says that good legislators have had more care for friendship than for justice. Now the ultimate point in the perfection of society is this. For in general, all associations that are forged and nourished by pleasure or profit, by public or private needs, are the less beautiful and noble, and the less friendships, in so far as they mix into friendship another cause and object and reward than friendship itself. Nor do the four ancient types—natural, social, hospitable, erotic—come up to real friendship, either separately or together.

From children toward fathers, it is rather respect. Friendship feeds on communication, which cannot exist between them because of their too great inequality, and might perhaps interfere with the duties of nature. For neither can all the secret thoughts of fathers be communicated to children, lest this beget an unbecoming intimacy, nor could the admonitions and corrections, which are one of the chief duties of friendship, be administered by children to fathers. There have been nations where by custom the children killed their fathers, and others where the fathers killed their children, to avoid the interference that they can sometimes cause each other; and by nature the one depends on the destruction of the other. There have been philosophers who disdained this natural tie, witness Aristippus: when pressed about the affection he owed his children for having come out of him, he began to spit, saying that that had come out of him just as well, and that we also bred lice and worms. And that other, whom Plutarch wanted to reconcile with his brother, said: "I don't think any more of him for having come out of the same hole."

Truly the name of brother is a beautiful name and full of affection, and for that reason he and I made our alliance a brotherhood. But that confusion of ownership, the dividing, and the fact that the richness of one is the poverty of the other, wonderfully softens and loosens the solder of brotherhood. Since brothers have to guide their careers along the same path and at the same rate, it is inevitable that they often jostle and clash with each other. Furthermore, why should the harmony and kinship which begets these true and perfect friendships be found in them? Father and son may be of entirely different dispositions, and brothers also. He is my son, he is my kinsman, but he is an unsociable man, a knave, or a fool. And then, the more they are friendships which law and natural obligation impose on us, the less of our choice and free will there is in them. And our free will has no product more properly its own than affection and friendship. Not that I have not experienced all the friendship that can exist in that situation, having had the best father that ever was, and the most indulgent, even in his extreme old age, and being of a family famous and exemplary, from father to son, in this matter of brotherly concord:

> Known to others
> For fatherly affection toward my brothers.
>   HORACE

To compare this brotherly affection with affection for women, even though it is the result of our choice—it cannot be done; nor can we put the love of women in the same category. Its ardor, I confess—

> Of us that goddess is not unaware
> Who blends a bitter sweetness with her care
>   CATULLUS

—is more active, more scorching, and more intense. But it is an impetuous and fickle flame, undulating and variable, a fever flame, subject to fits and lulls, that holds us only by one corner. In friendship it is a general and universal warmth, moderate and even, besides, a constant and settled warmth, all gentleness and smoothness, with nothing bitter and stinging about it. What is more, in love there is nothing but a frantic desire for what flees from us:

> Just as a huntsman will pursue a hare
> O'er hill and dale, in weather cold or fair;
> The captured hare is worthless in his sight;
> He only hastens after things in flight.
>   ARIOSTO

As soon as it enters the boundaries of friendship, that is to say harmony of wills, it grows faint and languid. Enjoyment destroys it, as having a fleshly end, subject to satiety. Friendship, on the contrary, is enjoyed according as it is desired; it is bred, nourished, and increased only in enjoyment, since it is spiritual, and the soul grows refined by practice. During the reign of this perfect friendship those fleeting affections once found a place in me, not to speak of my friend, who confesses only too many of them in these verses. Thus these two passions within me came to be known to each other, but to be compared, never; the first keeping its course in proud and lofty flight, and disdainfully watching the other making its way far, far beneath it.

As for marriage, for one thing it is a bargain to which only the entrance is free—its continuance being constrained and forced, depending otherwise than on our will—and a bargain ordinarily made for other ends. For another, there supervene a thousand foreign tangles to unravel, enough to break the thread and trouble the course of a lively affection; whereas in friendship there are no dealings or business except with itself. Besides, to tell the truth, the ordinary capacity of women is inadequate for that communion and fellowship which is the nurse of this sacred bond; nor does their soul seem firm enough to endure the strain of so tight and durable a knot. And indeed, but for that, if such a relationship, free and voluntary, could be built up, in which not only would the souls have this complete enjoyment, but the bodies would also share in the alliance, so that the entire man would be engaged, it is certain that the resulting friendship would be fuller and more complete. But this sex in no instance has yet succeeded in attaining it, and by the common agreement of the ancient schools is excluded from it.

And that other, licentious Greek love is justly abhorred by our morality. Since it involved, moreover, according to their practice, such a necessary disparity in age and such a difference in the lovers' functions, it did not correspond closely enough with the perfect union and harmony that we require here: *For what is this love of friendship? Why does no one love either an ugly youth, or a handsome old man?* [Cicero.] For even the picture the Academy paints of it will not contradict me, I think, if I say this on the subject: that this first frenzy which the son of Venus inspired in the lover's heart at the sight of the flower of tender youth, in which they allow all the insolent and passionate acts that immoderate ardor can produce, was simply founded on external beauty, the false image of corporeal generation. For it could not be founded on the spirit, the signs of which were still hidden, which was only at its birth and before the age of budding. If this frenzy seized a base heart, the means of his courtship were riches, presents, favor in advancement to dignities, and other such base merchandise, which were generally condemned. If it fell on a nobler heart, the means were also noble: philosophical instruction, precepts to revere religion, obey the laws, die for the good of the country; examples of valor, prudence, justice; the lover studying to make himself acceptable by the grace and beauty of his soul, that of his body being long since faded, and hoping by this mental fellowship to establish a firmer and more lasting pact.

When this courtship attained its effect in due season (for whereas they do not require of the lover that he use leisure and discretion in his enterprise, they strictly require it of the loved one, because he had to judge an inner beauty, difficult to know and hidden from discovery), then there was born in the loved one the desire of spiritual conception through the medium of spiritual beauty. This was the main thing here, and corporeal beauty accidental and secondary; quite the opposite of the lover. For this reason they prefer the loved one, and prove that the gods also prefer him, and strongly rebuke the poet Aeschylus for having, in the love of Achilles and Patroclus, given the lover's part to Achilles, who was in the first beardless bloom of his youth, and the handsomest of all the Greeks.

After this general communion was established, the stronger and worthier part of it exercising its functions and predominating, they say that there resulted from it fruits very useful personally and to the public; that it constituted the strength of the countries which accepted the practice, and the principal defense of equity and liberty: witness the salutary loves of Harmodius and Aristogeiton. Therefore they call it sacred and divine. And, by their reckoning, only the violence of tyrants and the cowardice of the common people are hostile to it. In short, all that can be said in favor of the Academy is that this was a love ending in friendship; which corresponds pretty well to the Stoic definition of love: *Love is the attempt to form a friendship inspired by beauty* [Cicero].

I return to my description of a more equitable and more equable kind of friendship. *Only those are to be judged friendships in which the characters have been strengthened and matured by age* [Cicero].

For the rest, what we ordinarily call friends and friendships are nothing but acquaintanceships and familiarities formed by some chance or convenience, by means of which our souls are bound to each other. In the friendship I speak of, our souls mingle and blend with each other so completely that they efface the seam that joined them, and cannot find it again. If you press me to tell why I loved him, I feel that this cannot be expressed, except by answering: Because it was he, because it was I.

Beyond all my understanding, beyond what I can say about this in particular, there was I know not what inexplicable and fateful force that was the mediator of this union. We sought each other before we met because of the reports we heard of each other, which had more effect on our affection than such reports would reasonably have; I think it was by some ordinance from heaven. We embraced each other by our names. And at our first meeting, which by chance came at a great feast and gathering in the city, we found ourselves so taken with each other, so well acquainted, so bound together, that from that time on nothing was so close to us as each other. He wrote an excellent Latin satire, which is published, in which he excuses and explains the precipitancy of our mutual understanding, so promptly grown to its perfection. Having so little time to last, and having begun so late, for we were both grown men, and he a few years older than I, it could not lose time and conform to the pattern of mild and regular friendships, which need so many precautions in the form of long preliminary association. Our friendship has no other model than itself, and can be compared only with itself. It is not one special consideration, nor two, nor three, nor four, nor a thousand: it is I know not what quintessence of all this mixture, which, having seized my whole will, led it to plunge and lose itself in his; which, having seized his whole will, led it to plunge and lose itself in mine, with equal hunger, equal rivalry. I say lose, in truth, for neither of us reserved anything for himself, nor was anything either his or mine.

When Laelius, in the presence of the Roman consuls—who, after condemning Tiberius Gracchus, prosecuted all those who had been in his confidence—came to ask Caius Blossius, who was Gracchus' best friend, how much he would have been willing to do for him, he answered: "Everything." "What, everything?" pursued Laelius. "And what if he had commanded you to set fire to our temples?" "He would never have commanded me to do that," replied Blossius. "But what if he had?" Laelius insisted. "I would have obeyed," he replied. If he was such a perfect friend to Gracchus as the histories say, he did not need to offend the consuls by this last bold confession, and he should not have abandoned the assurance he had of Gracchus' will. But nevertheless, those who charge that this answer is seditious do not fully understand this mystery, and fail to assume first what is true, that he had Gracchus' will up his sleeve, both by power over him and by knowledge of him. They were friends more than citizens, friends more than friends or enemies of their country or friends of ambition and disturbance. Having committed themselves absolutely to each other, they held absolutely the reins of each other's inclination; and if you assume that this team was guided by the strength and leadership of reason, as indeed it is quite impossible to harness it without that, Blossius' answer is as it should have been. If their actions went astray, they were by my measure neither friends to each other, nor friends to themselves.

For that matter, this answer has no better ring than would mine if someone questioned me in this fashion: "If your will commanded you to kill your daughter, would you kill her?" and I said yes. For that does not bear witness to any consent to do so, because I have no doubt at all about my will, and just as little about that of such a friend. It is not in the power of all the arguments in the world to dislodge me from the certainty I have of the intentions and judgments of my friend. Not one of his actions could be presented to me, whatever appearance it might have, that I could not immediately find the motive for it. Our souls pulled together in such unison, they regarded each other with such ardent affection, and with a like affection revealed themselves to each other to the very depths of our hearts, that not only did I know his soul as well as mine, but I should certainly have trusted myself to him more readily than to myself.

Let not these other, common friendships be placed in this rank. I have as much knowledge of them as another, and of the most perfect of their type, but I advise you not to confuse the rules of the two; you would make a mistake. You must walk in those other friendships bridle in hand, with prudence and precaution; the knot is not so well tied that there is no cause to mistrust it. "Love him," Chilo used to say, "as if you are to hate him some day; hate him as if you are to love him." This precept, which is so abominable in this sovereign and masterful friendship, is healthy in the practice of ordinary and customary friendships, in regard to which we must use the remark that Aristotle often repeated: "O my friends, there is no friend."

In this noble relationship, services and benefits, on which other friendships feed, do not even deserve to be taken into account; the reason for this is the complete fusion of our wills. For just as the friendship I feel for myself receives no increase from the help I give myself in time of need, whatever the Stoics say, and as I feel no gratitude to myself for the service I do myself; so the union of such friends, being truly perfect, makes them lose the sense of such duties, and hate and banish from between them these words of separation and distinction: benefit, obligation, gratitude, request, thanks, and the like. Everything actually being in common between them—wills, thoughts, judgments, goods, wives, children, honor, and life—and their relationship being that of one soul in two bodies, according to Aristotle's very apt definition, they can neither lend nor give anything to each other. That is why the lawmakers, to honor marriage with some imaginary resemblance to this divine union, forbid gifts between husband and wife, wishing thus to imply that everything should belong to each of them and that they have nothing to divide and split up between them.

If, in the friendship I speak of, one could give to the other, it would be the one who received the benefit who would oblige his friend. For each of them seeking above all things to benefit the other, the one who provides the matter and the occasion is the liberal one, giving his friend the satisfaction of doing for him what he most wants to do. When the philosopher Diogenes was short of money, he used to say that he asked it back of his friends, not that he asked for it. And to show how this works in practice, I will tell you an ancient example that is singular.

Eudamidas of Corinth had two friends, Charixenus, a Sicyonian, and Aretheus, a Corinthian. When he came to die, he being poor and his two friends rich, he made his will thus: "I leave this to Aretheus, to feed my mother and support her in her old age; this to Charixenus, to see my daughter married and give her the biggest dowry he can; and in case one of them should chance to die, I substitute the survivor in his place." Those who first saw this will laughed at it; but his heirs having been informed of it, accepted it with singular satisfaction. And when one of them, Charixenus, died five days later, and the place of substitute was opened to Aretheus, he supported the mother with great care, and of five talents he had in his estate, he gave two and a half to his only daughter for her marriage, and two and a half for the marriage of the daughter of Eudamidas, holding their weddings on the same day.

This example is quite complete except for one circumstance, which is the plurality of friends. For this perfect friendship I speak of is indivisible: each one gives himself so wholly to his friend that he has nothing left to distribute elsewhere; on the contrary, he is sorry that he is not double, triple, or quadruple, and that he has not several souls and several wills, to confer them all on this one object. Common friendships can be divided up: one may love in one man his beauty, in another his easygoing ways, in another liberality, in one paternal love, in another brotherly love, and so forth; but this friendship that possesses the soul and rules it with absolute sovereignty cannot possibly be double. If two called for help at the same time, which one would you run to? If they demanded conflicting services of you, how would you arrange it? If one confided to your silence a thing that would be useful for the other to know, how would you extricate yourself? A single dominant friendship dissolves all other obligations. The secret I have sworn to reveal to no other man, I can impart without perjury to the one who is not another man: he is myself. It is a great enough miracle to be doubled, and those who talk of tripling themselves do not realize the loftiness of the thing: nothing is extreme that can be matched. And he who supposes that of two men I love one just as much as the other, and that they love each other and me just as much as I love them, multiplies into a fraternity the most singular and unified of all things, of which even a single one is the rarest thing in the world to find.

The rest of this story fits in very well with what I was saying, for Eudamidas bestows upon his friends the kindness and favor of using them for his need. He leaves them heirs to this liberality of his, which consists of putting into their hands a chance to do him good. And without doubt the strength of friendship is shown much more richly in his action than in that of Aretheus.

In short, these are actions inconceivable to anyone who has not tasted friendship, and which make me honor wonderfully the answer of that young soldier to Cyrus, who asked him for how much he would sell a horse with which he had just won the prize in a race, and whether he would exchange him for a kingdom: "No indeed, Sire, but I would most willingly let him go to gain a friend, if I found a man worthy of such an alliance." That was not badly spoken, "if I found one"; for it is easy to find men fit for a superficial acquaintance. But for this kind, in which we act from the very bottom of our hearts, which holds nothing back, truly it is necessary that all the springs of action be perfectly clean and true.

In the relationships which bind us only by one small part, we need look out only for the imperfections that particularly concern that part. The religion of my doctor or my lawyer cannot matter. That consideration has nothing in common with the functions of the friendship they owe me. And in the domestic relationship between me and those who serve me, I have the same attitude. I scarcely inquire of a lackey whether he is chaste; I try to find out whether he is diligent. And I am not as much afraid of a gambling mule driver as of a weak one, or of a profane cook as of an ignorant one. I do not make it my business to tell the world what it should do—enough others do that—but what I do in it.

> That is my practice: do as you see fit.
> TERENCE

For the familiarity of the table I look for wit, not prudence; for the bed, beauty before goodness; in conversation, competence, even without uprightness. Likewise in other matters.

Just as the man who was found astride a stick, playing with his children, asked the man who surprised him thus to say nothing about it until he was a father himself, in the belief that the passion which would then be born in his soul would make him an equitable judge of such an act, so I should like to talk to people who have experienced what I tell. But knowing how far from common usage and how rare such a friendship is, I do not expect to find any good judge of it. For the very discourses that antiquity has left us on this subject seem to me weak compared with the feeling I have. And in this particular the facts surpass even the precepts of philosophy:

Nothing shall I, while sane, compare with a dear friend.
                                                                    HORACE

The ancient Menander declared that man happy who had been able to meet even the shadow of a friend. He was certainly right to say so especially if he spoke from experience. For in truth, if I compare all the rest of my life—though by the grace of God I have spent it pleasantly, comfortably, and, except for the loss of such a friend, free from any grievous affliction, and full of tranquillity of mind, having accepted my natural and original advantages without seeking other ones—if I compare it all, I say, with the four years which were granted me to enjoy the sweet company and society of that man, it is nothing but smoke, nothing but dark and dreary night. Since the day I lost him,

        Which I shall ever recall with pain,
    Ever with reverence—thus, Gods, did you ordain—
                                                                    VIRGIL

I only drag on a weary life. And the very pleasures that come my way, instead of consoling me, redouble my grief for his loss. We went halves in everything; it seems to me that I am robbing him of his share,

        Nor may I rightly taste of pleasures here alone,
        —So I resolved—when he who shared my life is gone.
                                                                    TERENCE

I was already so formed and accustomed to being a second self everywhere that only half of me seems to be alive now.

> Since an untimely blow has snatched away
> Part of my soul, why then do I delay,
> I the remaining part, less dear than he,
> And not entire surviving? The same day
> Brought ruin equally to him and me.
>
> HORACE

There is no action or thought in which I do not miss him, as indeed he would have missed me. For just as he surpassed me infinitely in every other ability and virtue, so he did in the duty of friendship.

> Why should I be ashamed or exercise control
> Mourning so dear a soul?
>
> HORACE

> Brother, your death has left me sad and lone;
> Since you departed all our joys have gone,
> Which while you lived your sweet affection fed;
> My pleasures all lie shattered, with you dead.
> Our soul is buried, mine with yours entwined;
> And since then I have banished from my mind
> My studies, and my spirit's dearest joys.
> Shall I ne'er speak to you, or hear your voice?
> Or see your face, more dear than life to me?
> At least I'll love you to eternity.
>
> CATULLUS

But let us listen a while to this boy of sixteen.

Because I have found that this work has since been brought to light, and with evil intent, by those who seek to disturb and change the state of our government without worrying whether they will improve it, and because they have mixed his work up with some of their own concoctions, I have changed my mind about putting it in here.[2] And so that the memory of the author

---

2. La Boétie's *Voluntary Servitude* was published in a revolutionary context by Protestants, in part in 1574 (*Le Reveille-Matin des François*), and in its entirety in 1576 (*Mémoires de l'Estat de France sous Charles Neufiesme*). Montaigne had presumably written most of this chapter before 1574 and changed his mind about publishing La Boétie's discourse when he learned of these publications.

In the 1580–88 editions of the *Essays*, Montaigne speaks of La Boétie as eighteen, not sixteen.

may not be damaged in the eyes of those who could not know his opinions and actions at close hand, I beg to advise them that this subject was treated by him in his boyhood, only by way of an exercise, as a common theme hashed over in a thousand places in books. I have no doubt that he believed what he wrote, for he was so conscientious as not to lie even in jest. And I know further that if he had had the choice, he would rather have been born in Venice than in Sarlat, and with reason. But he had another maxim sovereignly imprinted in his soul, to obey and submit most religiously to the laws under which he was born. There never was a better citizen, or one more devoted to the tranquillity of his country, or more hostile to the commotions and innovations of his time. He would much rather have used his ability to suppress them than to give them material that would excite them further. His mind was molded in the pattern of other ages than this.

Now, in exchange for this serious work, I shall substitute another, produced in that same season of his life, gayer and more lusty.

Bacon

OF FRIENDSHIP

Introduction

"It was truly said," Bacon writes in his essay "Of Counsel,"
"*optimi consiliarii mortui* [the best counselors are dead]. Books
will speak plain, when counselors blanch. Therefore it is good
to be conversant in them, specially the books of such as themselves have been actors upon the stage." This remark can be
understood as Bacon's recommendation of his book of *Essays*,
for Bacon aspired to be a counselor to the crown throughout
his life, first to Queen Elizabeth and then to King James. And
he was an "actor upon the stage," who served as Solicitor-
General and Lord Chancellor under King James. His essays
aim to provide the "dry light" of friendly counsel that a prince
needs so that he may "fitly play his own part."

Although Bacon read Montaigne, there are no signs of influence. The advice that Bacon gives about friendship is
shrewd and practical; he dispenses with any discussion of the
nature of friendship and proceeds immediately to its usefulness, speaking of the three "fruits" of friendship. His remarks about the first fruit, that friendship brings about "peace
in the affections," are especially noteworthy. Bacon is perhaps
the first philosopher to conceive of a need for friendship that
is amoral, in the sense that it is not the consequence of any
goodness, natural or acquired, in a person. The emotions of a
human being, he says, are like fluids under pressure, which
need to be discharged: this discharge takes place only through
the outlet of a friend.

One consequence of this is that a prince is necessarily
caught in a dilemma. If he has no friend, then he "cannibal-
izes his own heart" and risks going mad. If, however, he is to
have a friend, then he must first make someone his equal

(here Bacon uses the thesis of *Nicomachean Ethics* VIII.7, that persons must become equal before they can be friends), but then he endangers his rule.

Bacon observes that the need we have for friends is satisfied only by letting someone not related by blood into our confidence: "they were princes, that had wives, sons, nephew; and yet all these could not supply the comfort of friendship." But he does not attempt to explain this, except for his brief remark, at the end of the essay, that we cannot ask relatives to do things for us as freely as we ask friends, because of the various respects that must be shown to the former.

There are many compelling, though very compressed, passages in the essay: for example, Bacon's description of a friend as a general counselor, who has an eye to one's entire welfare, or his terse explanation of why a friend can contribute to one's character in ways that self-examination or reading a good book cannot. Perhaps his most striking suggestion is that self-knowledge involves clarification of one's thoughts (we speak of "knowing one's mind"), which depends necessarily on communicating, or at least pretending to communicate, those thoughts to another: "In a word, a man were better relate himself, to a statue, or picture, than to suffer his thoughts to pass in smother."

Bacon

OF FRIENDSHIP
XXVII

It had been hard for him that spake it, to have put more truth and untruth together, in few words, than in that speech; *whosoever is delighted in solitude, is either a wild beast, or a god.* For it is most true, that a natural and secret hatred, and aversation towards *society*, in any man, hath somewhat of the savage beast; but it is most untrue, that it should have any character, at all, of the divine nature; except it proceed, not out of a pleasure in *solitude*, but out of a love and desire, to sequester a man's self, for a higher conversation: such as is found, to have been falsely and fainedly, in some of the heathen; as *Epimenides* the Candian, *Numa* the Roman, *Empedocles* the Sicilian, and *Apollonius* of Tyana; and truly and really, in divers of the ancient hermits, and holy fathers of the church. But little do men perceive, what *solitude* is, and how far it extendeth. For a crowd is not company; and faces are but a gallery of pictures; and talk but a *tinkling cymbal*, where there is no *love*. The Latin adage meeteth with it a little; *magna civitas, magna solitudo;* because in a great town, *friends* are scattered; so that there is not that fellowship, for the most part, which is in less *neighborhoods*. But we may go further, and affirm most truly; that it is a mere, and miserable *solitude*, to want true *friends;* without which the world is but a wilderness: and even in this sense also of *solitude*, whosoever in the frame of his nature and affections, is unfit for *friendship*, he taketh it of the beast, and not from humanity.

A principal *fruit* of *friendship,* is the ease and discharge of the fullness and swellings of the heart, which passions of all kinds do cause and induce. We know diseases of stoppings, and suffocations, are the most dangerous in the body; and it is not much otherwise in the mind: you may take *sarsa* to open the liver; *steel* to open the spleen; *flowers* of *sulphur* for the lungs; *castoreum* for the brain; but no receipt openeth the heart, but a true *friend*; to whom you may impart, griefs, joys, fears, hopes, suspicions, counsels, and whatsoever lieth upon the heart, to oppress it, in a kind of civil shrift or confession.

It is a strange thing to observe, how high a rate, great kings and monarchs, do set upon this *fruit* of *friendship*, whereof we speak: so great, as they purchase it, many times, at the hazard of their own safety, and greatness. For princes, in regard of the distance of their fortune, from that of their subjects and servants, cannot gather this *fruit*; except (to make themselves capable thereof) they raise some persons, to be as it were companions, and almost equals to themselves, which many times sorteth to inconvenience. The modern languages give unto such persons, the name of *favorites*, or *privadoes*; as if it were matter of grace, or conversation. But the Roman name attaineth the true use, and cause thereof; naming them *participes curarum*; for it is that, which tieth the knot. And we see plainly, that this hath been done, not by weak and passionate *princes* only, but by the wisest, and most politic that ever reigned; who have oftentimes joined to themselves, some of their servants; whom both themselves have called *friends*; and allowed others likewise to call them in the same manner; using the word which is received between private men.

L. Sulla, when he commanded *Rome,* raised *Pompey* (after surnamed the *Great*) to that height, that *Pompey* vaunted himself for *Sulla's* overmatch. For when he had carried the *consulship* for a friend of his, against the pursuit of *Sulla,* and that *Sulla* did a little resent thereat, and began to speak great, *Pompey* turned upon him again, and in effect bade him be quiet; *for that more men adored the sun rising, than the sun setting.* With *Julius Caesar, Decimus Brutus* had obtained that interest, as he set him down, in his testament, for heir in remainder, after his *nephew.* And this was the man, that had power with him, to draw him forth to his death. For when *Caesar* would have discharged the senate, in regard of some ill presages, and specially a dream of *Calpurnia*; this man lifted him gently by the arm, out of his chair, telling him, he hoped he would not dismiss the senate, till his wife had dreamt a better dream. And it seemeth, his favor was so great, as *Antonius* in a letter, which is recited *verbatim,* in one of *Cicero's Philippics,* calleth him *venefica, witch*; as if he had enchanted *Cae-*

sar. Augustus raised *Agrippa* (though of mean birth) to that height, as when he consulted with *Maecenas,* about the marriage of his daughter *Julia, Maecenas* took the liberty to tell him; *that he must either marry his daughter to Agrippa, or take away his life, there was no third way, he had made him so great.* With *Tiberius Caesar, Sejanus* had ascended to that height, as they two were termed and reckoned, as a pair of friends. *Tiberius* in a letter to him saith; *haec pro amicitiâ nostrâ non occultavi:* and the whole Senate, dedicated an altar to *friendship,* as to a *goddess,* in respect of the great dearness of *friendship,* between them two. The like or more was between *Septimius Severus,* and *Plautianus.* For he forced his eldest son to marry the daughter of *Plautianus;* and would often maintain *Plautianus,* in doing affronts to his son: and did write also in a letter to the senate, by these words; *I love the man so well, as I wish he may over-live me.* Now if these princes, had been as a *Trajan,* or a *Marcus Aurelius,* a man might have thought, that this had proceeded of an abundant goodness of nature; but being men so wise, of such strength and severity of mind, and so extreme lovers of themselves, as all these were; it proveth most plainly, that they found their own felicity (though as great as ever happened to mortal men) but as an half piece, except they might have a *friend* to make it entire: and yet, which is more, they were *princes,* that had wives, sons, nephews; and yet all these could not supply the comfort of *friendship.*

It is not to be forgotten, what *Commineus* observeth, of his first master *Duke Charles* the *Hardy;* namely, that he would communicate his secrets with none; and least of all, those secrets, which troubled him most. Whereupon he goeth on, and saith, that towards his latter time; *that closeness did impair, and a little perish his understanding.* Surely *Commineus* might have made the same judgement also, if it had pleased him, of his second master *Lewis* the Eleventh, whose closeness was indeed his tormentor. The parable of *Pythagoras* is dark, but true; *cor ne edito; eat not the heart.* Certainly, if a man would give it a hard phrase, those that want *friends* to open themselves unto, are cannibals of their own *hearts.* But one thing is most admirable, (wherewith I will conclude this first *fruit* of *friendship*) which is, that this communicating of a man's self to his *friend,* works two contrary effects; for it redoubleth *joys,* and cutteth *griefs* in halves. For there is no man, that imparteth his *joys* to his *friend,* but he *joyeth* the more; and no man, that imparteth his *griefs* to his *friend,* but he *grieveth* the less. So that it is, in truth of operation upon a man's mind, of like virtue, as the *alchemists* use to attribute to their stone, for man's body; that it worketh all contrary effects, but still to the good, and benefit of nature. But yet, without praying in aid of *alchemists,* there is a manifest image of this, in the ordinary course of nature. For in bodies, *union* strengtheneth and cherisheth any natural action; and, on the other side, weakeneth and dulleth any violent impression: and even so is it of minds.

The second *fruit of friendship,* is healthful and sovereign for the *understanding,* as the first is for the *affections.* For *friendship* maketh indeed a *fair day* in the *affections,* from storm and tempests: but it maketh *daylight* in the *understanding,* out of darkness and confusion of thoughts. Neither is this to be understood, only of faithful counsel, which a man receiveth from his *friend;* but before you come to that, certain it is, that whosoever hath his mind fraught, with many thoughts, his wits and understanding do clarify and break up, in the communicating and discoursing with another: he tosseth his thoughts, more easily; He marshalleth them more orderly; He seeth how they look when they are turned into words; finally, he waxeth wiser than himself; and that more by an hour's discourse, than by a day's meditation. It was well said by *Themistocles* to the King of *Persia; that speech was like cloth of arras, opened, and put abroad; whereby the imagery doth appear in figure; whereas in thoughts, they lie but as in packs.* Neither is this second *fruit* of *friendship,* in opening the *understanding,* restrained only to such *friends,* as are able to give a man counsel: (they indeed are best) but even, without that, a man learneth of himself, and bringeth his own thoughts to light, and whetteth his wits as against a stone, which itself cuts not. In a word, a man were better relate himself, to a statue, or picture, than to suffer his thoughts to pass in smother.

Add now, to make this second *fruit* of *friendship* complete, that other point, which lieth more open, and falleth within vulgar observation; which is *faithful counsel* from a *friend. Heraclitus* saith well, in one of his enigmas; *dry light is ever the best.* And certain it is, that the light, that a man receiveth, by counsel from another, is drier, and purer, than that which cometh from his own understanding, and judgement; which is ever infused and drenched in his affections and customs. So as, there is as much difference, between the *counsel,* that a *friend* giveth, and that a man giveth himself, as there is between the *counsel* of a *friend,* and of a *flatterer*. For there is no such *flatterer*, as is a man's self; and there is no such remedy, against *flattery* of a man's self, as the liberty of a *friend*. *Counsel* is of two sorts; the one concerning *manners*, the other concerning *business*. For the first; the best preservative to keep the mind in health, is the faithful admonition of a *friend*. The calling of a man's self, to a strict account, is a medicine, sometime, too piercing and corrosive. Reading good books of *morality*, is a little flat, and dead. Observing our faults in others, is sometimes unproper for our case. But the best receipt (best (I say) to work, and best to take) is the admonition of a *friend*. It is a strange thing to behold, what gross errors, and extreme absurdities, many (especially of the greater sort) do commit, for want of a *friend*, to tell them of them; to the great damage, both of their fame, and fortune. For, as *S. James* saith, they are as men, *that look sometimes into a glass, and presently forget their own shape, and favor*. As for *business*, a man may think, if he will, that two eyes see no more than one; or that a gamester seeth always more than a looker on; or that a man in anger, is as wise as he, that hath said over the four and twenty letters; or that a musket may be shot off, as well upon the arm, as upon a rest; and such other fond and high imaginations, to think himself all in all. But when all is done, the help of good *counsel*, is that, which setteth *business* straight. And if any man think, that he will take *counsel*, but it shall be by pieces; asking *counsel* in one business of one man, and in another business of another man; it is well, (that is to say, better perhaps than if he asked none at all;) but he runneth two dangers: one, that he shall not be faithfully counseled; for it is a rare thing, except it be from a perfect and entire *friend*, to have counsel given, but such as shall be bowed and crooked to some ends, which he hath that giveth it. The other, that he shall have counsel given, hurtful, and unsafe, (though with good meaning) and mixed, partly of mischief, and partly of remedy: even as if you would call a physician, that is thought good, for the cure of the disease, you complain of, but is unacquainted with your body; and therefore, may put you in way for a present cure, but overthroweth your health in some other kind; and so cure the disease, and kill the patient. But a *friend*, that is wholly acquainted with a man's estate, will beware by furthering any present *business*, how he dasheth upon other inconvenience. And therefore, rest not upon *scattered counsels*; they will rather distract, and mislead, than settle, and direct.

After these two noble *fruits of friendship; (peace in the affections,* and *support of the judgement,*) followeth the last *fruit;* which is like the *pomegranate,* full of many kernels; I mean *aid,* and *bearing a part,* in all *actions,* and *occasions.* Here, the best way, to represent to life the manifold use of *friendship,* is to cast and see, how many things there are, which a man cannot do himself; and then it will appear, that it was a sparing speech of the ancients, to say, *that a friend is another himself:* for that a *friend* is far more than *himself.* Men have their time, and die many times in desire of some things, which they principally take to heart; the bestowing of a child, the finishing of a work, or the like. If a man have a true *friend,* he may rest almost secure, that the care of those things, will continue after him. So that a man hath as it were two lives in his desires. A man hath a body, and that body is confined to a place; but where *friendship* is, all offices of life, are as it were granted to him, and his deputy. For he may exercise them by his *friend.* How many things are there, which a man cannot, with any face or comeliness, say or do himself? A man can scarce allege his own merits with modesty, much less extol them: a man cannot sometimes brook to supplicate or beg: and a number of the like. But all these things, are graceful in a *friend's* mouth, which are blushing in a man's own. So again, a man's person hath many proper relations, which he cannot put off. A man cannot speak to his son, but as a father; to his wife, but as a husband; to his enemy, but upon terms: whereas a *friend* may speak, as the case requires, and not as it sorteth with the person. But to enumerate these things were endless: I have given the rule, where a man cannot fitly play his own part: if he have not a *friend,* he may quit the stage.

Kant

LECTURE ON
FRIENDSHIP

Introduction

Immanuel Kant's longest continuous treatment of friendship
is in a lecture that was part of a course on ethics which he offered at the University of Königsberg from 1775 to 1780. It
should be noted that the lecture is not a polished work, since
it was not prepared for publication. It lacks the system and
coherence of a treatise, as well as the hidden artifice of an apparently desultory moral essay.

Kant explains friendship as a means of reconciling two conflicting "motives to action in man": self-love and love of humanity. They conflict in the sense that choosing to act on the
one implies losing what one gains by acting on the other:
when you act out of self-love, you lose moral merit; when you
act out of love of humanity, you are neglecting your own happiness. There is, Kant says, an ideal resolution of the conflict
in the Idea of friendship: If each of two friends loves the other
as himself, the happiness of each is taken care of by the
other, and each gains moral merit, because each acts for the
other.

Hence Kant interprets the maxim that "a friend is another
self" to mean that, in the Ideal of friendship, each friend loves
the other as if he were himself, that is to say, *in place of* himself. However, Kant seems to hold that the resolution of the
conflict that one finds in the Ideal of friendship is unattainable
in practice: "absolute conformity is impossible," he says.

Friendship is divided into three types by Kant, as by Aristotle, but Kant's division is based on something like different
principles of action (needs, tastes, and dispositions), rather

than different objects of love. One sees in Kant for the first time a concern with the historical evolution of friendship: as a society develops economically, friendships of need become impossible; as it develops morally, particular friendships give way to universal friendship. Although Kant says of a close friendship that "This is the whole end of man, through which he can enjoy his existence," his view seems to be that friendship is something inferior which needs to give way to a higher type of social regard. "Friendship is not of heaven but of the earth," he says, "the complete moral perfection of heaven must be universal; but friendship is not universal."

The lecture is tinged with an evident reserve. Friendship, according to Kant, is "man's refuge in this world from his distrust of his fellows"; however, we are warned that "We must so conduct ourselves towards a friend that there is no harm done if he should turn enemy. We must give him no handle against us." We must especially be on our guard that we "place no weapon in the hands of a hot-headed friend who might be capable of sending us to the gallows in a moment of passion."

Kant

LECTURE ON FRIENDSHIP

Friendship is the hobby-horse of all rhetorical moralists; it is nectar and ambrosia to them.

There are two motives to action in man. The one—self-love—is derived from himself, and the other—the love of humanity—is derived from others and is the moral motive. In man these two motives are in conflict. If the purposes of self-love did not demand our attention, we would love others and promote their happiness. On the other hand, we recognize that acts of self-love have no moral merit, but have at most the sanction of the moral law, while acts prompted by our love of mankind and by our desire to promote the happiness of the human race, are most meritorious. Yet we attach particular importance to whatever promotes the worth of our own person. Here friendship comes in; but how are we to proceed? Are we first, from our self-love, to secure our own happiness, and having done that, look to the happiness of our fellows; or should the happiness of others be our first concern? In the first case we subordinate the happiness of others to our own, the inclination towards our own happiness becomes stronger and stronger, the pursuit of our own happiness has no term, and so care for the happiness of others is altogether suppressed; in the second case, we think of others and our own happiness loses ground in the race. If men, however, were so minded that each one looked to the happiness of others, then the welfare of each would be secured by the efforts of his fellows. If we felt that others would care for our happiness as we for theirs, there would be no reason to fear that we should be left behind. The happiness I gave to another would be returned to me. There would be an exchange of welfare and no one would suffer, for another would look after my happiness as well as I looked after his. It might seem as if I should be the loser by caring for the happiness of others, but if this care were reciprocated, there would be no loss; and the happiness of each would be promoted by the generosity of the others. This is the Idea of friendship, in which self-love is superseded by a generous reciprocity of love.

Let us now examine the other side of the picture. Let us see what would happen if every man concerned himself only with his own happiness and was indifferent to the happiness of others. Everyone is then entitled to care for his own happiness. There is no merit in this, though it has the sanction of the moral rule. Provided that, in furthering my own, I do not hinder my neighbour in his pursuit of happiness, I commit no moral fault, although I achieve no moral merit.

But if I had to choose between friendship and self-love, which should I choose? On moral grounds I should choose friendship, but on practical grounds self-love, for no one could see to my happiness so well as I could myself. In either case, however, my choice would be bad. If I chose only friendship, my happiness would suffer; if I chose only self-love, there would be no moral merit or worth in my choice.

Friendship is an Idea, because it is not derived from experience. Empirical examples of friendship are extremely defective. It has its seat in the understanding. In ethics, however, it is a very necessary Idea. Let us take this opportunity to define the significance of the terms 'an Idea' and 'an Ideal'. We require a standard for measuring degree. The standard may be either natural or arbitrary, according as the quantity is or is not determined by means of concepts a priori. What then is the determinate standard by means of which we measure quantities which are determined a priori? The standard in such cases is the upper limit, the maximum possible. Where this standard is employed as a measure of lesser quantities, it is an Idea; when it is used as a pattern, it is an Ideal. Now if we compare the affectionate inclinations of men, we find that the degrees and proportions in which men distribute their love as between themselves and their fellows vary greatly. The maximum reciprocity of love is friendship, and friendship is an Idea because it is the measure by which we can determine reciprocal love. The greatest love I can have for another is to love him as myself. I cannot love another more than I love myself. But if I am to love him as I love myself I must be sure that he will love me as he loves himself, in which case he restores to me that with which I part and I come back to myself again. This Idea of friendship enables us to measure friendship and to see the extent to which it is defective. When, therefore, Socrates remarks, 'My dear friends, there are no friends', he implies thereby that there is no friendship which fully conforms to the Idea of friendship. And he is right; for any such absolute conformity is impossible; but the Idea is true. Assume that I choose only friendship, and that I care only for my friend's happiness in the hope that he cares only for mine. Our love is mutual; there is complete restoration. I, from generosity, look after his happiness and he similarly looks after mine; I do not throw away my happiness, but surrender it to his keeping, and he in turn surrenders his into my hands; but this Idea is valuable only for reflection; in practical life such things do not occur.

But if every one cared only for himself and never troubled about any one else, there would be no friendship. The two things must, therefore, be combined. Man cares for his own happiness and for that of others also. But as in this matter no limits are fixed and the degrees and proportions cannot be defined, the measure of friendship in the mixture cannot be determined by any law or formula. I am bound to look to my wants and to my satisfaction. If I cannot secure the happiness of my neighbour otherwise than by refraining from satisfying the needs of life, no one can place upon me the obligation of looking to his happiness and showing friendship towards him. But as each of us has his own measure of need and can raise the standard at will, the point at which the satisfaction of needs should give place to friendship is indeterminate. There is no question, however, that many of our needs, or things we have made our needs, are of such a nature that we can well sacrifice them for friendship.

There are three types of friendship, based respectively on need, taste, and disposition.

The friendship of need comes about when men can trust one another in the mutual provision for the needs of life. It was the original form of friendship amongst men, and is encountered mostly in the crudest social conditions. When savages go hunting, each of them has at heart and endeavours to promote the same interests as his colleagues; they are friends. The simpler the needs of a group of men the more frequent is this kind of friendship amongst them; and in proportion as their needs increase the frequency of such friendship diminishes. When the stage of luxury, with its multiplicity of needs, is reached, man has so many of his own affairs to absorb his attention that he has little time to attend to the affairs of others. At that stage, therefore, such friendship does not exist; it is not even wanted; for if one of the participants knows that the other seeks his friendship as a means for satisfying some of his needs, the friendship becomes interested and ceases. In such friendship one of the participants may be active, the other passive; the one may really provide for the needs of the other; where that happens the active friend is generous and the passive friend is the reverse. That being so, no true man will importune a friend with his troubles; he will rather bear them himself than worry his friend with them. If, therefore, the friendship is noble on both sides, neither friend will impose his worries upon the other. Nevertheless, the friendship of need is presupposed in every friendship, not for enjoyment, but for confidence. In every true friend I must have the confidence that he would be competent to care for my affairs and to further my necessities, though I must never demand the proof of my confidence in order to enjoy it. If I know and can assume with confidence that my friend will really help me in need, I have a true friend. But as I am also a true friend of his, I ought not to expect any such thing of him or place him in any quandary; I must have confidence only; rather than make demands, I ought to bear my own troubles; he again must have the same confidence in me, but must also refrain from demanding proof. On the one hand, therefore, friendship presupposes a benevolent disposition and a helping hand in need, and on the other abstention from abusing it by making calls upon it. My friend is magnanimous in being well disposed towards me, wishing me well and being ready to help me in my need; I, again, must be magnanimous in refraining from making demands upon him. Friendship which goes to the length of making good a friend's losses is very rare and is a very delicate and sensitive thing. The reason is that we cannot lay such demands upon another. The finest sweets of friendship are its dispositions of good-will; and on these we must avoid encroaching. The delight of friendship does not consist in the discovery that there is a shilling for me in a stranger's money-box. There is another reason, that it changes the relationship. The relation of friendship is a relation of equality. A friend who bears my losses becomes my benefactor and puts me in his debt. I feel shy in his presence and cannot look him boldly in the face. The true relationship is cancelled and friendship ceases.

The friendship of taste is a pseudo-friendship. It consists in the pleasure we derive from each other's company and not from each other's happiness. Persons of the same station and occupation in life are less likely to form such a friendship than persons of different occupations. One scholar will not form a friendship of taste with another; because their capacities are identical; they cannot entertain or satisfy one another, for what one knows, the other knows too. But a scholar can form such a friendship with a business-man or a soldier. Provided the scholar is not a pedant and the business-man not a blockhead, each of them can talk entertainingly to the other about his own subject. I am not attracted to another because he has what I already possess, but because he can supply some want of mine by supplementing that in which I am lacking. In other words, variety and not uniformity is the source of the friendship of taste.

There remains the third type of friendship, the friendship of disposition or sentiment. There is no question here of any service, or of any demand. The friendship is one of pure, genuine disposition, and is friendship in the absolute sense. There is no proper expression in German for the friendship of sentiment. There are dispositions of the feelings which are not dispositions to actual service; on these the friendship of sentiment is based. The point of special importance is this. In ordinary social intercourse and association we do not enter completely into the social relation. The greater part of our disposition is withheld; there is no immediate outpouring of all our feelings, dispositions and judgments. We voice only the judgments that seem advisable in the circumstances. A constraint, a mistrust of others, rests upon all of us, so that we withhold something, concealing our weaknesses to escape contempt, or even withholding our opinions. But if we can free ourselves of this constraint, if we can unburden our heart to another, we achieve complete communion. That this release may be achieved, each of us needs a friend, one in whom we can confide unreservedly, to whom we can disclose completely all our dispositions and judgments, from whom we can and need hide nothing, to whom we can communicate our whole self. On this rests the friendship of dispositions and fellowship. It can exist only between two or three friends. We all have a strong impulse to disclose ourselves, and enter wholly into fellowship; and such self-revelation is further a human necessity for the correction of our judgments. To have a friend whom we know to be frank and loving, neither false nor spiteful, is to have one who will help us to correct our judgment when it is mistaken. This is the whole end of man, through which he can enjoy his existence. But even between the closest and most intimate of friends there are still some things which call for reserve, for the other's sake more than for one's own. There can be perfect and complete intimacy only in matters of disposition and sentiment, but we have certain natural frailties which ought to be concealed for the sake of decency, lest humanity be outraged. Even to our best friend we must not reveal ourselves, in our natural state as we know it ourselves. To do so would be loathsome.

To what extent do we make things better for ourselves by making friends? It is not man's way to embrace the whole world in his good-will; he prefers to restrict it to a small circle. He is inclined to form sects, parties, societies. The most primitive societies are those based on family connexion, and there are men who move only in the family circle. Then there are religious sects. These also are societies, associations formed by men for the cultivation of their common religious views and sentiments. This is on the face of it a laudable purpose, but it tends to harden the heart against and to ostracize those who stand outside the pale of the particular sect; and any tendency to close the heart to all but a selected few is detrimental to true spiritual goodness, which reaches out after a good-will of universal scope. Friendship, likewise, is an aid in overcoming the constraint and the distrust man feels in his intercourse with others, by revealing himself to them without reserve. In this form of association also we must guard against shutting out from our heart all who are not within the charmed circle. Friendship is not of heaven but of the earth; the complete moral perfection of heaven must be universal; but friendship is not universal; it is a peculiar association of specific persons; it is man's refuge in this world from his distrust of his fellows, in which he can reveal his disposition to another and enter into communion with him.

If men complain of the lack of friendship, it is because they themselves have no friendly disposition and no friendly heart. They accuse others of being unfriendly, but it is they themselves who, by demands and importunities, turn their friends from them. We shun those who, under the cloak of friendship, make a convenience of us. But to make a general complaint about the lack of friends is like making a general complaint about the lack of money. The more civilized man becomes, the broader his outlook and the less room there is for special friendships; civilized man seeks universal pleasures and a universal friendship, unrestricted by special ties; the savage picks and chooses according to his taste and disposition, for the more primitive the social culture the more necessary such associations are. But such friendship presupposes weaknesses on both sides; it presupposes that neither party should be open to reproach by the other. If each has something to condone in the other, and neither need reproach himself, then there is equality between them, and neither can assert a superiority.

What then is that adaptation of man to man that constitutes the bond of friendship? Not an identity of thought; on the contrary, difference in thought is a stronger foundation for friendship, for then the one makes up the deficiencies of the other. Yet on one point they must agree. Their intellectual and moral principles must be the same, if there is to be complete understanding between them. Otherwise, there will always be discrepancy in their decisions and they will never agree. Every one seeks to deserve friendship. Uprightness of disposition, sincerity, trustworthiness, conduct devoid of all falsehood and spite, and a sweet, cheerful and happy temper, these are the elements which make up the character of a perfect friend; and once we have made ourselves fit objects of friendship we may be sure that we shall find some one who will take a liking to us and choose us for a friend, and that on closer contact our friendship will grow and become more and more intimate.

But as men are not transparent to each other, it may be that we fail to find what we imputed to our friend and sought in him. So friendships may come to an end. In friendships of taste the relationship loses its basis when with the process of time taste changes and finds new objects, and so a new friend supplants the old. The friendship of disposition is rare because men seldom have principles. Friends drift apart because there was no friendship of disposition between them.

The friendship of disposition calls for the following remarks. The name of friendship should inspire respect; and if by any chance a friend should turn into an enemy, we must still reverence the old friendship and never show that we are capable of hate. To speak ill of our friends is not merely wrong in itself, because it proves that we have no respect for friendship, that we have chosen our friends badly and that we are ungrateful to them; it is also wrong because it is contrary to the rule of prudence; for it leads those who hear us to wonder whether, if ever they became our friends and we subsequently became estranged, they would not be spoken of in the same strain, and so they turn from our friendship. We must so conduct ourselves towards a friend that there is no harm done if he should turn into an enemy. We must give him no handle against us. We ought not, of course, to assume the possibility of his becoming an enemy; any such assumption would destroy confidence between us; but it is very unwise to place ourselves in a friend's hands completely, to tell him all the secrets which might detract from our welfare if he became our enemy and spread them abroad; it is imprudent not only because he might thereby do us an injury if he became an enemy, but also because he might fail to keep our secrets through inadvertence. In particular, we ought to place no weapon in the hands of a hot-headed friend who might be capable of sending us to the gallows in a moment of passion, though he would implore our pardon as soon as he had cooled down.

Is every man a possible friend for us? No. I can be a friend of mankind in general in the sense that I can bear good-will in my heart towards everyone, but to be the friend of everybody is impossible, for friendship is a particular relationship, and he who is a friend to everyone has no particular friend. And yet there are men of the world whose capacity to form friendships with anyone might well earn them the title of everybody's friends. Such citizens are very rare. They are men of a kindly disposition, who are always prepared to look on the best side of things. The combination of such goodness of heart with taste and understanding characterizes the friend of all men, and in itself constitutes a high degree of perfection. But as a rule, men are inclined to form particular relationships because this is a natural impulse and also because we all start with the particular and then proceed to the general. A man without a friend is isolated. Friendship develops the minor virtues of life.

Emerson

FRIENDSHIP

Introduction

Ralph Waldo Emerson published his first series of *Essays* in 1841, nine years after he resigned as pastor of the Second Church in Boston. His sermons were laced with philosophical ideas he had developed through reading Kant, Fichte, and Schelling, as well as Goethe, Wordsworth, and Coleridge. His *Essays* are philosophical sermons, designed to provoke self-examination, which inspire and exhort to a higher ideal.

The rehabilitation, or perhaps discovery, of Emerson as a philosopher—which has been so ably undertaken recently by Stanley Cavell[1]—might have been less necessary had Emerson written books of aphorisms, more or less loosely arranged, as did Nietzsche and Wittgenstein, for then it would be clearer what demands are placed on the reader. The essay form, and Emerson's masterful prose, make it seem that an argument lies on the surface, and when we do not find it, we conclude that the work has little philosophical significance.

Many of Emerson's *Essays* are written from his journals and refined in his correspondence. The essay "Friendship" seems, in fact, to have been composed by Emerson's reflecting on his own intimate friendships with Margaret Fuller, Caroline Sturgis, and Samuel Grey Ward. Whereas Cicero merely dedicated his dialogue on friendship to a friend, Emerson wrote his essay through writing to friends about his friendships with them.

Emerson understood "Friendship" to be literally an *essay*, an experiment. The experiment has, as its structure, the characteristic themes of "New England Transcendentalism": that the

1. See the bibliography under the heading "Emerson".

218

Divine is present in all, and especially in human beings; that nature is a symbol; that the world is passing away and intimates a higher reality; that mediation, tradition, conformity, and imitation ought to be cast aside as deceptions. But its aim is to search out and uncover the cant, self-deception, softness, and infirmity which, when acquiesced in, hinders us from seeking that "select and sacred relation which is a kind of absolute."

This absolute, for Emerson, is common and ordinary: "The end of friendship is a commerce the most strict and homely that can be joined." Montaigne's ideal of friendship was rare and incommunicable; Kant's was in principle unattainable. Emerson "cannot forgive the poet if he spins his thread too fine." The elements of friendship can be found among "plough-boys and tin-peddlars." And friendship is to be pursued, not so much by starting something new, as by receiving what one has already been given with a detached and patient reverence.

Emerson seems to hold that we can escape solipsism only by practicing sincerity with a friend: "I who alone am, I who see nothing in nature whose existence I can affirm with equal evidence to my own, behold now the semblance of my being, in all its height, variety, and curiosity, reiterated in a foreign form." And this seems to be the source of the characteristic delight of friendship: the joy that "the *not mine* is *mine*."

Emerson

FRIENDSHIP

We have a great deal more kindness than is ever spoken. Maugre all the selfishness that chills like east winds the world, the whole human family is bathed with an element of love like a fine ether. How many persons we meet in houses, whom we scarcely speak to, whom yet we honor, and who honor us! How many we see in the street, or sit with in church, whom, though silently, we warmly rejoice to be with! Read the language of these wandering eye-beams. The heart knoweth.

The effect of the indulgence of this human affection is a certain cordial exhilaration. In poetry and in common speech the emotions of benevolence and complacency which are felt towards others are likened to the material effects of fire; so swift, or much more swift, more active, more cheering, are these fine inward irradiations. From the highest degree of passionate love to the lowest degree of good-will, they make the sweetness of life.

Our intellectual and active powers increase with our affection. The scholar sits down to write, and all his years of meditation do not furnish him with one good thought or happy expression; but it is necessary to write a letter to a friend,—and forthwith troops of gentle thoughts invest themselves, on every hand, with chosen words. See, in any house where virtue and self-respect abide, the palpitation which the approach of a stranger causes. A commended stranger is expected and announced, and an uneasiness betwixt pleasure and pain invades all the hearts of a household. His arrival almost brings fear to the good hearts that would welcome him. The house is dusted, all things fly into their places, the old coat is exchanged for the new, and they must get up a dinner if they can. Of a commended stranger, only the good report is told by others, only the good and new is heard by us. He stands to us for humanity. He is what we wish. Having imagined and invested him, we ask how we should stand related in conversation and action with such a man, and are uneasy with

fear. The same idea exalts conversation with him. We talk better
than we are wont. We have the nimblest fancy, a richer memory,
and our dumb devil has taken leave for the time. For long hours
we can continue a series of sincere, graceful, rich communications, drawn from the oldest, secretest experience, so that they
who sit by, of our own kinsfolk and acquaintance, shall feel a
lively surprise at our unusual powers. But as soon as the stranger
begins to intrude his partialities, his definitions, his defects into
the conversation, it is all over. He has heard the first, the last
and best he will ever hear from us. He is no stranger now.
Vulgarity, ignorance, misapprehension are old acquaintances.
Now, when he comes, he may get the order, the dress and the
dinner,—but the throbbing of the heart and the communications
of the soul, no more.

What is so pleasant as these jets of affection which make a
young world for me again? What so delicious as a just and firm
encounter of two, in a thought, in a feeling? How beautiful, on
their approach to this beating heart, the steps and forms of the
gifted and the true! The moment we indulge our affections, the
earth is metamorphosed; there is no winter and no night; all
tragedies, all ennuis vanish,—all duties even; nothing fills the
proceeding eternity but the forms all radiant of beloved persons.
Let the soul be assured that somewhere in the universe it should
rejoin its friend, and it would be content and cheerful alone for
a thousand years.

I awoke this morning with devout thanksgiving for my friends,
the old and the new. Shall I not call God the Beautiful, who daily
showeth himself so to me in his gifts? I chide society, I embrace
solitude, and yet I am not so ungrateful as not to see the wise,
the lovely and the noble-minded, as from time to time they pass
my gate. Who hears me, who understands me, becomes mine,—
a possession for all time. Nor is Nature so poor but she gives me
this joy several times, and thus we weave social threads of our
own, a new web of relations; and, as many thoughts in succes-
sion substantiate themselves, we shall by and by stand in a new
world of our own creation, and no longer strangers and pilgrims
in a traditionary globe. My friends have come to me unsought.
The great God gave them to me. By oldest right, by the divine
affinity of virtue with itself, I find them, or rather not I, but the
Deity in me and in them derides and cancels the thick walls of
individual character, relation, age, sex, circumstance, at which

he usually connives, and now makes many one. High thanks I owe you, excellent lovers, who carry out the world for me to new and noble depths, and enlarge the meaning of all my thoughts. These are new poetry of the first Bard,—poetry without stop,—hymn, ode and epic, poetry still flowing, Apollo and the Muses chanting still. Will these too separate themselves from me again, or some of them? I know not, but I fear it not; for my relation to them is so pure that we hold by simple affinity, and the Genius of my life being thus social, the same affinity will exert its energy on whomsoever is as noble as these men and women, wherever I may be.

I confess to an extreme tenderness of nature on this point. It is almost dangerous to me to "crush the sweet poison of misused wine" of the affections. A new person is to me a great event and hinders me from sleep. I have often had fine fancies about persons which have given me delicious hours; but the joy ends in the day; it yields no fruit. Thought is not born of it; my action is very little modified. I must feel pride in my friend's accomplishments as if they were mine, and a property in his virtues. I feel as warmly when he is praised, as the lover when he hears applause of his engaged maiden. We over-estimate the conscience of our friend. His goodness seems better than our goodness, his nature finer, his temptations less. Every thing that is his,—his name, his form, his dress, books and instruments,—fancy enhances. Our own thought sounds new and larger from his mouth.

Yet the systole and diastole of the heart are not without their analogy in the ebb and flow of love. Friendship, like the immortality of the soul, is too good to be believed. The lover, beholding his maiden, half knows that she is not verily that which he worships; and in the golden hour of friendship we are surprised with shades of suspicion and unbelief. We doubt that we bestow on our hero the virtues in which he shines, and afterwards worship the form to which we have ascribed this divine inhabitation. In strictness, the soul does not respect men as it respects itself. In strict science all persons underlie the same condition of an infinite remoteness. Shall we fear to cool our love by mining for the metaphysical foundation of this Elysian temple? Shall I not be as real as the things I see? If I am, I shall not fear to know them for what they are. Their essence is not less beautiful than their appearance, though it needs finer organs for its apprehension. The root of the plant is not unsightly to science, though for chaplets and festoons we cut the stem short. And I must hazard the production of the bald fact amidst these pleasing reveries, though it should prove an Egyptian skull at our banquet. A man who stands united with his thought conceives magnificently of himself. He is conscious of a universal success, even though bought by uniform particular failures. No advantages, no powers, no gold or force, can be any match for him. I cannot choose but rely on my own poverty more than on your wealth. I cannot make your consciousness tantamount to mine. Only the star dazzles; the planet has a faint, moonlike ray. I hear what you say of the admirable parts and tried temper of the party you praise, but I see well that, for all his purple cloaks, I shall not like him, unless he is at least a poor Greek like me. I cannot deny it, O friend, that the vast shadow of the Phenomenal includes thee also in its pied and painted immensity,—thee also, compared with whom all else is shadow. Thou art not Being, as Truth is, as Justice is,—thou art not my soul, but a picture and effigy of that. Thou hast come to me lately, and already thou art seizing thy hat and cloak. Is it not that the soul puts forth friends as the tree puts forth leaves, and presently, by the germination of new buds, extrudes the old leaf? The law of nature is alternation for evermore. Each electrical state superinduces the opposite. The soul environs itself with friends that it may enter into a grander self-acquaintance or solitude; and it goes alone for a season that it may exalt its conversation or society. This method betrays itself along the whole history of our personal relations. The instinct of affection revives the hope of union with our mates, and the returning sense of insulation recalls us from the chase. Thus every man passes his life in the search after friendship, and if he should record his true sentiment, he might write a letter like this to each new candidate for his love:—

DEAR FRIEND,

If I was sure of thee, sure of thy capacity, sure to match my mood with thine, I should never think again of trifles in relation to thy comings and goings. I am not very wise; my moods are quite attainable, and I respect thy genius; it is to me as yet unfathomed; yet dare I not presume in thee a perfect intelligence of me, and so thou art to me a delicious torment. Thine ever, or never.

Yet these uneasy pleasures and fine pains are for curiosity and not for life. They are not to be indulged. This is to weave cobweb, and not cloth. Our friendships hurry to short and poor conclusions, because we have made them a texture of wine and dreams, instead of the tough fibre of the human heart. The laws of friendship are austere and eternal, of one web with the laws of nature and of morals. But we have aimed at a swift and petty benefit, to suck a sudden sweetness. We snatch at the slowest fruit in the whole garden of God, which many summers and many winters must ripen. We seek our friend not sacredly, but with an adulterate passion which would appropriate him to ourselves. In vain. We are armed all over with subtle antagonisms, which, as soon as we meet, begin to play, and translate all poetry into stale prose. Almost all people descend to meet. All association must be a compromise, and, what is worst, the very flower and aroma of the flower of each of the beautiful natures disappears as they approach each other. What a perpetual disappointment is actual society, even of the virtuous and gifted! After interviews have been compassed with long foresight we must be tormented presently by baffled blows, by sudden, unseasonable apathies, by epilepsies of wit and of animal spirits, in the heyday of friendship and thought. Our faculties do not play us true, and both parties are relieved by solitude.

I ought to be equal to every relation. It makes no difference how many friends I have and what content I can find in conversing with each, if there be one to whom I am not equal. If I have shrunk unequal from one contest, the joy I find in all the rest becomes mean and cowardly. I should hate myself, if then I made my other friends my asylum:—

> "The valiant warrior famousèd for fight,
> After a hundred victories, once foiled,
> Is from the book of honor razèd quite
> And all the rest forgot for which he toiled."

Our impatience is thus sharply rebuked. Bashfulness and apathy are a tough husk in which a delicate organization is protected from premature ripening. It would be lost if it knew itself before any of the best souls were yet ripe enough to know and own it. Respect the *naturlangsamkeit* which hardens the ruby in a million years, and works in duration in which Alps and Andes come and go as rainbows. The good spirit of our life has no heaven which is the price of rashness. Love, which is the essence of God, is not for levity, but for the total worth of man. Let us not have this childish luxury in our regards, but the austerest worth; let us approach our friend with an audacious trust in the truth of his heart, in the breadth, impossible to be overturned, of his foundations.

The attractions of this subject are not to be resisted, and I leave, for the time, all account of subordinate social benefit, to speak of that select and sacred relation which is a kind of absolute, and which even leaves the language of love suspicious and common, so much is this purer, and nothing is so much divine.

I do not wish to treat friendships daintily, but with roughest courage. When they are real, they are not glass threads or frostwork, but the solidest thing we know. For now, after so many ages of experience, what do we know of nature or of ourselves? Not one step has man taken toward the solution of the problem of his destiny. In one condemnation of folly stand the whole universe of men. But the sweet sincerity of joy and peace which I draw from this alliance with my brother's soul is the nut itself whereof all nature and all thought is but the husk and shell. Happy is the house that shelters a friend! It might well be built, like a festal bower or arch, to entertain him a single day. Happier, if he know the solemnity of that relation and honor its law! He who offers himself a candidate for that covenant comes up, like an Olympian, to the great games where the first-born of the world are the competitors. He proposes himself for contests where Time, Want, Danger, are in the lists, and he alone is victor who has truth enough in his constitution to preserve the delicacy of his beauty from the wear and tear of all these. The gifts of fortune may be present or absent, but all the speed in that contest depends on intrinsic nobleness and the contempt of trifles. There are two elements that go to the composition of friendship, each so sovereign that I can detect no superiority in either, no reason why either should be first named. One is truth. A friend is a person with whom I may be sincere. Before him I may think aloud. I am arrived at last in the presence of a man so real and equal that I may drop even those undermost garments of dissimulation, courtesy, and second thought, which men never put off, and may deal with him with the simplicity and wholeness with which one chemical atom meets another. Sincerity is the luxury allowed, like diadems and authority, only to the highest rank; *that* being permitted to speak truth, as having none above it to court or conform unto. Every man alone is sincere. At the entrance of a second person, hypocrisy begins. We parry and fend the approach of our fellow-man by compliments, by gossip, by amusements, by affairs. We cover up our thought from him under a hundred folds. I knew a man who under a certain religious frenzy cast off this drapery, and omitting all compliment and commonplace, spoke to the conscience of every person he encountered, and that with great insight and beauty. At first he was resisted, and all men agreed he was mad. But persisting— as indeed he could not help doing—for some time in this course, he attained to the advantage of bringing every man of his ac- quaintance into true relations with him. No man would think of speaking falsely with him, or of putting him off with any chat of markets or reading-rooms. But every man was constrained by so much sincerity to the like plaindealing, and what love of nature, what poetry, what symbol of truth he had, he did certainly show him. But to most of us society shows not its face and eye, but its side and its back. To stand in true relations with men in a false age is worth a fit of insanity, is it not? We can seldom go erect. Almost every man we meet requires some civility—requires to be humored; he has some fame, some talent, some whim of religion or philanthropy in his head that is not to be questioned, and which spoils all conversation with him. But a friend is a sane man who exercises not my ingenuity, but me. My friend gives me entertainment without requiring any stipulation on my part. A friend therefore is a sort of paradox in nature. I who alone am, I who see nothing in nature whose existence I can affirm with equal evidence to my own, behold now the semblance of my being, in all its height, variety and curiosity, reiterated in a foreign form; so that a friend may well be reckoned the master- piece of nature.

The other element of friendship is tenderness. We are holden to men by every sort of tie, by blood, by pride, by fear, by hope, by lucre, by lust, by hate, by admiration, by every circumstance and badge and trifle,—but we can scarce believe that so much character can subsist in another as to draw us by love. Can another be so blessed and we so pure that we can offer him tenderness? When a man becomes dear to me I have touched the goal of fortune. I find very little written directly to the heart of this matter in books. And yet I have one text which I cannot

choose but remember. My author says,—"I offer myself faintly
and bluntly to those whose I effectually am, and tender myself
least to him to whom I am the most devoted." I wish that friendship should have feet, as well as eyes and eloquence. It must
plant itself on the ground, before it vaults over the moon. I wish
it to be a little of a citizen, before it is quite a cherub. We chide
the citizen because he makes love a commodity. It is an exchange
of gifts, of useful loans; it is good neighborhood; it watches with
the sick; it holds the pall at the funeral; and quite loses sight of
the delicacies and nobility of the relation. But though we cannot
find the god under this disguise of a sutler, yet on the other hand
we cannot forgive the poet if he spins his thread too fine and
does not substantiate his romance by the municipal virtues of
justice, punctuality, fidelity and pity. I hate the prostitution of
the name of friendship to signify modish and worldly alliances.
I much prefer the company of ploughboys and tin-peddlers to
the silken and perfumed amity which celebrates its days of encounter by a frivolous display, by rides in a curricle and dinners
at the best taverns. The end of friendship is a commerce the most
strict and homely that can be joined; more strict than any of
which we have experience. It is for aid and comfort through all
the relations and passages of life and death. It is fit for serene
days and graceful gifts and country rambles, but also for rough
roads and hard fare, shipwreck, poverty and persecution. It
keeps company with the sallies of the wit and the trances of
religion. We are to dignify to each other the daily needs and
offices of man's life, and embellish it by courage, wisdom and
unity. It should never fall into something usual and settled, but
should be alert and inventive and add rhyme and reason to what
was drudgery.

Friendship may be said to require natures so rare and costly,
each so well tempered and so happily adapted, and withal so
circumstanced (for even in that particular, a poet says, love demands that the parties be altogether paired), that its satisfaction
can very seldom be assured. It cannot subsist in its perfection,
say some of those who are learned in this warm lore of the heart,
betwixt more than two. I am not quite so strict in my terms,
perhaps because I have never known so high a fellowship as
others. I please my imagination more with a circle of god-like
men and women variously related to each other and between
whom subsists a lofty intelligence. But I find this law of *one*

to one peremptory for conversation, which is the practice and consummation of friendship. Do not mix waters too much. The best mix as ill as good and bad. You shall have very useful and cheering discourse at several times with two several men, but let all three of you come together and you shall not have one new and hearty word. Two may talk and one may hear, but three cannot take part in a conversation of the most sincere and searching sort. In good company there is never such discourse between two, across the table, as takes place when you leave them alone. In good company the individuals merge their egotism into a social soul exactly co-extensive with the several consciousnesses there present. No partialities of friend to friend, no fondnesses of brother to sister, of wife to husband, are there pertinent, but quite otherwise. Only he may then speak who can sail on the common thought of the party, and not poorly limited to his own. Now this convention, which good sense demands, destroys the high freedom of great conversation, which requires an absolute running of two souls into one.

No two men but being left alone with each other enter into simpler relations. Yet it is affinity that determines *which* two shall converse. Unrelated men give little joy to each other, will never suspect the latent powers of each. We talk sometimes of a great talent for conversation, as if it were a permanent property in some individuals. Conversation is an evanescent relation,—no more. A man is reputed to have thought and eloquence; he cannot, for all that, say a word to his cousin or his uncle. They accuse his silence with as much reason as they would blame the insignificance of a dial in the shade. In the sun it will mark the hour. Among those who enjoy his thought he will regain his tongue.

Friendship requires that rare mean betwixt likeness and un-likeness that piques each with the presence of power and of consent in the other party. Let me be alone to the end of the world, rather than that my friend should overstep, by a word or a look, his real sympathy. I am equally balked by antagonism and by compliance. Let him not cease an instant to be himself. The only joy I have in his being mine, is that the *not mine* is *mine.* I hate, where I looked for a manly furtherance or at least a manly resistance, to find a mush of concession. Better be a nettle in the side of your friend than his echo. The condition which high friendship demands is ability to do without it. That high office requires great and sublime parts. There must be very two, before there can be very one. Let it be an alliance of two large, formidable natures, mutually beheld, mutually feared, before yet they recognize the deep identity which, beneath these disparities, unites them.

He only is fit for this society who is magnanimous; who is sure that greatness and goodness are always economy; who is not swift to intermeddle with his fortunes. Let him not intermeddle with this. Leave to the diamond its ages to grow, nor expect to accelerate the births of the eternal. Friendship demands a religious treatment. We talk of choosing our friends, but friends are self-elected. Reverence is a great part of it. Treat your friend as a spectacle. Of course he has merits that are not yours, and that you cannot honor if you must needs hold him close to your person. Stand aside; give those merits room; let them mount and expand. Are you the friend of your friend's buttons, or of his thought? To a great heart he will still be a stranger in a thousand particulars, that he may come near in the holiest ground. Leave it to girls and boys to regard a friend as property, and to suck a short and all–confounding pleasure, instead of the noblest benefit.

Let us buy our entrance to this guild by a long probation. Why should we desecrate noble and beautiful souls by intruding on them? Why insist on rash personal relations with your friend? Why go to his house, or know his mother and brother and sisters? Why be visited by him at your own? Are these things material to our covenant? Leave this touching and clawing. Let him be to me a spirit. A message, a thought, a sincerity, a glance from him, I want, but not news, nor pottage. I can get politics and chat and neighborly conveniences from cheaper companions. Should not the society of my friend be to me poetic, pure, universal and great as nature itself? Ought I to feel that our tie is profane in comparison with yonder bar of cloud that sleeps on the horizon, or that clump of waving grass that divides the brook? Let us not vilify, but raise it to that standard. That great defying eye, that scornful beauty of his mien and action, do not pique yourself on reducing, but rather fortify and enhance. Worship his superiorities; wish him not less by a thought, but hoard and tell them all. Guard him as thy counterpart. Let him be to thee for ever a sort of beautiful enemy, untamable, devoutly revered, and not a trivial conveniency to be soon outgrown and cast aside. The hues of the opal, the light of the diamond, are not to be seen if the eye is too near. To my friend I write a letter and from him I receive a letter. That seems to you a little. It suffices me. It is a spiritual gift, worthy of him to give and of me to receive. It profanes nobody. In these warm lines the heart will trust itself, as it will not to the tongue, and pour out the prophecy of a godlier existence than all the annals of heroism have yet made good.

Respect so far the holy laws of this fellowship as not to prejudice its perfect flower by your impatience for its opening. We must be our own before we can be another's. There is at least this satisfaction in crime, according to the Latin proverb;—you can speak to your accomplice on even terms. *Crimen quos inquinat, æquat.* To those whom we admire and love, at first we cannot. Yet the least defect of self-possession vitiates, in my judgment, the entire relation. There can never be deep peace between two spirits, never mutual respect, until in their dialogue each stands for the whole world.

What is so great as friendship, let us carry with what grandeur of spirit we can. Let us be silent,—so we may hear the whisper of the gods. Let us not interfere. Who set you to cast about what you should say to the select souls, or how to say any thing to such? No matter how ingenious, no matter how graceful and bland. There are innumerable degrees of folly and wisdom, and for you to say aught is to be frivolous. Wait, and thy heart shall speak. Wait until the necessary and everlasting overpowers you, until day and night avail themselves of your lips. The only reward of virtue is virtue; the only way to have a friend is to be one. You shall not come nearer a man by getting into his house. If unlike, his soul only flees the faster from you, and you shall never catch a true glance of his eye. We see the noble afar off and they repel us; why should we intrude? Late,—very late,—we perceive that no arrangements, no introductions, no consuetudes or habits of society would be of any avail to establish us in such relations with them as we desire,—but solely the uprise of nature in us to the same degree it is in them; then shall we meet as water with water; and if we should not meet them then, we shall not want them, for we are already they. In the last analysis, love is only the reflection of a man's own worthiness from other men. Men have sometimes exchanged names with their friends, as if they would signify that in their friend each loved his own soul.

The higher the style we demand of friendship, of course the less easy to establish it with flesh and blood. We walk alone in the world. Friends such as we desire are dreams and fables. But a sublime hope cheers ever the faithful heart, that elsewhere, in other regions of the universal power, souls are now acting, enduring and daring, which can love us and which we can love. We may congratulate ourselves that the period of nonage, of follies, of blunders and of shame, is passed in solitude, and when we are finished men we shall grasp heroic hands in heroic hands. Only be admonished by what you already see, not to strike leagues of friendship with cheap persons, where no friendship can be. Our impatience betrays us into rash and foolish alliances which no god attends. By persisting in your path, though you forfeit the little you gain the great. You demonstrate yourself, so as to put yourself out of the reach of false relations, and you draw to you the first-born of the world,—those rare pilgrims whereof only one or two wander in nature at once, and before whom the vulgar great show as spectres and shadows merely.

It is foolish to be afraid of making our ties too spiritual, as if so we could lose any genuine love. Whatever correction of our popular views we make from insight, nature will be sure to bear us out in, and though it seem to rob us of some joy, will repay us with a greater. Let us feel if we will the absolute insulation of man. We are sure that we have all in us. We go to Europe, or we pursue persons, or we read books, in the instinctive faith that these will call it out and reveal us to ourselves. Beggars all. The persons are such as we; the Europe, an old faded garment of dead persons; the books, their ghosts. Let us drop this idolatry. Let us give over this mendicancy. Let us even bid our dearest friends farewell, and defy them, saying 'Who are you? Unhand me: I will be dependent no more.' Ah! seest thou not, O brother, that thus we part only to meet again on a higher platform, and only be more each other's because we are more our own? A friend is Janus-faced; he looks to the past and the future. He is the child of all my foregoing hours, the prophet of those to come, and the harbinger of a greater friend.

I do then with my friends as I do with my books. I would have them where I can find them, but I seldom use them. We must have society on our own terms, and admit or exclude it on the slightest cause. I cannot afford to speak much with my friend. If he is great he makes me so great that I cannot descend to converse. In the great days, presentiments hover before me in the firmament. I ought then to dedicate myself to them. I go in that I may seize them, I go out that I may seize them. I fear only that I may lose them receding into the sky in which now they are only a patch of brighter light. Then, though I prize my friends, I cannot afford to talk with them and study their visions, lest I lose my own. It would indeed give me a certain household joy to quit this lofty seeking, this spiritual astronomy or search of stars, and come down to warm sympathies with you; but then I know well I shall mourn always the vanishing of my mighty gods. It is true, next week I shall have languid moods, when I can well afford to occupy myself with foreign objects; then I shall regret the lost literature of your mind, and wish you were by my side again. But if you come, perhaps you will fill my mind only with new visions; not with yourself but with your lustres, and I shall not be able any more than now to converse with you. So I will owe to my friends this evanescent intercourse. I will receive from them not what they have but what they are. They shall give me that which properly they cannot give, but which emanates from them. But they shall not hold me by any relations less subtile and pure. We will meet as though we met not, and part as though we parted not.

It has seemed to me lately more possible than I knew, to carry a friendship greatly, on one side, without due correspondence on the other. Why should I cumber myself with regrets that the receiver is not capacious? It never troubles the sun that some of his rays fall wide and vain into ungrateful space, and only a small part on the reflecting planet. Let your greatness educate the crude and cold companion. If he is unequal, he will presently pass away; but thou art enlarged by thy own shining, and no longer a mate for frogs and worms, dost soar and burn with the gods of the empyrean. It is thought a disgrace to love unrequited. But the great will see that true love cannot be unrequited. True love transcends the unworthy object and dwells and broods on the eternal, and when the poor interposed mask crumbles, it is not sad, but feels rid of so much earth and feels its independency the surer. Yet these things may hardly be said without a sort of treachery to the relation. The essence of friendship is entireness, a total magnanimity and trust. It must not surmise or provide for infirmity. It treats its object as a god, that it may deify both.

Kierkegaard

YOU SHALL LOVE YOUR *NEIGHBOUR*

Introduction

Søren Kierkegaard's aim in the following selection from his *Works of Love* is to present the reader with a choice. The choice is between "poetic love"—erotic love and friendship—and "love of neighbour". The former is a love of mood and inclination; the latter is spiritual. The former is partial and transient; the latter makes no distinctions and is eternal. In friendship we love the "other *self*"; in love of neighbor we love the "other *you*".

Aristotle had characterized close friendship as a kind of excess of affection (1158a11–14; 1171a8–14); Kierkegaard claims that excess is characteristic of *all* friendship. "All passion," he says, "whether it attacks or defends itself, fights in one manner only: either—or: 'Either I exist and am the highest or I do not exist at all—either all or nothing.' " Hence the pure form of friendship is shown towards one other person only; any friendship that reaches out to many is a confusion. On the other hand, love of neighbor extends to all without distinction. Thus the choice presented to us is between *love of one and only one* and *love of all*.

Once Kierkegaard has isolated friendship in its pure form, he goes on to argue that it is essentially selfishness: "Self-love and passionate preferences are essentially the same." He argues for this by pointing to various characteristics of friendship that indicate that it is nothing other than selfishness: the friend is another *self*; friendship "self-ignites" just as self-love does; jealousy is always fundamentally present in friendship; friendship requires reciprocity, which is to say, love returned

233

to the *self*; friendship presupposes that we admire the other, but this implies that we love *ourselves* for correctly admiring someone so admirable; and friendship is willful and hence selfish because it is arbitrary and not under a law. Kierkegaard suggests that, rather than being a remedy for self-love, friendship can even stimulate selfishness by giving clarity and definition to a previously inchoate self-love.

Kierkegaard's critique of friendship as selfishness is especially powerful because he presents what appears to be a practicable and inspiring alternative to friendship, which nevertheless preserves many features usually attributed to friendship. For example, friends are said to be equals, but Kierkegaard argues that you cannot truly regard another as an equal unless you love him in just the same way as you love everyone else. Again, a friend is supposedly another self, but in fact someone who is merely a friend is not yet truly a self: "Only in love to one's neighbour is the self, which loves, spiritually qualified simply as spirit and his neighbour as purely spiritual."

Kierkegaard

YOU SHALL LOVE
YOUR *NEIGHBOUR*
II B

The objection is often made against Christianity—though in different manners and moods, with various passions and purposes—that it displaces erotic love and friendship. Then, again, men have wanted to defend Christianity and to that end appealed to its doctrine that one ought to love God with his whole heart and his neighbour as himself. When the argument is carried on in this manner, it is quite indifferent whether one agrees or disagrees, just as a fight with air and an agreement with air are equally meaningless. One should rather take pains to clarify the point of contention in order calmly to admit in the defence that Christianity has thrust erotic love and friendship from the throne, the love rooted in mood and inclination, preferential love, in order to establish spiritual love in its place, love to one's neighbour, a love which in all earnestness and truth is inwardly more tender in the union of two persons than erotic love is and more faithful in the sincerity of close relationship than the most famous friendship. One must rather take pains to make very clear that the praise of erotic love and friendship belong to paganism, that the *poet* really belongs to paganism since his task belongs to it—in order with the sure spirit of conviction to give to Christianity what belongs to Christianity, love to one's neighbour, of which love not a trace is found in paganism. One must rather take care to discern and divide rightly, in order, if possible, to occasion the individual to choose, instead of confusing and combining and thereby hindering the individual from getting a definite impression of which is which. Above all, one must refrain from defending Christianity, rather than consciously or unconsciously wanting to uphold everything—also what is non-Christian.

Everyone who earnestly and with insight thinks on these things will easily see that the question for discussion must be posed in this way: are erotic love and friendship the highest love or must this love be dethroned? Erotic love and friendship are related to passion, but all passion, whether it attacks or defends itself, fights in one manner only: either—or: "Either I exist and am the highest or I do not exist at all—either all or nothing." Confusion and bewilderment (which paganism and the poet are opposed to just as much as Christianity is) develops when the defence amounts to this—that Christianity certainly teaches a higher love but *in addition* praises friendship and erotic love. To talk thus is a double betrayal—inasmuch as the speaker has neither the spirit of the poet nor the spirit of Christianity. Concerning relationships of the spirit, one cannot—if one wants to avoid talking foolishly—talk like a shopkeeper who has the best grade of goods and in addition a medium grade, which he can *also* highly recommend as being almost as good. No, if it is certain that Christianity teaches that love to God and one's neighbour is true love, then it is also certain that as it has thrust down "every proud obstacle to the knowledge of God and takes every thought captive to obey Christ"—that it likewise has also thrust down erotic love and friendship. Would it not be remarkable—if Christianity were such a confusing and bewildering subject as many a defence (often worse than any attack) would make it into—would it not be remarkable, then, that in the whole New Testament there is not found a word about love in the sense in which the poet sings of it and paganism defined it; would it not be remarkable that in the whole New Testament there is not found a single word about friendship in the sense in which the poet sings of it and paganism cultivated it. Or let the poet who himself understands what it is to be a poet go through what the New Testament teaches about love, and he will be plunged into despair because he will not find a single word which could inspire him. And if, for all that, any so-called poet did find a word and used it, then it would be a deceitful, guilt-laden use, for instead of respecting Christianity, he would be stealing a precious word and distorting the meaning in his use of it. Let the poet search the New Testament for a word about friendship which could please him, and he will search vainly unto despair.

But let a Christian search, one who wants to love his neighbour; he certainly will not search in vain; he will find each word stronger and more authoritative than the last, serving to kindle this love in him and to keep him in this love . . .

Therefore we will test the Christian conviction on the poet. What does the poet teach about love and friendship? The question is not about this or that particular poet, but only about the poet, that is, only about him as far as he is faithful as a poet to himself and to his task. If such a so-called poet has lost faith in the artistic worth of erotic love and friendship and in its interpretation and has supplanted it by something else, he is not a poet, and perhaps the something else which he sets in its place is not Christian either, and the whole thing is a blunder. Erotic love is based on disposition which, explained as inclination, has its highest, its unconditional, artistically unconditional, unique expression in that there is only one beloved in the whole world, and that only this one time of erotic love is genuine love, is everything, and the next time nothing. Usually one says, proverbially, that the first try does not count. Here, on the other hand, the one time is unconditionally the whole; the next time is unconditionally the ruin of everything. This is poesy, and the emphasis rests decisively in the highest expression of passionateness—to be or not to be. To love a second time is not really to love, and to poetry this is an abomination. If a so-called poet wants to make us believe that erotic love can be repeated in the same person, if a so-called poet wants to occupy himself with gifted foolishness, which presumably would exhaust passion's mysteriousness in the *why* of cleverness, then he is not a poet. Nor is that Christian which he puts in place of the poetic. Christian love teaches love of all men, unconditionally all. Just as decidedly as erotic love strains in the direction of the one and only beloved, just as decidedly and powerfully does Christian love press in the opposite direction. If in the context of Christian love one wishes to make an exception of a single person whom he does not want to love, such love is not "also Christian love" but is decidedly not Christian love. Yet there is this kind of confusion in so-called Christendom—the poets have given up the passion of erotic love, they yield, they slacken the tension of passion, they strike a bargain (by adding on) and are of the opinion that a man, in the sense of erotic love, can love many times, so that consequently there are many beloveds. Christian love also yields, slackens the tension of eternity, strikes compromises, and is of the opinion that when one loves a great deal, then it is Christian love. Thus *both* poetic and Christian love have become confused, and the replacement is *neither* the poetic *nor* the Christian. Passion always has this unconditional characteristic—that it excludes the third; that is to say, a third factor means confusion. To love without passion is an impossibility. Therefore the distinction between erotic love and Christian love is the one possible eternal distinction in passion. Another difference between erotic love and Christian love can not be imagined. If, therefore, one occasionally presumes to understand his life with the help of the poet and with the help of Christianity's explanation, presumes the ability to understand these two explanations together—and then in such a way that meaning would come into his life—then he is under a delusion. The poet and Christianity explain things in opposite ways. The poet idolises the inclinations and is therefore quite right—since he always has only erotic love in mind—in saying that to command love is the greatest foolishness and the most preposterous kind of talk. Christianity, which constantly thinks only of Christian love, is also quite right when it dethrones inclination and sets this *shall* in its place.

The poet and Christianity give explanations which are quite opposed, or more accurately expressed, the poet really explains nothing, for he explains love and friendship—in riddles. He explains love and friendship as riddles, but Christianity explains love eternal. From this one again sees that it is an impossibility to love according to both explanations simultaneously, for the greatest possible contradiction between the two explanations is this, that the one is no explanation and the other is the explanation.

As the poet understands them, love and friendship contain no ethical task. Love and friendship are good fortune. Poetically understood (and certainly the poet is an excellent judge of fortune) it is good fortune, the highest good fortune, to fall in love, to find the one and only beloved; it is good fortune, almost as great, to find the one and only friend. Then the highest task is to be properly grateful for one's good fortune. But the task can never be an *obligation* to find the beloved or to find this friend. This is out of the question—something the poet well understands. Consequently, the task is dependent upon whether fortune will give one the task; but ethically understood this is simply a way of saying that there is no task at all. On the other hand, when one has the *obligation* to love his neighbour, then there is the task, the ethical task, which is the origin of all tasks. Just because Christianity is the true ethic, it knows how to shorten deliberations and cut short prolix introductions, to remove all provisional waiting and preclude all waste of time. Christianity is involved in the task immediately, because it has brought the task along. There is, indeed, great debate going on in the world about what should be .called the highest good. But whatever it is called at the moment, whatever variations there are, it is unbelievable how many prolixities are involved in grasping it. Christianity, however, teaches a man immediately the shortest way to find the highest good: shut your door and pray to God— for God is still the highest. And when a man will go out into the world, he can go a long way—and go in vain—he can wander the world around—and in vain—all in order to find the beloved or the friend. But Christianity never suffers a man to go in vain, not even a single step, for when you open the door which you shut in order to pray to God, the first person you meet as you go out is your neighbour whom you *shall* love. Wonderful! Perhaps a girl tries inquisitively and superstitiously to find out her fate, to get a glimpse of her intended, and deceptive cleverness makes her believe that when she has done this and this and that, she shall recognise him by his being the first person she sees on such and such a day. I wonder, then, if it should be so difficult to get to see one's neighbour also—if one does not make it difficult for himself to see him—for Christianity has made it for ever impossible to make a mistake about him. There is in the whole world not a single person who can be recognised with such ease and certainty as one's neighbour. You can never confuse him with anyone else, for indeed all men are your neighbour. If you confuse another man with your neighbour, there is essentially no mistake in this, for the other man is your neighbour also; the mistake lies in you, that you will not understand who your neighbour is. If you save a man's life in the dark, supposing him to be your friend, but he is your neighbour, this again is no mistake; alas, the mistake would be only in your wanting to save only your friend. If your friend complains that, in his opinion, you did for a neighbour what he thought you would do only for him, be at rest, it is your friend who makes the mistake.

The point at issue between the poet and Christianity may be

stated precisely in this way: *erotic love and friendship are preferential and the passion of preference.* Christian love is self-renunciation's love and therefore trusts in this *shall.* To exhaust these passions would make one's head swim. But the most passionate boundlessness of preference in excluding others is to love only the one and only; self-renunciation's boundlessness in giving itself is not to exclude a single one.

In other times when men were still earnest about understanding Christianity in relationship to life, they thought Christianity was in some way opposed to erotic love because it is based upon spontaneous inclinations. They thought that Christianity, which as spirit has made a cleft between body and spirit, despised love as sensuality. But this was a misunderstanding, an extravagance of spirituality. Moreover, it may easily be shown that Christianity is far from unreasonably wishing to turn the sensuous against a man by teaching him extravagance. Does not Paul say it is better to marry than to burn! No, for the very reason that Christianity in truth is spirit, it understands the sensuous as something quite different from what men bluntly call the sensual. Just as it has not forbidden men to eat and drink, so has it not been scandalised by a drive men have not given themselves. Sensuality, the flesh, Christianity understands as selfishness. No conflict between body and spirit can be imagined, unless there is a rebellious spirit on the side of the body with which the spirit then struggles. In the same way no conflict can be thought of as existing between spirit and a stone, between spirit and a tree. Therefore self-love, egocentricity, is sensuality. Consequently Christianity has misgivings about erotic love and friendship because preference in passion or passionate preference is really another form of self-love. Paganism had never dreamed of this. Because paganism never had an inkling of self-renunciation's love of one's neighbour, whom one *shall* love, it therefore reckoned thus: self-love is abhorrent because it is love of self, but erotic love and friendship, which are passionate preferences for other people, are genuine love. But Christianity, which has made manifest what love is, reckons otherwise. Self-love and passionate preferences are essentially the same; but love of one's neighbour—that is genuine love. To love the beloved, asks Christianity—is that loving, and adds, "Do not the pagans do likewise?" If because of this someone thinks that the difference between Christianity and paganism is that in Christianity the beloved and the friend are loved with an entirely different tenderness and fidelity than in paganism, he misunderstands. Does not paganism also offer examples of love and friendship so perfect that the poet instructively goes back to them? But no one in paganism loved his neighbour—no one suspected that there was such a being. Therefore what paganism called love, in contrast to self-love, was preference. But if passionate preference is essentially another form of self-love, one again sees the truth in the saying of the worthy father, "The virtues of paganism are glittering vices."

That passionate preference is another form of self-love will now be shown, together with its opposite, that self-renunciation's love loves one's neighbour, whom one *shall* love. Just as self-love centres exclusively about this *self*—whereby it is self-love, just so does erotic love's passionate preference centre around the one and only beloved and friendship's passionate preference around the friend. The beloved and the friend are therefore called, remarkably and significantly enough, the *other-self*, the *other-I*—for one's neighbour is the *other-you*, or more accurately, the third-man of equality. The other-self, the other-I. But wherein lies self-love? It lies in the I, in the self. Would not self-love, then, still remain in loving the other-self, the other-I? Certainly one need not be an extraordinary judge of human nature in order with the help of these clues to make discoveries about erotic love and friendship, discoveries provocative for others and humiliating for one's self. The fire in self-love is spontaneously ignited; the I ignites itself by itself. But in erotic love and friendship, poetically understood, there is also self-ignition. Truly enough one may say that it is only occasionally—and then morbidly—that jealousy *shows* itself, but this is no proof that it is not always fundamentally present in love and friendship. Test it. Bring a neighbour between the lover and the beloved as the middle term whom one shall love; bring a neighbour between friend and friend as the middle term whom one shall love— and you will immediately see jealousy. Nevertheless *neighbour* is definitely the middle-term of self-renunciation which steps in between self-love's I and I and also comes between erotic love's and friendship's I and the other-I. That it is self-love when a faithless person jilts the beloved and leaves the friend in the lurch, paganism saw also—and the poet sees it. But only Christianity sees as self-love the devotion of the lover's surrender to the one and only, whereby the beloved is held firmly. Yet how can *devotion* and *boundless abandon* be *self-love?* Indeed, when it is devotion to the other-I, the other-myself.—Let a poet describe what erotic love in a person must be if it is to be called erotic love. He will say much that we shall not dwell upon here, but then he will add: "and there must be admiration; the lover must admire the beloved." The neighbour, however, has never been presented as an object of admiration. Christianity has never taught that one must admire his neighbour—one shall love him. Consequently there must be admiration in erotic love's relationship, and the greater, the more intense the admiration is, the better, says the poet. Now, to admire another person certainly is not self-love, but to be loved by the one and only object of admiration, must not this relationship turn back in a selfish way to the I which loves—loves its other-I? It is this way with friendship, too. To admire another person certainly is not love, but to be the one and only friend of this rarest object of admiration, must not this relationship turn back in a doubtful way to the I from which it proceeded? Is it not an obvious danger for self-love to have a one and only object for its admiration when in return this one and only object of admiration makes one the one and only object of his own love or his friendship?

Love of one's neighbour, on the other hand, is self-renouncing love, and self-renunciation casts out all preferential love just as it casts out all self-love—otherwise self-renunciation would also make distinctions and would nourish preference for preference. If passionate preference had no other selfishness about it, it still would have this, that consciously or unconsciously there is a wilfulness about it—unconsciously insofar as it is in the power of natural predispositions, consciously insofar as it utterly surrenders itself to this power and consents to it. However hidden, however unconscious this wilfulness is in its impassioned yielding to its "one and only," the arbitrariness is nevertheless there. The one and only object is not found by obedience to the royal law, "You shall love," but by choosing, yes, by unconditionally selecting a one and only individual, but Christian love also has a one and only object, one's neighbour, but one's neighbour is as far as possible from being only one person, one and only, infinitely removed from this, for one's neighbour is all men. When the lover or the friend can love only this one person in the whole world (something delightful to the poet's cars), there is in this tremendous devotion a tremendous wilfulness, and the lover in this onrushing, inordinate devotion really relates himself to himself in self-love. Self-renunciation would eradicate this self-loving and self-willing by the "You shall" of the eternal. And self-renunciation, which presses in as a judge to try self-love, is therefore double-edged in that it cuts off both sides equally. It knows very well that there is a self-love which one may call faithless self-love, but it knows just as well that there is a self-love which may be called devoted self-love. The task of self-renunciation is therefore a double one, relating itself to the difference between these two variants. For the faithless self-love which wants to shirk there is the task: devote yourself. For the devoted self-love, the task is: give up this devotion. That which delights the poet indescribably, namely, that the lover says, "I cannot love anyone else, I cannot give up loving, I cannot give up this love, for it would be the death of me and I would die of love"— this does not satisfy self-renunciation at all and it will not tolerate that such a devotion be honoured by the name of love, since it is self-love. Thus self-renunciation first judges and then sets the task: love your neighbour; him *shall* you love.

Wherever Christianity is, there is also self-renunciation, which is Christianity's essential form. In order to be related to Christianity one must first and foremost become sober, but self-renunciation is precisely the way by which a human being becomes sober in an eternal sense. On the other hand, wherever Christianity is absent, the intoxication of self-feeling is the most intense, and the height of this intoxication is most admired. Love and friendship are the very height of self-feeling, the I intoxicated in the other-I. The more securely the two I's come together to become one I, the more this united I selfishly cuts itself off from all others. At the peak of love and friendship the two really become one self, one I. This is explainable only because in this exclusive love there are natural determinants (tendencies, inclinations) and self-love, which selfishly can unite the two in a new selfish self. Spiritual love, on the other hand, takes away from myself all natural determinants and all self-love. Therefore love for my neighbour cannot make me one with the neighbour in a united self. Love to one's neighbour is love between two individual beings, each eternally qualified as spirit. Love to one's neighbour is spiritual love, but two spirits are never able to become a single self in a selfish way. In erotic love and friendship the two love one another in virtue of differences or in virtue of likenesses

which are grounded in differences (as when two friends love one
another on the basis of likeness in customs, character, occupation, education, etc., consequently on the basis of the likeness
by which they are different from other men or in which they are
like each other as different from other men). In this way the two
can selfishly become one self. Neither one of them has yet the
spiritual qualifications of a *self*; neither has yet learned to love
himself Christianly. In erotic love the I is qualified as body-
psyche-spirit, the beloved qualified as body-psyche-spirit. In
friendship the I is qualified as psyche-spirit and the friend is
qualified as psyche-spirit. Only in love to one's neighbour is the
self, which loves, spiritually qualified simply as spirit and his
neighbour as purely spiritual. Therefore what was said at the
beginning of this discourse does not hold good at all for erotic
love and friendship, that only one human being recognised as
one's neighbour is necessary in order to cure a man of self-
love—if in this human being he loves his neighbour. In love and
friendship one's neighbour is not loved but one's other-self, or
the first I once again, but more intensely. Although self-love is
condemnable, frequently it seems as if men do not have strength
enough to agree about self-love; then it really makes its first open
appearance when the other-self has been found and the two I's
find in this relationship strength for the self-feeling of self-love.
If anyone thinks that by falling in love or by finding a friend he
has learned Christian love, he is in profound error. No, if one is
in love and in such a way that the poet will say of him, "He is
really in love"—yes, then the command of love can be changed
a little when it is spoken to him and yet the same thing will be
said. The command of love can say to him: love your neighbour
as you love your beloved. And yet, does he not love the beloved
as himself, as required by the command which speaks of one's
neighbour? Certainly he does, but the beloved whom he loves
as himself is not his neighbour; the beloved is his other-I. Whether
we talk of the first-I or the other-I, we do not come a step closer
to one's neighbour, for one's neighbour is the first-*Thou*. The one
whom self-love in the strictest sense loves is also basically the
other-I, for the other-I is oneself, and this is indeed self-love. In
the same way it is self-love to love the other-I which is the
beloved or the friend. Just as self-love in the strictest sense has
been characterised as self-deification, so love and friendship (as
the poet understands it, and with his understanding this love

stands and falls) are essentially idolatry. Fundamentally love to God is decisive; from this arises love to one's neighbour; but of this paganism was not aware. Men left God out; men considered erotic love and friendship to be love and shunned self-love. But the Christian love-command requires one to love God above all and then to love one's neighbour. In love and friendship preference is the middle term; in love to one's neighbour God is the middle term. Love God above all else and then love your neighbour and in your neighbour every man. Only by loving God above all else can one love his neighbour in the next human being. The next human being—he is one's neighbour—this the next human being in the sense that the next human being is every other human being. Understood in this way, the discourse was right when it stated at the beginning that if one loves his neighbour in a single other human being he loves all men.

Love to one's neighbour is therefore eternal equality in loving, but this eternal equality is the opposite of exclusive love or preference. This needs no elaborate development. Equality is just this, not to make distinctions, and eternal equality is absolutely not to make the slightest distinction, is unqualifiedly not to make the slightest distinction. Exclusive love or preference, on the other hand, means to make distinctions, passionate distinctions, unqualifiedly to make distinctions.

Has not Christianity, then, since by its "You shall" it thrust love and friendship from the throne, set something far higher in its place? Something far higher—yet let us speak with caution, with the caution of orthodoxy. Men have confused Christianity in many ways, but among them is this way of calling it the highest, the deepest, and thereby making it appear that the purely human was related to Christianity as the high or the higher to the highest or supremely highest. But this is a deceptive way of speaking which untruthfully and improperly lets Christianity in a meddlesome way try to ingratiate itself with human curiosity and craving for knowledge. Is there anything at all for which humanity as such—is there anything for which the natural man has greater desire than for the highest! When a mere newsmonger blazons abroad that his newest news is of the highest significance, then the gathering of hangers-on proceeds merrily in the world, which from time immemorial has had an indescribable partiality for and has felt a deep need of—being deceived. No, Christianity is certainly the highest and the supremely highest, but, mark well, to the natural man it is an offence. He who in describing Christianity as the highest omits the middle term, offence, sins against it: he commits an effrontery, more abominable than if a modest housewife were to dress like a strip-teaser, even more appalling than if John, the rigorous judge, were to dress like a Beau Brummel. Christianity is in itself too profound, in its movements too serious, for dancing and skipping in such free-wheeling frivolity of talk about the higher, the highest, the supremely highest. Through offence goes the way to Christianity. By this is not meant that the approach to Christianity should make one offended by Christianity—this would be another way of hindering oneself from grasping Christianity—but offence guards the approach to Christianity. Blessed is he who is not offended by it.

So it is also with this command to love one's neighbour. Only acknowledge it, or if it is disturbing to you to have it put in this way, I will admit that many times it has thrust me back and that I am yet very far from the illusion that I fullfill this command, which to flesh and blood is offence, and to wisdom foolishness. Are you, my reader, perhaps what is called an educated person? Well, I too am educated. But if you think to come closer to this highest by the help of *education,* you make a great mistake. Precisely at this point the error is rooted, for we all desire education, and education repeatedly has *the highest* in its vocabulary. Yes, no bird which has learned only one word cries out more continuously this single word and no crow caws more continuously its own name than education cries out about the highest. But Christianity is by no means *the highest* of education, and Christianity disciplines precisely by this repulsion of offence. This you can easily see, for do you believe that your education or the enthusiasm of any man for gaining an education has taught either of you to love your neighbour? Alas, have not this education and the enthusiasm with which it is coveted rather developed a new kind of distinction, a distinction between the educated and the non-educated? Only observe what is said among the educated about love and friendship, the degree of similarity in education a friend must have, how educated a girl must be and precisely in what way. Read the poets, who hardly know how to defend their frankness against the mighty domination of education, who hardly dare believe in the power of love to break the bonds of all distinctions. Does it seem to you that such talk or such poetry or a life attuned to such talk and such poetry brings a man closer to loving his neighbour? Here again the marks of offence stand out. Imagine the most educated person, one of whom we all admiringly say: "He is so educated." Then think of Christianity, which says to him: "You shall love your neighbour!" Of course, a certain courteousness in social intercourse, a politeness towards all men, a friendly condescension to the poor, a frank attitude towards the mighty, a beautifully controlled freedom of spirit—yes, that is education—do you think it is also loving one's neighbour?

One's neighbour is one's equal. One's neighbour is not the beloved, for whom you have passionate preference, nor your friend, for whom you have passionate preference. Nor is your neighbour, if you are well educated, the well-educated person with whom you have cultural equality—for with your neighbour you have before God the equality of humanity. Nor is your neighbour one who is of higher social status than you, that is, insofar as he is of higher social status he is not your neighbour, for to love him because he is of higher status than you can very easily be preference and to that extent self-love. Nor is your neighbour one who is inferior to you, that is, insofar as he is inferior he is not your neighbour, for to love one because he is inferior to you can very easily be partiality's condescension and to that extent self-love. No, to love one's neighbour means equality. It is encouraging in your relationship to people of distinction that in them you *shall* love your neighbour. In relation to those inferior it is humbling that in them you are not to love the inferior but *shall* love your neighbour. If you do this there is salvation, for you *shall* do it. Your neighbour is every man, for on the basis of distinctions he is not your neighbour, nor on the basis of likeness to you as being different from other men. He is your neighbour on the basis of equality with you before God; but this equality absolutely every man has, and he has it absolutely.

Elizabeth Telfer

FRIENDSHIP

Introduction

In her essay "Friendship"—the first serious work by an English-speaking philosopher on that subject since Emerson—Elizabeth Telfer begins by attempting to state necessary and sufficient conditions for a relationship's being a friendship, a section that should be compared with Aristotle's definition at *Ethics* 1155b28–56a5. She helpfully distinguishes three types of 'shared activity' in a friendship: reciprocated services, mutual contact, and joint pursuits. Such activity, she says, is a necessary condition of friendship—a claim which ought to be compared with Aristotle's rather different one, that it is the state of character making us disposed to do such activities that is necessary (see *Ethics* VIII.5).

The element of choice in a friendship is nicely related by Telfer to the 'mutual awareness' of the relationship that Aristotle observed was necessary. She says that friends choose to be friends primarily through consenting to a shared understanding of their relationship.

Telfer's argument (in part 2 of her essay) that we do have special duties to friends is likewise usefully compared with *Ethics* VIII.9–12. Although Telfer on several occasions points to duties among family members to buttress her argument, she distinguishes sharply between familial relationships and friendship. Her concern is with relationships which we choose to enter into. Such relationships may "arise naturally," she says, but she seems not to allow the existence of *natural friendships* in Aristotle's sense.

Kierkegaard had criticized friendship as being partial; Telfer agrees with that criticism on different grounds. She holds the view that friendships are inherently unjust yet justified because they promote the general well-being of society: "this is a case where the utility of a practice is high enough to compensate for the fact that some measure of injustice is involved in it." Both our duties to our friends and our deciding to form friendships in the first place, can be given a rule-utilitarian justification: "more happiness overall is produced," she says, "if each man makes the welfare of a few others his special concern." It seems difficult, on such a view, to make sense of the notion of loving one's friends "for their own sake" (to use Aristotle's phrase). But it is unclear whether Telfer, in the end, wishes to preserve that notion in her account of friendship.

Elizabeth Telfer

FRIENDSHIP

It is often said that friendships are among the most important constituents of a worth-while life. I wish to examine this view by trying to answer three questions about friendship: what it is, how morality bears on it, and why it is thought to be important.

1   The Nature of Friendship

We can begin our answer to the first question with the obvious point that there is a certain type of activity which all friends, *qua* friends, engage in: the performing of services of all kinds for some other person. Suppose, however, that a man fetches coal and shopping and clears the snow for the lonely old lady next door. This kind of case would not really be one of friendship, for, while she might say, 'My neighbour's been a real *friend* to me this winter', we would normally distinguish between 'befriending' or 'being a friend to' and 'being friends' or 'being a friend of'. In the situation described we would not speak of the existence of a friendship or say that the pair were friends or that he was a friend of hers (as distinct from a friend to her). His conduct is in some ways like that of a friend, but the situation is not one of *friendship*, and it is the latter concept with which we are concerned.

It might be suggested that what is missing in the example is reciprocity. But the old lady and her neighbour do not become friends simply because in return for his fetching and shovelling she knits him socks. What are missing are two other types of activity, which are not so much reciprocal as actually *shared:* those activities the main point of which is that they involve contact

Meeting of the Aristotelian Society at 5/7, Tavistock Place, London, W.C.1, on Monday, 24th May 1971, at 7.30 p.m.

250

with the friend, such as talking together or exchanging letters;
and joint engagement in pursuits which the friends would in any
case perform quite apart from the friendship—notably leisure
pursuits, but also sometimes work, worship and so on. My thesis, then, is that there are three types of activity which are all
necessary conditions of friendship: reciprocal services, mutual
contact and joint pursuits. I shall henceforth refer to these necessary conditions collectively, as the 'shared activity' condition for
friendship.

The 'shared activity' condition, however, is not a sufficient
condition for friendship. This becomes clear if we imagine a
case where the condition is fulfilled. Consider, for example,
the situation where two neighbours, each living alone, perform
services for each other, go to the pictures together, and drop in
on each other to chat in the evenings. Would we be able to say
that the pair were friends, simply on the strength of this situation? I think it is clear that we would not, on the ground that
friendship depends, not only on the performance of certain *actions*, but also on their being performed for certain specific *reasons*—out of friendship, as we say, rather than out of duty or
pity or indeed self-interest. These reasons can, I think, be seen
as a set of long-term *desires*, which motivate and hence explain
actions done out of friendship. My contention is that the existence of the relevant desires is a second necessary condition for
friendship. Let us examine these desires—which we may call the
passions of friendship—in more detail.

The first element in the passions of friendship is affection;
friends must have affection for, or be fond of, each other. (This
passion is not of course peculiar to friendship; for example, it is
also felt by colleagues of long standing, or by members of the
same family.) I define 'affection' as a desire for another's welfare
and happiness *as a particular individual*. This desire is thus to be
distinguished both from sense of duty and from benevolence.
For these motives prompt us to seek others' good in general,
whereas we want to say that those who feel affection feel a
concern for another which they do not feel for everyone. It is
this concern which normally motivates services performed out
of friendship, whereas befriending is motivated by benevolence,
pity or sense of duty. This special concern for friends also gives
rise to reactions of special pleasure at their good fortune, pain at
their misfortune, anger with those who injure them, and so on.

Two points about affection may be briefly noted before we consider other passions of friendship. The first concerns its relation with benevolence and sense of duty. We have said that benevolence and sense of duty are to be distinguished from affection because affection is for the individual. But surely, it may be argued, the benevolent and the dutiful man also concern themselves with the individual? The answer here is to distinguish between two kinds of concern for the individual. To say that the benevolent or dutiful man concerns himself with the individual is to say that he sees each individual as making separate claims which may not only compete with the majority interest but also differ in content from those of other individuals. But the concern of affection is not for *each* individual, but for *this* individual rather than others.

The second point I wish to make about affection is that it does not seem to have any necessary connexion with the particular character of him for whom it is felt. If asked to explain why we are fond of someone, we *may* mention characteristics in him which stimulate affection, but it makes equally good sense to give an historical explanation—'I've known him for a long time' or 'I looked after him when he was ill'—or a biological one such as 'He's my brother, after all'. Affection is in this sense *irrational*, and because of this may survive radical changes in the character of its object. Thus we often continue to be fond of someone when we no longer like or respect him, and such a situation is not considered in any way odd.

The second element in the passions which are part of friendship, and one which distinguishes it from many other relationships which involve affection, is a desire on the part of the friends for each others' company, as distinct from a desire for company as such. It will normally be this desire which leads friends to seek contact with each other and to share pursuits, and which also gives rise to our pleasure when we see friends, regret at parting, and so on. It is the presence of this desire which distinguishes a case of friendship from those where a man keeps company with another out of loneliness, or pity, or sense of duty.

Is this desire for another's company irrational in the same way as affection is? I think not, at least where it is part of *friendship* and not of being in love, infatuation, *etc*. These latter states also involve a desire for the other's company. But whereas it is characteristic of them that a sufferer from them may intelligibly say 'I don't know what it is about him/her that draws me, but I cannot be without him/her' we would not speak of friendship unless the friends are prepared to *explain* the desire for each other's company, and to do so in terms of two particular attitudes towards each other: liking, and the sense of a bond or of something in common.

Now both these attitudes are rational, in the sense that they are necessarily based on beliefs about the nature of the friend: we *like* a person and feel we *are like* him because of what we think he is *like*. The degree of rationality which this involves, however, is rather limited. For even where we *can* give our reasons for liking someone or feeling a bond with him, we cannot further justify these reasons, or always explain why they operate in one case and not in another apparently similar. And we may find it very difficult to *state* our reasons at all. In such a case the most we might be prepared to say is that there must be qualities in the friend, even if we cannot 'pin them down', such that if he ceased to have them we would cease to like or feel akin to him. Let me say a little more about these two attitudes.

Liking is a difficult phenomenon to analyse. Although it is a *reason* for seeking someone's company, it is not simply *equivalent* to enjoyment of his company, as might at first seem, as we can for a time enjoy the company of people whom we do not basically like—indeed, certain kinds of unpleasant people have their own fascination. It seems rather to be a quasi-aesthetic attitude, roughly specifiable as 'finding a person to one's taste', and depends partly on such things as his physical appearance, mannerisms, voice and speech, and style of life; partly on his traits of character, moral and other. The relative importance of these features as a basis for liking obviously depends on the liker.

This account of liking tends to suggest that before we can like someone we have to tot up items in his nature and strike a balance between the attractive and the unattractive aspects of it. But in reality our reaction, like a reaction to a picture, is to a whole personality seen as a unified thing. This is why we often find it very difficult to say what it is we like about a person. Sometimes what we like is partly the way in which everything about the person seems to 'hang together' and be part of a unified style; sometimes we enjoy a contrast, for example that between a mild unassuming exterior and an iron determination. Of course, the fact that we like a personality as a unity or whole does not rule out the possibility that we may dislike some individual features intensely. But in such a case we characteristically feel that these features are not merely objectionable in themselves, but also somehow mar, or intrude upon, a whole that is otherwise pleasing; and this fact sharpens our vexation.

The sense of a bond, or the sense that we have something in common with another person, is a quite separate reason for seeking his company from the existence of liking. For people can be ill-at-ease with those whom they like, and explain why they are *not* friends with them, contrary to others' expectation, by saying 'I like him, but I can't seem to communicate with him' or 'We don't talk the same language' or 'We don't seem to have much in common'. The bond may be shared interests or enthusiasms or views, but it may also be a similar style of mind or way of thinking which makes for a high degree of empathy.

In the light of this discussion we can I think reject the notion that we need to think of our friends as good people, as Plato and Aristotle sometimes seem to assume. For there seems no *necessary* incompatibility between fondness, liking, and a sense of a bond, on the one hand, and disapproval of some qualities in a person, on the other. (Indeed, we can even have a kind of admiration or liking for the very qualities of which we at the same time disapprove.) On the other hand, some moral defects arouse distaste as well as disapproval and so prevent liking. And one of the strongest bonds may well be, even if not matched virtue and mutual admiration as in Aristotle, at least similar moral seriousness and shared moral purpose. Again, to say that we need not think of our friends as good people is not to say that friendship with a thoroughly bad person is morally permissible, or to deny that some moral defects may make a person incapable of friendship.

One reason why Aristotle insists that friendship (at any rate, the truest form of friendship) must be between good men is that he thinks that to care for someone because he is virtuous is to care for him for his own sake, whereas to care for him because he is useful or pleasant is not.[1] Now if Aristotle means merely that it is not true friendship to care for someone for what you can get out of him, we agree. But he seems rather to mean that

1. Aristotle *Nicomachean Ethics* 1156a 10–19, 1156b 6–12.

to care for a man because of his virtue is to care for him 'in himself', rather than because of contingent and changeable facts about him, and that 'caring for him in himself' in this sense is one of the requirements of friendship.

Now it is clear that Aristotle is mistaken in supposing that a man's virtue is not a contingent and changeable fact—as indeed he later admits.[2] But his other assumption—that we care for friends 'in themselves' rather than for any contingent facts about them—has a certain plausibility. How far is it valid? It is false if it means that qualities in the friend cannot be *reasons* for friendship. For liking and the sense of a bond, which are necessary conditions of friendship, both depend on the friend's nature. It follows that if the friends change in such a way that they cease to like each other or to have anything in common, the friendship is at an end—not in the sense that it would be wise or usual to break it off, but by definition. It may be that 'Love is not love which alters when it alteration finds'; but friendship, which is based on and dependent on reasons, is different.

But there are two senses in which Aristotle's requirement *is* valid, as can be seen in the light of my earlier discussion. First, there is an element in friendship—affection—which does not have the same dependence on the nature of the friend as liking and sense of a bond. It *may* fade if the friend alters, but there is no logical reason why it should do so, and often it in fact does not. Secondly, even liking, although it depends on qualities which others may also have, is nevertheless a reaction to an individual, not a type. Thus if I like James because he is witty, gentle, and good at making things, I like him, not as one example of a witty, gentle and craftsmanlike person, for whom another such might be substituted, but as an individual whose uniqueness defies complete classification.[3]

My account so far of friendship is in terms of two necessary conditions: shared activities and the passions of friendship. But it might well be objected that this account fails to do justice to an important aspect of friendship, that of commitment and choice. Indeed, an objector might go further, and say that to give the status of a necessary condition to the passions of friendship is

2. *Op. cit.* 1165b 12–22.
3. This discussion of liking owes much to W. G. Maclagan, "Respect for Persons as a Moral Principle", Part 1 *Philosophy* 1960.

incompatible with the plain fact that we can speak of choosing to be someone's friend. His argument is that since we can speak of choosing to be someone's friend, but cannot choose our feelings, the presence of certain feelings cannot be a necessary condition for friendship. Their rôle, he would maintain, is rather that of *reasons* for friendship, reasons why I might choose to be someone's friend. Similarly, if my inclinations alter, this may be a reason for breaking off the friendship, but it does not *mean* that the friendship is broken off. Such an objector might compare friendship in this respect to marriage, which is normally entered upon on the basis of certain feelings but which exists whether or not these feelings obtain. He might go on to say that in friendship, as in marriage, it makes sense to ask which feelings do justify entering upon the friendship, and again which changes of feelings (if any) justify breaking it off.

My reply to this objection is first of all to recall the case where the usual passions of friendship do not obtain, but the behaviour does—where, for example, A helps B and does things with him, not out of spontaneous inclination, but out of pity or sense of duty. My claim is that if B comes to realise A's real motives he would naturally say, not 'You shouldn't have become my friend', but 'You don't really regard me as a friend at all'. Again, if A ceases to like B or to feel any bond with him, but goes on acting as before 'for auld lang syne', as it were, B on becoming aware of the situation would I think say 'You don't really think of me as a friend any more.'

To some extent, of course, I am stipulating, rather than reporting, that the presence of the inclinations is a necessary part of friendship. I think the word may sometimes be used to describe a relationship analogous to marriage. But perhaps I can make the stipulation more palatable by pointing out that, even on my analysis so far, choice necessarily enters into friendship. For although the right passions are a necessary condition of friendship they are not by themselves a sufficient condition. A man who possesses these passions has still to act on them—actually to help instead of merely wanting to, for example—and insofar as he acts he is necessarily making choices. In this way my two necessary conditions are compatible with, and themselves imply, *choice* in friendship—though they also imply that we cannot choose to be a friend of just anyone, since the relevant passions cannot be summoned up at will.

It might plausibly be maintained, however, that we speak of

choosing our friends in a stronger sense than that already cov-
ered by the two necessary conditions of shared activities and
passions of friendship. For the existence of what I have called
shared activities need not imply more than a series of unconnected choices, not seen by the chooser as forming any pattern. But
choosing a friend seems to mean forming a long-term *policy* of
action: making one decision to act in general in the ways we have
described, not making many decisions on particular occasions.

Is it a necessary condition of friendship that we should choose
our friends, in this stronger sense? It seems clear that we need
not (though we may) make a conscious decision of the kind I
have just described; we can speak of people as gradually *becoming*
friends, or of friendship as *springing up*, thus suggesting that
there need not be any definite beginning to the friendship. But
nevertheless I would claim that a weaker version of this condition
is necessary: namely, that the existence of the passions of friendship in both parties, and the practice on both sides of acting
on them, once established, be *acknowledged* by the parties. This
acknowledgement involves, not so much the *formation* of a policy,
as endorsement of or consent to a policy which is by then en-
shrined in practice. This is part of what is meant by *commitment*
in friendship.

I have claimed that there are three necessary conditions for
friendship: shared activities, the passions of friendship, and acknowledgement of the fulfilment of the first two conditions,
constituting an acknowledgement of and consent to the special
relationship. I now add that I regard these as not only individu-
ally necessary but also jointly sufficient for friendship.

2   Friendship and Duty

But friends can also be said to be committed in a quite different
sense from that which I have been discussing: friendship is seen
as giving rise to *duties* and corresponding rights. Examples of
such duties, as commonly conceived, are: to help the friend
when under attack (physical or verbal) or in need or trouble of
any kind; to proffer advice and criticism, not only when asked
for but also when not asked for but needed. The notion of duties
to friends, however, is by no means unproblematic, and before
I can consider these duties further I must discuss three arguments
to the effect that it does not make sense to speak of duties to
friends.

The first argument can be dismissed fairly briskly. It is to the effect that friendship is an involuntary relationship, and no duties can be founded on an involuntary relationship. I have already denied that friendship is involuntary in the relevant sense. But in any case we should query the assumption that no duties can arise from an involuntary relationship. Cannot children be said to have duties to their parents, or siblings to each other?

The second reason for rejecting the notion of duties to friends is more problematic. It is that to speak of duty implies the possibility that the action may be against the grain, whereas we spontaneously want to help our friends. We cannot meet this difficulty simply by saying that we can often speak of duties in situations where we also in fact wish to do the actions, as in the case of duties to family. For whether or not we wish to help our families is a contingent matter, whereas I have made it part of the very definition of friendship that we should want to help our friends.

This difficulty about duties to friends can I think be circumvented by stressing two points. First, the existence of friendship, while it implies general goodwill, need not imply that the friends wish each other well at all times and in all respects. Thus it is quite compatible with friendship for a man to lose concern temporarily for a friend—perhaps as the result of a quarrel—or to find that some aspect of his friend's behaviour always tries his patience. In these cases it makes perfectly good sense to say that caring for his friend goes against the grain. Secondly, some of our duties to our friends are extremely disagreeable (such as telling them unpleasant 'home truths'). There is thus a point in speaking of duty in that our natural concern for our friends' welfare, though prompting us in the right direction, is not so strong that all the required actions come easily to us.

The third objection which may be raised to the conception that we have duties to friends is that duties belong to impersonal relationships, whereas friendship is a personal relationship. The force of this objection, however, obviously depends on what sense of 'personal' and 'impersonal' is in question. Let us therefore consider in what senses friendship may be said to be personal, and whether any of them preclude us from speaking of 'duties of friendship'.[4]

4. This discussion of senses of "personal" and "impersonal" is based on that in R. S. Downie, *Roles and Values*, pp. 134–8 (Methuen 1971).

First, friendship is personal in that it necessarily involves knowledge by acquaintance. But in this it does not differ from many relationships which obviously involve duties: for example, that of husband and wife.

Secondly, friendship is personal in that it necessarily involves what we may call a 'reactive' attitude: that which regards another human being, not as an object to be manipulated causally, but as a *person*, *i.e.*, a rational agent capable of self-determination.[5] But our relationships with all adult sane human beings should be, and normally are, personal in this sense; it therefore cannot be incompatible with the existence of duties.

Thirdly, we may say that friendship is personal in that it is 'part of one's private life'. But the notion of private life itself needs elucidation. It may mean anything which is not connected with one's work. In this sense relationships with one's family, friends, fellow-churchmen, fellow-clubmen, mistress, are all part of one's private life. Or one may use the term in a sense relative to one's interlocutor, meaning roughly 'whatever I choose to keep apart from you'. In this sense family life may be private life to one's colleagues, friendships and love affairs to one's family. But 'private life' in both these senses can include relationships in which we normally speak of duties, so we cannot base an argument against the conception of duties to friends on the idea that friendship is part of private life.

Fourthly, we may say that friendship is personal in that it is part of one's 'non-official life', as contrasted with 'official life' in which what to do is in some way fixed or laid down. It might then be argued that the official sphere (which would include not only work, or most forms of it, but also membership of organizations such as clubs, churches and political parties, and of relationships which are governed by law and convention such as marriage and parenthood) is that in which it makes sense to speak of duty. The non-official sphere, on the other hand, to which belong friendships, companionships and acquaintance-ships, and love affairs, is outside the scope of duty. This argument from the non-official nature of friendship seems to have a certain plausibility. But it in fact comprises two different claims, which must be considered separately.

First, then, the claim may be that duties belong to conventional

5. For the notion of a reactive attitude see P. F. Strawson, "Freedom and Resentment", *Proceedings of the British Academy* 1962.

or institutional relationships, whereas friendship is a natural relationship. To support the claim examples are adduced of relationships involving duties: for example, that of husband to wife (and *vice versa*), schoolmaster to pupils, treasurer of club to club members, and so on. In all these cases the rôle is *defined* in terms of a set of duties: one cannot explain what a husband is without explaining the rights and duties of marriage. But friendship can be explained entirely in natural terms (in the kind of way we explained it in our first section). Hence, it may be argued, friendship is not a duty-relationship.

But this argument is confused. For there are cases of *natural* relationships, such as that between parent and child, which give rise to duties just as much as do the conventional relationships. The difference is that, whereas the statement that husbands have duties to wives is analytic, the statement that parents have duties to children is synthetic. If then friendship is a natural relationship, it may well involve duties in the same way as parenthood does—duties whose precise content will depend on the nature of the particular society. We incur these duties as a result of making friends just as we incur the duties of parents as a result of having children.

The second claim based on the non-official nature of friendship may be developed as a criticism of our reply to the first. It may be argued that parenthood, although like friendship in being a natural rather than a conventional relationship, is nevertheless official in a sense in which friendship is not, because society *recognizes* the duties of parenthood. This recognition is shown both by the legal enforcement of some very important duties, and by the more informal sanctions of disapproval which are brought to bear on parents who neglect non-legal duties to their children. Nothing of this kind—the argument goes on—happens in the case of friendship, and therefore we cannot speak of duties to friends.

This second argument assumes that duties are always dependent on the attitudes of society. But this assumption does not seem to be correct. We may grant that the precise content of one's duties may vary from society to society, since people's needs vary in different societies and are met in different ways by different social arrangements. But it does not follow that we have no duties except those recognized by society. For example it makes sense to say that parents had a duty to educate their daughters as well as their sons, even at the time when society did not recognize this duty, because the daughters had a need which was not being met at all. In the same way we might have duties to friends, which society does not recognize, in view of some need which is not otherwise met.

I conclude then that the personal nature of friendship, however this is interpreted, does not rule out the possibility of our having duties to friends.

It is possible, however, to attack the notion of duties to friends from a quite different point of view. This attack would grant that it *makes sense* to speak of duties to friends, but hold that we are *mistaken* in thinking that we in fact have such duties, because the alleged duties to friends cannot be properly grounded or justified. It might of course be retorted that further defence of the view that friends have special duties to each other is neither possible nor necessary; it is just an ultimate moral principle that we have special duties to friends. But it does not seem to be self-evident that we have special duties to a small group of people, simply because we care about them and seek their company. In any case, those who oppose the idea of duties to friends might well go on to argue that friendship seems *prima facie* to involve a kind of *injustice,* in that it means giving preferential treatment to those who differ neither in need nor in desert—in other words that, so far from being duties, our services to friends might be construed as positively immoral.

Faced with these arguments, the defenders of the duties of friendship will point out first of all that not all services to friends are in any sense exclusive of services to others. Thus we can distinguish between the expenditure on our friends of time or money which might otherwise have been spent on others, and the proffering of advice or criticism which is *not* thereby rendered unavailable for others. It is only in the first type of case that the issue of the morality of preferential treatment for friends arises sharply. And even there the alleged duties to help our friends are acknowledged to be severely restricted in various ways by the demands of other specific duties.

But these restrictions still leave an area in which no duty arising out of another rôle is in question but in which there may be a choice between helping a friend and helping a stranger. Suppose, for example, a man could spend an evening helping to decorate either a friend's flat or that of an old age pensioner, or could

spend spare cash either on a loan to friends or on contributions
to Oxfam. Most people would say that the friends had, if not a
prior claim, at least a competing claim, and our present problem
is to defend this view.

A plausible line of defence seems to be an appeal to a Rule-
Utilitarian position. Thus it might be argued that many sets
of rights and duties which set up special claims not obviously
required by justice, are justified by the conduciveness of their
observance to the general good. If for example a parent is asked
why he should support his child, he will reply that it is one of
the duties of a parent. If he is then asked *why* parents should be
held to have special duties to their children, instead of their being
the responsibility of the State or of grand-parents, he will say
that it is best for all concerned that parents should have special
responsibility for children. In the same way, then, we may suggest that the general welfare is best served by our regarding
friends as having a special claim on us. We may defend this view
on the grounds that more happiness overall is produced if each
man makes the welfare of a few others his special concern, for
two reasons: he will be able to be more effective if he concentrates
his energies, and he will be able to know more precisely what
the needs of a small group are.

Now the first of these arguments does not by itself support
the view that we have special duties to *friends*, but only the view
that we should choose *a* small group as special recipients of our
benevolence. But if we add the second argument, about the
knowledge of needs, we can defend the view that the special
group we choose should be that of our friends. It is not only that
we have a good deal of contact with our friends and get to know
their needs that way, for this fact applies equally to our family
or to colleagues at work. But we also have a special understanding of our friends' needs, in virtue not only of the *rapport* which
by definition exists between friends but also of a sharpened
awareness, which results from the special concern friends in any
case have for each other.

We can thus advance beyond the point made earlier, that there
is nothing self-contradictory in the idea of duties towards those
for whom we already feel a special concern, and assert that the
existence of this concern is part of the *justification* for the claim
that we have special duties to friends. As we have just seen, a

special concern, in making us especially aware of others' needs, gives us the duties that are attendant on special knowledge of needs. But it also gives us a special degree of *power* to help, and in this way also gives us special duties. This is because a man can have a duty to do only what he is able to do, and in some cases he is able, as a result of the strength of his concern for a friend, to do for him what he *could* not do (and hence could not have a duty to do) for anyone else.

It might be argued at this point that I have not met the objection that it is *unjust* to view friends as having special claims; for since friendship is, and is bound to be, very unevenly distributed, the rights which it confers will also be unevenly distributed. I think the only possible answer is that this is a case where the utility of a practice is high enough to compensate for the fact that some measure of injustice is involved in it. But in any case when we speak of duties to friends we are clearly speaking of *prima facie* duties, which would be overridden by a stronger claim.

I can now briefly sum up the conclusions of this section. I have tried to show that various arguments, purporting to show that it does not make sense to speak of duties to friends, are not cogent: those from the alleged involuntariness of friendship, from the constraining nature of duty, and from the personalness, in either the 'knowledge by acquaintance' or the 'reactive' or the 'private life' sense, of the relationship of friendship. I considered at more length the notion that friendship is separated from duty by being personal in the sense of 'non-official'. I suggested there that we could speak of the duties of friendship even though they are both non-institutional and unsupported by social sanctions. I then raised a new type of problem, that of *grounding* the alleged duties to friends. I have tried to show that this can be done in terms of the general good.

3   *The Value of Friendship*

It may be said that the train of thought so far has been that, *if* we have friends, *then* we have certain duties to them. But this does not constitute a demonstration of the value of friendship itself, any more than it shows the value of parenthood to say that if people produce children then they have a duty towards them.

Now some people will say that there is no point in raising the question what the *good* of friendship is, since people cannot help having friends in any case. But this is not strictly true, as we have seen; commitment to friendship is a voluntary matter. It may be true that people cannot help forming vaguer and looser associations, and that they cannot help having the *passions* of friendship towards various other people. But this does not amount to the inevitability of friendship itself.

It may be said that if our emotional make-up is such as to incline us to want to make friends, then this in itself constitutes a *prima facie* case for the goodness of friendship. For how can we show something to be good (it may be maintained) except by showing that it meets deep-seated desires?

But this argument is cogent only if the desires in question—the passions of friendship—are unavoidable; whereas it seems clear that, even if we cannot ourselves get rid of them once we have them, we can foster or inhibit their development in children. Certain kinds of early environment make people less inclined to form strong attachments later, and whether this is a good or bad thing depends on whether friendship itself is a good or a bad thing. Nor can we settle the question by saying that a person who cannot make friends is considered psychologically unhealthy. For we would not include a capacity for friendship in our requirement for psychological health unless we already assumed that friendship is a good thing, so we cannot defend friendship in the name of mental health without going round in a circle.

Why, then, is friendship always considered a good thing—perhaps one of the chief blessings of life? Part of the reason has been given already in my previous section. It is true that my account of the duties of friendship did not raise the question of the value of friendship itself, but rather asked whether, given that we have friends, we are to regard ourselves as having duties to them. But we can use the conclusions of the account as part of a justification of friendship itself. Friendship, we may say, promotes the general happiness by providing a degree and kind of consideration for others' welfare which cannot exist outside it, and which compensates by its excellence for the 'unfairness' of the unequal distribution of friendship. For even those who have no friends are (we may suppose) better off than they would be if there were no such thing as friendship, since the understanding developed by it and the mutual criticism involved in it will improve the way friends deal with people outside the relationship.

But we value friendship for reasons other than its general serviceability to society. To see what these are, we may start from Aristotle's account of why the happy man needs friends[6]— though he tends to assume, as we have seen, that friendship worthy of the name must be between good people. He suggests first that friends are *useful* to a man both to help him in his need and to be recipients of his beneficence in his prosperity. These points have both been partially dealt with earlier; but we would say, not that a man must have friends in order to receive or give *any* help (as Aristotle seems to suggest) but rather that there are particular services which a man can receive only from friends and perform only for them.

Secondly, Aristotle suggests friendship is *pleasant*. He sees this pleasure mainly in terms of the *good* man's pleasure at his equally good friend's virtuous actions. But the joys of friendship are many and various. Notably, of course, there is the pleasure of the friend's company and of shared activity with someone of kindred outlook. Nor need the fact that we gain this pleasure mean that the friendship is 'for the sake of pleasure'. We may begin a friendship because we enjoy someone's company, but soon we enjoy his company because he is a friend.

Now an appeal to pleasure as a justification of friendship may not seem to be on very safe ground, for friendship, like any other attachment we may form, increases our potentiality for pain as well as for pleasure. It could well be argued that from the point of view of the balance of pleasure over pain we would do better to play safe by eschewing friendship. But this pessimistic view does not take into account the full range of the pleasures of friendship. It is true that we can set the pleasure of making a new friend against the sorrow of losing an old one, or the pleasure of a friend's company against the pain of his absence, or the plea- sure of discovering his excellences against the pain of disillusion- ment with him. But there are some pleasures of friendship which have no corresponding pains. These are the pleasures which arise from doing things with a friend, as opposed to doing them alone or with others. What we are doing may be in any case enjoyable—playing games, playing music, conversation, philos-

6. Aristotle, *op. cit.* 1169b 3–1170b 19.

ophy—in which case the presence of the friend enhances the pleasure. Or what we do may in itself be unattractive, but become fun—indeed, be turned into a kind of game—when shared with a friend: for example, spring-cleaning or moving house.

This discussion of the pleasures of friendship points to a third value in friendship, noted indirectly by Aristotle: friendship is *life-enhancing*, it makes us have life 'more abundantly'. This happens in various different ways. First, it increases our stake in the world, and hence our capacity for emotions. We have already noticed this point in terms of the increased capacity for pleasure and pain, but it applies also to the whole range of emotions: hope, fear, anger, pride and so on. Friendship makes us 'more alive' because it makes us *feel* more.

Secondly, friendship enhances many of our *activities*, by intensifying our absorption in them, and hence the quality of our performance of them. The increased absorption is partly a by-product (or rather perhaps an aspect) of the increased pleasure which joint activity with friends produces, since (as Aristotle says) pleasure taken in an activity intensifies it. But I think collaboration with friends may also produce an increased emotional commitment to the activity which is separable from the effects of enhanced pleasure.

Thirdly, friendship enlarges our *knowledge*. I have already spoken of the increased knowledge of human needs and wishes which springs from close association with some one other person. But friendship can enlarge our knowledge throughout the whole gamut of human experience, by enabling us in some measure to adopt the viewpoint of another person through our sympathetic identification with him. Through friendship we can know what it is like to feel or think or do certain things which we do not feel, think or do ourselves. And our knowledge is not merely knowledge by description, but knowledge by acquaintance, derived from our sympathetic sharing of his experience.

We might compare this effect of friendship with that of reading a great work of literature. C. S. Lewis, trying to answer the question 'What is the good of Literature?', says "We want to be more than ourselves . . . we want to see with other eyes, to imagine with other imaginations, to feel with other hearts, as well as with our own.

". . . It is not a question of knowing [in the sense of gratifying our rational curiosity about other people's psychology] at all. It is *connaître* not *savoir;* it is *erleben:* we become these other selves."[7] This empathy with the authors of literature is exactly like the empathy with friends which I have tried to describe, and indeed C. S. Lewis himself compares in this respect the effects of love with those of literature.

Friendship, then, contributes to the well-being of society and to the profit, pleasure and life-enhancement of the friends. But this strong justification of friendship need not show that a particular person is mistaken in deciding it is not for him. He might legitimately do this either because he feels that his temperament makes him unlikely to be a satisfactory friend or because he feels called upon to embark on some absorbing project which will leave no time or energy for friendship.

Perhaps I might conclude by pointing out that too much dwelling on the values of friendship has its own dangers. It may lead people to concentrate on looking for *friendships* rather than friends, and to value the other person as a possible term in a relationship rather than as himself. But it may well be that this attitude, which is wrong in itself and hurtful if detected, is also self-defeating: in other words, that we attain the valuable relationship of friendship only when we cease to think about it and concentrate on the friend himself.

---

7. C. S. Lewis, *An Experiment in Criticism,* pp. 137, 139 (Cambridge University Press 1961).

BIBLIOGRAPHY

Socrates and Plato

Gadamer, Hans-Georg, "*Logos* and *Ergon* in Plato's *Lysis*," in *Dialogue and Dialectic*, New Haven, 1980, 1–20.

Kosman, A., "Platonic Love," in W.H. Werkmeister, ed., *Facets of Plato's Philosophy*, Assen, 1976 (*Phronesis* suppl. 2).

Plato, *Phaedrus* and *Symposium*.

Versenyi, L., "Plato's *Lysis*," *Phronesis*, 20, 1975, 185–98.

Vlastos, Gregory, "The Individual as Object of Love in Plato," in *Platonic Studies*, 2nd edn., Princeton, 1981.

Xenophon, *Memorabilia*, II.ii–x.

Plato and Aristotle

Annas, Julia, "Plato and Aristotle on Friendship and Altruism," *Mind*, 86, 1977, 532–54.

Nussbaum, Martha, *The Fragility of Goodness*, Cambridge, 1986.

Price, A.W., *Love and Friendship in Plato and Aristotle*, Oxford, 1989.

Aristotle

Alpern, Kenneth D., "Aristotle on the Friendship of Utility and Pleasure," *Journal of the History of Philosophy*, 21, 1983, 303–16.

Annas, Julia, "Self-Love in Aristotle," *Southern Journal of Philosophy Supplement*, 27, 1988, 1–18.

Aristotle, *Eudemian Ethics*, book VII.

Cooper, John M., "Aristotle on the Forms of Friendship," *Review of Metaphysics*, 30, 1976–7, 619–48.

_____, "Friendship and the Good in Aristotle," *Philosophical Review*, 86, 1977, 290–315.

Fortenbaugh, W.W., "Aristotle's Analysis of Friendship," *Phronesis*, 20, 1975, 51–62.

Hardie, W.F.R., *Aristotle's Ethical Theory*, 2nd edn., Oxford, 1980, ch. xv.

Kahn, Charles H., "Aristotle and Altruism," *Mind*, 90, 1981, 20–40.

Millgram, E., "Aristotle on Making Other Selves," *Canadian Journal of Philosophy*, 17, 1987, 361–76.

Sherman, Nancy, "Aristotle on Friendship and the Shared Life," *Philosophy and Phenomenological Research*, 47, 1987, 589–613.

—————, *The Fabric of Character*, Oxford, 1989.

Walker, A.D.M., "Aristotle's Account of Friendship in the *Nicomachean Ethics*," *Phronesis*, 24, 1979, 180–96.

Cicero

Cicero, Marcus T., *De Finibus*, esp. II.xxiv and III.xxi.

Mitsis, Phillip, *Epicurus' Ethical Theory: The Pleasures of Invulnerability*, Ithaca, 1988, ch. 3, "Friendship and Altruism."

Seneca

Seneca, *Ad Lucilium Epistulae Morales*, iii, "On True and False Friendship," xxxv, "On the Friendship of Kindred Minds," ciii, "On the Dangers of Association with Our Fellow-Man," and cix, "On the Fellowship of Wise Men."

Aelred

Fiske, Adel M., "Aelred of Rievaulx's Idea of Friendship and Love," *Cîteaux*, 13, 1962, 5–17 and 97–132.

—————, *Friends and Friendship in the Monastic Tradition*, Cuernavaca, 1970.

McGuire, Brian P., *Friendship and Community: The Monastic Experience*, 350–1250, Kalamazoo, 1988.

Thomas Aquinas

Aquinas, Thomas, *De Caritate* ("On Charity"), trans. L.H. Kendzierski, Milwaukee, 1984.

Bobick, Joseph, "Aquinas on Friendship with God," *New Scholasticism*, 60, 1986, 257–781.

Bond, Leo, "A Comparison between Human and Divine Friendship," *Thomist*, 3, 1941, 54–94.

Jones, L. Gregory, "Theological Transformation of Aristotelian

Friendship in the Thought of St. Thomas Aquinas," *New Scholasticism*, 61, 373–99, 1987.

Porter, Jean, " '*De Ordine Caritatis*': Charity, Friendship, and Justice in Thomas Aquinas' Summa Theologiae," *Thomist*, 53, 1989, 197–213.

Montaigne

Hallie, Philip P., *The Scar of Montaigne*, Middletown, Conn., 1966.

Kant

Kant, Immanuel, *The Metaphysical Principles of Virtue*, trans. J. Ellington, Indianapolis, 1964, §46.

Reich, Klaus, "Kant and Greek Ethics," *Mind*, N.S. 48, 1939, 446–63.

Emerson

Cavell, Stanley, *The Senses of Walden*, expanded edn., San Francisco, 1981.

Emerson, Ralph Waldo, "Love," in *Essays: First Series*, Boston, 1903.

Norton, Charles Eliot, ed., *Letters from Ralph Waldo Emerson to a Friend*, 1838–53, Boston, 1899.

Rusk, Ralph L., ed., *The Letters of Ralph Waldo Emerson*, New York, 1939.

Kierkegaard

Kierkegaard, Søren, *Works of Love*, IIA, "You *Shall* Love," and IIC., "*You* Shall Love Your Neighbor."

Telfer (contemporary work)

Badhwar, Neera K., "Friends as Ends in Themselves," *Philosophy and Phenomenological Research*, 48, 1–23, 1987.

Chong, Kim-Chong, "Egoism, Desires, and Friendship," *American Philosophical Quarterly*, 21, 1984, 349–58.

Derrida, Jacques, "The Politics of Friendship," trans. Gabriel Motzkin, *Journal of Philosophy*, 85, 1988, 632–44.

Friedman, Marilyn, "Feminism and Modern Friendship: Dislocating the Community," *Ethics*, 99, 1989, 275–90.

Gilbert, Paul, "Friendship and the Will," *Philosophy*, 61, 1986, 61–70.

Grene, Marjorie, "In and On Friendship," in A. Donagan, ed., *Human Nature and Natural Knowledge*, Dordrecht, 1986.

Hampshire, Stuart, "Morality and Convention," in A. Sen and B. Williams, eds., *Utilitarianism and Beyond*, Cambridge, 1982, 145–58.

Kekes, John, "Civility and Society," *History of Philosophy Quarterly*, 1, 1984, 429–44.

Kupfer, Joseph, "Can Parents and Children Be Friends?", *American Philosophical Quarterly*, 27, 1990, 15–26.

Moravcsik, J.M.E., "The Perils of Friendship and Conceptions of the Self," in J. Dancy, ed., *Human Agency*, Stanford, 1988.

Thomas, Laurence, "Friendship," *Synthese*, 72, 1987, 217–36.

Whiting, Jennifer, "Friends and Future Selves," *Philosophical Review*, 45, 1986, 547–80.

Wollheim, Richard, *The Thread of Life*, Cambridge, 1984, pp. 275–80.

Friendship, Consequentialism, and Deontology

Badhwar, Neera K., "Friendship, Justice, and Supererogation," *American Philosophical Quarterly*, 22, 1985, 123–32.

Berger, Fred R., "Love, Friendship, and Utility: On Practical Reason and Reductionism," in A. Donagan, ed., *Human Nature and Natural Knowledge*, Dordrecht, 1986.

Blum, Lawrence A., *Friendship, Altruism, and Morality*, London, 1980.

Railton, Peter, "Alienation, Consequentialism, and the Demands of Morality," *Philosophy and Public Affairs*, 13, 1984, 134–71.

Regan, Tom, "A Refutation of Utilitarianism," *Canadian Journal of Philosophy*, 13, 1983, 141–59.

Stocker, Michael, "The Schizophrenia of Modern Ethical Theories," *Journal of Philosophy*, 73, 1976, 453–66.

Wilcox, William H., "Egoists, Consequentialists, and Their Friends," *Philosophy and Public Affairs*, 16, 1987, 73–84.

Williams, B., "Persons, Character, and Morality," in his *Moral Luck*, Cambridge, 1981.

Other Philosophical Writing about or Relating to Friendship

Augustine, *Confessions*, IV.4–15; VI.
Epictetus, *Discourses*, II.xxii, "Of Friendship."
Ferguson, Adam, *Principles of Moral and Political Science*, London, 1792, I, 26–36.
McTaggart, *The Nature of Existence*, Cambridge, 1927, vol. II, ch. XLI, "Emotion," 144–69.
Plutarch, *Moralia*, "How to Tell a Flatterer from a Friend," "On Having Many Friends," "On Brotherly Love," and "On Affection for Offspring."
Reid, Thomas, *Essays on the Active Powers of the Human Mind*, Edinburgh, 1895, III.ii.4, "Of the Particular Benevolent Affections."
Scheler, Max, *The Nature of Sympathy*, trans., Peter Heath, Hamden, Conn., 1970.
Sidgwick, Henry, *The Methods of Ethics*, 7th edn., Indianapolis, 1981, III.iv, "Benevolence."

On Egoism and Altruism

Bradley, F.H. "Selfishness and Self-Sacrifice," in *Ethical Studies*, Oxford, 1927.
Broad, C.D. *Five Types of Ethical Theory*, London, 1930.
Butler, Joseph, "Upon the Love of Our Neighbor," Sermon XI, in *Fifteen Sermons Preached at the Rolls Chapel*, London, 1913.
Nagel, Thomas, *The Possibility of Altruism*, Princeton, 1973.
Parfit, Derek, *Reasons and Persons*, Oxford, 1984.
Sidgwick, Henry, *The Methods of Ethics*, 7th edn., Indianapolis, 1981, "Concluding Chapter."
Williams, Bernard, "Egoism and Altruism," in his *Problems of the Self*, Cambridge University Press, 1973.
Zemach, Eddy, "Love Thy Neighbor as Thyself, or Egoism and Altruism," *Midwest Studies in Philosophy*, 3, 1978, 148–58.

Theological Discussion of Agape, Eros, and Friendship

D'Arcy, M.C., *The Mind and the Heart of Love*, London, 1954.
Lewis, C.S., *The Four Loves*, London, 1960.

Meilander, Gilbert C., *Friendship: A Study in Theological Ethics*, Notre Dame, 1981.

Newman, John H., "Love of Relations and Friends," *Parochial and Plain Sermons*, London, 1908, vol. ii, sermon v.

Nygren, Anders, *Agape and Eros*, trans. Philip S. Watson, New York, 1969.

de Rougemont, Denis, *Love in the Western World*, New York, 1940.

de Sales, St. Francis, *Introduction to the Devout Life*, trans. J. K. Ryan, Garden City, N.Y., 1972, Part III, §§ 19–22.

Taylor, Jeremy, "Discourse on the Nature and Offices of Friendship," *Works*, vol. 1, R. Heber, ed., London, 1847.